DATA STRUCTURES AND ALGORITHMS WITH C++

100+ Coding Q&A

Yasin Cakal

Code of Code

CONTENTS

INTRODUCTION

The "Data Structures and Algorithms with C++" book is designed to provide a comprehensive understanding of data structures and algorithms and how to implement them using C++. This book is suitable for both beginners and experienced programmers and aims to give them the knowledge and skills they need to become proficient in data structures and algorithms.

Throughout the book, readers will learn about a wide range of data structures such as arrays, stacks, queues, linked lists, skip lists, hash tables, binary search trees, Cartesian trees, B-trees, red-black trees, splay trees, AVL trees, and KD trees. These data structures are fundamental to computer science and are used in many applications.

Additionally, readers will learn about a wide range of algorithms such as Quicksort, Mergesort, Timsort, Heapsort, bubble sort, insertion sort, selection sort, tree sort, shell sort, bucket sort, radix sort, counting sort, and cubesort. These algorithms are widely used in various fields and a good understanding of them can help you to write efficient and optimized code.

This book also covers algorithm design techniques such as greedy algorithms, dynamic programming, divide and conquer, backtracking, and randomized algorithms. These techniques are used to design and analyze algorithms. They are important to understand and can help you to improve your problem-solving abilities.

Hands-on exercises and examples are included to help readers practice the concepts they learn. By working through these exercises and examples, readers can solidify their understanding of the material and gain experience in implementing data structures and algorithms in C++.

This book will also cover the Time and Space Complexity of the algorithm and Data Structures, so that readers can understand the trade-offs of choosing one over the other. Understanding the time and space complexity of an algorithm is essential for making informed decisions when designing and implementing solutions to problems.

By the end of this book, readers will have a solid understanding of data structures and algorithms and how to use them effectively in C++. This course is perfect for anyone who wants to improve their skills as a developer or prepare for a career in computer science or data science. If you're ready to begin your journey towards mastering data structures and algorithms with C++, this book is perfect for you. Start now and begin your journey towards mastering data structures and algorithms with C++.

INTRODUCTION TO DATA STRUCTURES AND ALGORITHMS

OVERVIEW OF DATA STRUCTURES AND ALGORITHMS WITH C++

Data structures and algorithms are fundamental concepts in computer science. Data structures are used to store and organize data in a structured way so that it can be easily accessed and manipulated. Algorithms are the set of instructions used to solve a problem. Both data structures and algorithms are essential for designing and coding efficient and complex computer programs.

This article provides an overview of data structures and algorithms for the course Data Structures and Algorithms with C++. It covers the basic principles of data structures and algorithms, as well as the different types of data structures and algorithms, and how to implement them in C++.

What are Data Structures and Algorithms?

Data structures and algorithms are two of the most important concepts in computer science. Data structures are the way data is organized and stored in a computer so it can be easily accessed and manipulated. Algorithms are the set of instructions used to solve a problem.

Data structures are the building blocks of algorithms. They provide the structure that allows algorithms to work efficiently. Data structures are used to store and organize data, while algorithms provide the instructions for manipulating the data.

Data structures and algorithms are essential for designing and coding efficient and complex computer programs. Without them, it would be impossible to create programs that are able to handle large amounts of data or to solve complex problems.

Types of Data Structures

There are several different types of data structures, each with its own advantages and disadvantages. Some of the most common data structures include arrays, linked lists, stacks, queues, trees, and graphs.

Arrays are the simplest type of data structure. They are used to store a collection of elements, such as numbers or characters, that are all of the same type. Arrays are easy to manipulate and are well-suited for storing large amounts of data.

Linked lists are another type of data structure. They are used to store a collection of elements, such as numbers or characters, that are all of the same type. Linked lists are more complex than arrays, but they are better suited for storing large amounts of data.

Stacks and queues are data structures that are used to store data in a specific order.

Stacks are used to store data in a Last-In-First-Out (LIFO) order, while queues are used to store data in a First-In-First-Out (FIFO) order.

Trees and graphs are more complex data structures. Trees are used to store data in a hierarchical structure, while graphs are used to store data in a network structure.

Types of Algorithms

Algorithms are the set of instructions used to solve a problem. There are several different types of algorithms, such as search algorithms, sorting algorithms, and graph algorithms.

Search algorithms are used to find an item in a data structure. These algorithms are used to search for a specific item in an array, linked list, stack, queue, tree, or graph.

Sorting algorithms are used to sort a collection of elements. These algorithms are used to sort an array, linked list, stack, queue, tree, or graph in a specific order.

Graph algorithms are used to find the shortest path between two nodes in a graph. These algorithms are used to solve problems such as the traveling salesman problem and the shortest path problem.

Implementing Data Structures and Algorithms in C++

Data structures and algorithms can be implemented in any programming language, but they are most commonly implemented in C++. C++ is a powerful programming language that is well-suited for implementing data structures and algorithms.

C++ has a powerful set of tools that make it easy to implement data structures and algorithms. It has built-in data types and classes that can be used to store and manipulate data. It also has powerful functions and templates that make it easy to implement algorithms.

Conclusion

Data structures and algorithms are essential for designing and coding efficient and complex computer programs. This article provides an overview of data structures and algorithms for the course Data Structures and Algorithms with C++. It covers the basic principles of data structures and algorithms, as well as the different types of data structures and algorithms, and how to implement them in C++.

Exercises

What is the difference between a data structure and an algorithm?

Name three different types of data structures.

What is the purpose of a sorting algorithm?

How can data structures and algorithms be implemented in C++?

What is the purpose of a graph algorithm?

Solutions

What is the difference between a data structure and an algorithm?

The difference between a data structure and an algorithm is that a data structure is used to store and organize data in a structured way so that it can be easily accessed and manipulated, while an algorithm is the set of instructions used to solve a problem.

Name three different types of data structures.

Three different types of data structures are arrays, linked lists, and trees.

What is the purpose of a sorting algorithm?

The purpose of a sorting algorithm is to sort a collection of elements, such as numbers or characters, in a specific order.

How can data structures and algorithms be implemented in C++?

Data structures and algorithms can be implemented in C++ using the built-in data types and classes, as well as powerful functions and templates.

What is the purpose of a graph algorithm?

The purpose of a graph algorithm is to find the shortest path between two nodes in a graph.

IMPORTANCE OF DATA STRUCTURES AND ALGORITHMS IN PROGRAMMING WITH C++

Data structures and algorithms are fundamental building blocks of computer programming. They are the basic building blocks that allow developers to create efficient, robust, and scalable software applications. While understanding the fundamentals of programming is important, the ability to effectively utilize data structures and algorithms is essential for creating efficient and effective software applications. In this article, we will discuss the importance of data structures and algorithms in programming, and how they are applied in C++ programming.

What are Data Structures and Algorithms?

Data structures are the means by which data is organized and stored in a computer system. They enable developers to store and access data in an efficient and organized manner. Data structures can range from the simple arrays and linked lists to more complex trees, graphs, and hash tables.

Algorithms are step-by-step instructions that enable computers to solve problems. They provide a set of instructions that allow computers to solve complex problems quickly and efficiently. Algorithms are used in a variety of computer programming tasks, including sorting, searching, and optimization.

Importance of Data Structures and Algorithms in Programming

Data structures and algorithms are fundamental to all aspects of computer programming. They are used to store and access data, solve problems, and optimize code performance.

Data Structures

Data structures are used to store and access data in an efficient and organized manner. They enable developers to organize data in a way that is easy to access and modify. Additionally, data structures can be used to organize and store data in a way that minimizes memory usage. This is especially important for applications that require large amounts of data to be stored or manipulated.

Algorithms

Algorithms are used to solve complex problems quickly and efficiently. They provide a set of instructions that allow computers to solve complex problems quickly and accurately. Algorithms are used in a variety of programming tasks, including sorting, searching, and optimization. Additionally, algorithms can be used to analyze data sets and identify trends and patterns.

Data Structures and Algorithms in Programming with C++

Data structures and algorithms are essential components of programming with the C++ language. C++ is a powerful language that provides developers with a variety of tools to create efficient and robust software applications.

Data Structures

C++ provides developers with a variety of data structures to store and access data in an organized and efficient manner. These data structures include arrays, linked lists, stacks, queues, trees, and hash tables. Each of these data structures has its own advantages and disadvantages, and can be used to store and access data in an efficient manner.

Algorithms

C++ also provides developers with a variety of algorithms to solve complex problems quickly and accurately. These algorithms include sorting algorithms, searching algorithms, optimization algorithms, and graph algorithms. Each of these algorithms can be used to solve different types of problems, and can be used to analyze data sets and identify trends and patterns.

Conclusion

Data structures and algorithms are fundamental components of programming with C++. They are used to store and access data in an efficient and organized manner, and to solve complex problems quickly and accurately. Understanding the fundamentals of data structures and algorithms is essential for creating efficient and effective software applications.

Exercises

What is a data structure?

What is an algorithm?

What are the benefits of using data structures in programming?

What are the benefits of using algorithms in programming?

What are some of the data structures and algorithms used in C++ programming?

Solutions

What is a data structure?

A data structure is a means by which data is organized and stored in a computer system.

What is an algorithm?

An algorithm is a set of step-by-step instructions that allow computers to solve complex problems quickly and accurately.

What are the benefits of using data structures in programming?

Data structures enable developers to store and access data in an efficient and organized manner, and to minimize memory usage.

What are the benefits of using algorithms in programming?

Algorithms provide a set of instructions that allow computers to solve complex problems quickly and accurately, and to analyze data sets and identify trends and patterns.

What are some of the data structures and algorithms used in C++ programming?

Data structures used in C++ programming include arrays, linked lists, stacks, queues, trees, and hash tables. Algorithms used in C++ programming include sorting algorithms, searching algorithms, optimization algorithms, and graph algorithms.

HOW TO CHOOSE THE RIGHT DATA STRUCTURE OR ALGORITHM FOR A GIVEN PROBLEM WITH C++

Choosing the right data structure or algorithm is an essential part of any software development project. When building software, it is important to understand the tradeoffs between different data structures and algorithms and to select the best one for the given problem. This article will explain how to choose the right data structure or algorithm for a given problem with C++.

Data Structures

Before we dive into choosing the right data structure or algorithm for a given problem with C++, let's first discuss data structures. Data structures are the building blocks of any software project. They are the way that data is stored and manipulated in order to achieve a desired outcome. Some of the most commonly used data structures in C++ include arrays, linked lists, stacks, queues, and trees.

Each data structure has its own advantages and disadvantages. For example, arrays are great for storing data in a static fashion, but they can be difficult to modify and may require a lot of memory. Linked lists, on the other hand, are great for dynamic data, but can be slow to search through. It is important to understand the strengths and weaknesses of each data structure in order to choose the right one for the given problem.

Algorithms

In addition to data structures, algorithms are also important when building software. Algorithms are a set of instructions that are used to solve a problem. There are many different algorithms that can be used to solve the same problem, each with its own strengths and weaknesses. Some of the most commonly used algorithms in C++ include sorting, searching, and graph algorithms.

Like data structures, each algorithm has its own advantages and disadvantages. For example, sorting algorithms are great for organizing data, but can be slow to execute. Searching algorithms are great for finding specific data, but can be memory intensive. It is important to understand the strengths and weaknesses of each algorithm in order to choose the right one for the given problem.

Selecting the Right Data Structure or Algorithm

Now that we have discussed data structures and algorithms, let's talk about how to choose the right one for a given problem. The first step is to understand the problem. It is important to understand the requirements of the problem, as well as any constraints or limitations. Once you have a good understanding of the problem, you can begin to evaluate different data structures and algorithms to determine which one is best suited for the given problem.

When evaluating data structures and algorithms, it is important to consider the time complexity and space complexity of each option. Time complexity measures how long a data structure or algorithm takes to complete a task, while space complexity measures how much memory is required to store the data. It is important to consider both time and space complexity when making your decision.

In addition to time and space complexity, it is also important to consider the efficiency of each data structure or algorithm. Efficiency measures how quickly a data structure or algorithm can complete a task. It is important to choose a data structure or algorithm that is both fast and efficient in order to ensure that the program runs as quickly and efficiently as possible.

Finally, it is important to consider the scalability of each data structure or algorithm. Scalability measures how well a data structure or algorithm can handle large amounts of data. It is important to choose a data structure or algorithm that is both fast and efficient, as well as one that can handle large amounts of data.

Conclusion

Choosing the right data structure or algorithm for a given problem with C++ is an essential part of any software development project. It is important to understand the tradeoffs between different data structures and algorithms and to select the best one for the given problem. This article has discussed how to choose the right data structure or algorithm for a given problem with C++ by considering the time complexity, space complexity, efficiency, and scalability of each option. With the right knowledge and understanding of data structures and algorithms, you will be able to make the best decision for your software development project.

Exercises

What is the difference between a data structure and an algorithm?

What is time complexity and why is it important?

What is space complexity and why is it important?

What is efficiency and why is it important?

What is scalability and why is it important?

Solutions

What is the difference between a data structure and an algorithm?

The difference between a data structure and an algorithm is that a data structure is a way of organizing and storing data, while an algorithm is a set of instructions used to solve a problem.

What is time complexity and why is it important?

Time complexity is a measure of how long a data structure or algorithm takes to complete a task. It is important because it helps to determine which data structure or algorithm is best suited for the given problem.

What is space complexity and why is it important?

Space complexity is a measure of how much memory is required to store the data. It is important because it helps to determine which data structure or algorithm is best suited for the given problem.

What is efficiency and why is it important?

Efficiency is a measure of how quickly a data structure or algorithm can complete a task. It is important because it helps to determine which data structure or algorithm is best suited for the given problem.

What is scalability and why is it important?

Scalability is a measure of how well a data structure or algorithm can handle large amounts of data. It is important because it helps to determine which data structure or algorithm is best suited for the given problem.

BASIC C++ CONCEPTS REVIEW

VARIABLES AND DATA TYPES IN C++

Data Structures and Algorithms with C++ is an essential course for understanding the fundamentals of programming. This course focuses on introducing students to the fundamentals of algorithms and data structures, as well as the C++ programming language. One of the most important topics covered in this course is variables and data types in C++. This article will discuss the different types of variables and data types in C++ and provide code examples to help explain the concepts.

What are Variables?

A variable is a named location in memory that stores a value. It is used in programming to store data values, such as numbers or strings. Variables are essential for writing programs, as they allow for the storage of data and help the programmer to reference and modify it.

In C++, each variable has a type associated with it. The type of a variable determines the size and layout of the variable's memory and the type of operations that can be performed on it. The type of a variable is determined when it is declared, and it cannot be changed once it has been declared.

For example, the following code declares a variable named "x" and assigns it the type "int" (integer):

```
int x;
```

Types of Variables

In C++, there are two types of variables: static and dynamic. Static variables are declared outside of any function and exist throughout the program. They cannot be changed and are used to store constant values.

Dynamic variables, on the other hand, are declared inside a function and are used to store values that can be changed. They are only available within the scope of the function in which they were declared.

Data Types

In C++, there are two types of data types: primitive and non-primitive. Primitive data types are the most basic types of data and include integers, floating-point numbers, characters, and booleans. Non-primitive data types include arrays, structures, and classes.

Primitive Data Types

Integer Data Type

The integer data type is used for storing whole numbers. It can be either signed or unsigned and can range from -2^{31} to $2^{31} - 1$.

The following code declares an integer variable named "x" and assigns it the value 10:

```
int x = 10;
```

Floating-Point Data Type

The floating-point data type is used for storing numbers with decimal points. It is usually represented using the "float" or "double" data types.

The following code declares a floating-point variable named "y" and assigns it the value 3.14:

```
float y = 3.14;
```

Character Data Type

The character data type is used for storing characters, such as letters, numbers, and symbols. It is usually represented using the "char" data type.

The following code declares a character variable named "c" and assigns it the value 'A':

```
char c = 'A';
```

Boolean Data Type

The boolean data type is used for storing true or false values. It is usually represented using the "bool" data type.

The following code declares a boolean variable named "b" and assigns it the value true:

```
bool b = true;
```

Non-Primitive Data Types

Array Data Type

The array data type is used for storing a collection of values of the same type. It is usually represented using the "array" data type.

The following code declares an array variable named "arr" and assigns it the values 1, 2, and 3:

```
int arr[3] = {1, 2, 3};
```

Struct Data Type

The struct data type is used for storing a collection of different types of values. It is usually represented using the "struct" data type.

The following code declares a struct variable named "myStruct" and assigns it the values 10 and 'A':

```
struct myStruct {
 int x;
```

```
 char c;
} myStruct = { 10, 'A' };
```

Class Data Type

The class data type is used for defining a type of object that has its own data and functions. It is usually represented using the "class" data type.

The following code declares a class variable named "MyClass" and assigns it the values 10 and 'A':

```
class MyClass {
 public:
  int x;
  char c;
} myObject = { 10, 'A' };
```

Conclusion

In this article, we discussed the different types of variables and data types in C++. We discussed the primitive data types (integer, floating point, character, and boolean) and the non-primitive data types (array, struct, and class). We also provided code examples to help explain the concepts.

Exercises

Declare a floating-point variable called "f" and assign it the value 3.14.

Declare a character variable called "c" and assign it the value 'A'.

Declare an array variable called "arr" and assign it the values 1, 2, and 3.

Declare a struct variable called "myStruct" and assign it the values 10 and 'A'.

Declare a class variable called "MyClass" and assign it the values 10 and 'A'.

Solutions

Declare a floating-point variable called "f" and assign it the value 3.14.
```
float f = 3.14;
```

Declare a character variable called "c" and assign it the value 'A'.
```
char c = 'A';
```

Declare an array variable called "arr" and assign it the values 1, 2, and 3.
```
int arr[3] = {1, 2, 3};
```

Declare a struct variable called "myStruct" and assign it the values 10 and 'A'.
```
struct myStruct {
 int x;
 char c;
} myStruct = { 10, 'A' };
```

Declare a class variable called "MyClass" and assign it the values 10 and 'A'.

```cpp
class MyClass {
 public:
  int x;
  char c;
} myObject = { 10, 'A' };
```

CONTROL FLOW STATEMENTS IN C++

Control flow statements are an important part of programming in any language, including C++. They allow a programmer to control the execution of a program based on certain conditions that are set within the code. Control flow statements are used to create loops, make decisions, and perform other tasks. In this article, we will explore the various control flow statements in C++ and learn how to use them effectively.

What is a Control Flow Statement?

A control flow statement is a command in a programming language that tells a program how to behave. Control flow statements are used to create loops, make decisions, and perform other tasks. Control flow statements are used to determine which code will be executed and in what order. The most common control flow statements in C++ are the if statement, the switch statement, the while loop, and the for loop.

The if Statement

The if statement is one of the most commonly used control flow statements in C++. It is used to evaluate a condition, and depending on the result of the evaluation, a certain set of instructions will be executed. Here is an example of an if statement in C++:

```
if (condition) {
  // code to be executed
}
```

The condition can be an expression that evaluates to true or false, such as an equality comparison. The code inside the brackets will be executed only if the condition is true.

The switch Statement

The switch statement is another control flow statement in C++. It is used to execute a block of code depending on the value of a variable or expression. The switch statement is similar to the if statement, but it is more efficient in certain situations. Here is an example of a switch statement in C++:

```
switch (expression) {
  case value1:
    // code to be executed if expression = value1
    break;
  case value2:
    // code to be executed if expression = value2
```

```
    break;
  default:
    // code to be executed if expression does not equal any of the cases
}
```

The expression can be any type of variable, such as an int, char, or string. The switch statement will then evaluate the expression and run the corresponding code for the case that matches the value of the expression.

The while Loop

The while loop is another control flow statement in C++ that is used to execute a block of code multiple times. The while loop will continue to execute the code until the condition evaluates to false. Here is an example of a while loop in C++:

```
while (condition) {
  // code to be executed
}
```

The condition can be any expression that evaluates to true or false. The code inside the brackets will be executed only if the condition is true. The while loop will keep executing the code until the condition evaluates to false.

The for Loop

The for loop is another control flow statement in C++ that is similar to the while loop, but it is more efficient in certain situations. The for loop is used to execute a block of code multiple times, but it also allows the programmer to set a specific number of iterations. Here is an example of a for loop in C++:

```
for (int i = 0; i < 10; i++) {
  // code to be executed
}
```

The for loop will execute the code inside the brackets 10 times. The int i is a counter that is set to zero and incremented by one each time the loop is executed. The loop will continue to execute until the counter is equal to 10.

Conclusion

In this article, we explored the various control flow statements in C++ and learned how to use them effectively. We examined the if statement, the switch statement, the while loop, and the for loop. Control flow statements are an important part of programming in C++ and are used to create loops, make decisions, and perform other tasks.

Exercises

Write a program that uses a for loop to print out the numbers from 1 to 10.

Write a program that uses a while loop to print out the numbers from 1 to 10.

Write a program that uses an if statement to print out the numbers from 1 to 10 if the variable x is greater than 5.

Write a program that uses a switch statement to print out the numbers from 1 to 10 depending on the value of the variable x.

Write a program that uses a for loop to print out the numbers from 1 to 10, and then prints out "Done" once the loop is finished.

Solutions

Write a program that uses a for loop to print out the numbers from 1 to 10.

```cpp
#include <iostream>
int main() {
  for (int i = 1; i <= 10; i++) {
    std::cout << i << std::endl;
  }
  return 0;
}
```

Write a program that uses a while loop to print out the numbers from 1 to 10.

```cpp
#include <iostream>
int main() {
  int i = 1;
  while (i <= 10) {
    std::cout << i << std::endl;
    i++;
  }
  return 0;
}
```

Write a program that uses an if statement to print out the numbers from 1 to 10 if the variable x is greater than 5.

```cpp
#include <iostream>
int main() {
  int x = 6;
  if (x > 5) {
    for (int i = 1; i <= 10; i++) {
      std::cout << i << std::endl;
    }
  }
  return 0;
}
```

Write a program that uses a switch statement to print out the numbers from 1 to 10 depending on the value of the variable x.

```cpp
#include <iostream>
int main() {
  int x = 5;
```

```cpp
switch (x) {
  case 1:
    for (int i = 1; i <= 10; i++) {
      std::cout << i << std::endl;
    }
    break;
  case 2:
    for (int i = 1; i <= 10; i++) {
      std::cout << i << std::endl;
    }
    break;
  case 3:
    for (int i = 1; i <= 10; i++) {
      std::cout << i << std::endl;
    }
    break;
  case 4:
    for (int i = 1; i <= 10; i++) {
      std::cout << i << std::endl;
    }
    break;
  case 5:
    for (int i = 1; i <= 10; i++) {
      std::cout << i << std::endl;
    }
    break;
  }
  return 0;
}
```

Write a program that uses a for loop to print out the numbers from 1 to 10, and then prints out "Done" once the loop is finished.

```cpp
#include <iostream>
int main() {
  for (int i = 1; i <= 10; i++) {
    std::cout << i << std::endl;
  }
  std::cout << "Done" << std::endl;
  return 0;
}
```

CLASSES AND OBJECTS IN C++

Welcome to the course "Data Structures and Algorithms with C++". In this course, we will be covering the fundamentals of classes and objects in C++. Classes and objects are a fundamental concept in object-oriented programming (OOP). These concepts are used to create and manipulate data structures and algorithms in C++.

In this article, we will be discussing the fundamentals of classes and objects in C++. We will explain how they are used and how they can be used to create and manipulate data structures and algorithms. We will also look at some examples of how classes and objects in C++ can be used to create complex data structures and algorithms.

What are Classes and Objects?

To understand classes and objects in C++, we must first understand the concept of object-oriented programming (OOP). OOP is a programming paradigm that is based on the concept of objects. An object is a self-contained unit which contains both data and methods. The data contained in an object is known as its attributes, while the methods are known as its behaviours.

Classes are the blueprints for objects. A class defines the attributes and behaviours of an object. An object is then created based on the class definition. This object will have the same attributes and behaviours as defined by the class.

In C++, classes are defined using the class keyword. The class definition consists of a list of attributes and methods. The attributes are declared using the private keyword and the methods are declared using the public keyword.

Class Example

Let's now look at an example of a class in C++. We will be creating a class called Point which represents a point in two-dimensional space.

```
// Point.h
class Point {
private:
        int x;
        int y;
public:
        Point();
        Point(int x, int y);
        int getX();
        int getY();
        void setX(int x);
```

```
        void setY(int y);
};
```

In this class, we have declared two attributes (x and y) and six methods (Point(), Point(int x, int y), getX(), getY(), setX(), and setY()). The attributes are declared using the private keyword and the methods are declared using the public keyword.

Object Example

Now that we have defined our Point class, we can create an object based on this class. We will create an object called myPoint which represents the point (2, 3).

```
// main.cpp
#include "Point.h"
int main() {
        Point myPoint(2, 3);
        return 0;
}
```

In this example, we have created an object called myPoint based on the Point class. This object has the attributes x and y with the values 2 and 3 respectively.

Using Classes and Objects

Now that we have looked at how to define classes and objects in C++, let's now look at how they can be used to create and manipulate data structures and algorithms. Classes and objects are commonly used to create abstract data types (ADTs), which are user-defined data types that can be used to represent data in a program.

For example, we can use our Point class to create an abstract data type called Vector. A Vector is a mathematical object which represents a directed line segment in two-dimensional space.

```
// Vector.h
class Vector {
private:
        Point start;
        Point end;
public:
        Vector();
        Vector(Point start, Point end);
        Point getStart();
        Point getEnd();
        void setStart(Point start);
        void setEnd(Point end);
        double length();
};
```

In this class, we have declared two attributes (start and end) and seven methods (Vector(), Vector(Point start, Point end), getStart(), getEnd(), setStart(), setEnd(), and length()). The attributes are both Point objects, and the methods are used to manipulate and calculate the length of the Vector.

Classes and objects are also used to create data structures and algorithms. For example, we can use our Vector class to create an algorithm for calculating the length of a Vector.

```cpp
// Vector.cpp
#include "Vector.h"
Vector::Vector() {
        start = Point();
        end = Point();
}
Vector::Vector(Point start, Point end) {
        this->start = start;
        this->end = end;
}
Point Vector::getStart() {
        return start;
}
Point Vector::getEnd() {
        return end;
}
void Vector::setStart(Point start) {
        this->start = start;
}
void Vector::setEnd(Point end) {
        this->end = end;
}
double Vector::length() {
        int xDiff = end.getX() - start.getX();
        int yDiff = end.getY() - start.getY();
        return sqrt(xDiff*xDiff + yDiff*yDiff);
}
```

In this example, we have implemented the length() method of the Vector class. This method calculates the length of the Vector by calculating the difference in the x and y coordinates of start and end, and then computing the square root of the sum of these differences.

Conclusion

In this article, we have looked at the fundamentals of classes and objects in C++. We have discussed how they can be used to create and manipulate data structures and algorithms. We have also looked at some examples of how classes and objects can be used to create abstract data types and algorithms.

Exercises

Write a class called Rectangle which represents a rectangle in two-dimensional space. The class should have two attributes (width and height) and four methods

(Rectangle(), Rectangle(int width, int height), getWidth(), getHeight(), setWidth(), and setHeight()).

Write a method for the Rectangle class called area() which calculates and returns the area of the Rectangle.

Write a class called Student which represents a student in a school. The class should have three attributes (name, age, and grade) and four methods (Student(), Student(string name, int age, int grade), getName(), getAge(), getGrade(), and setGrade()).

Write a method for the Student class called getAverageGrade() which calculates and returns the average grade of the Student.

Write a class called Circle which represents a circle in two-dimensional space. The class should have two attributes (radius and center) and three methods (Circle(), Circle(int radius, Point center), getRadius(), getCenter(), and setRadius()).

Solutions

Write a class called Rectangle which represents a rectangle in two-dimensional space. The class should have two attributes (width and height) and four methods (Rectangle(), Rectangle(int width, int height), getWidth(), getHeight(), setWidth(), and setHeight()).

```cpp
// Rectangle.h
class Rectangle {
private:
        int width;
        int height;
public:
        Rectangle();
        Rectangle(int width, int height);
        int getWidth();
        int getHeight();
        void setWidth(int width);
        void setHeight(int height);
};
```

Write a method for the Rectangle class called area() which calculates and returns the area of the Rectangle.

```cpp
// Rectangle.cpp
#include "Rectangle.h"
Rectangle::Rectangle() {
        width = 0;
        height = 0;
}
Rectangle::Rectangle(int width, int height) {
```

```cpp
        this->width = width;
        this->height = height;
}
int Rectangle::getWidth() {
        return width;
}
int Rectangle::getHeight() {
        return height;
}
void Rectangle::setWidth(int width) {
        this->width = width;
}
void Rectangle::setHeight(int height) {
        this->height = height;
}
double Rectangle::area() {
        return width * height;
}
```

Write a class called Student which represents a student in a school. The class should have three attributes (name, age, and grade) and four methods (Student(), Student(string name, int age, int grade), getName(), getAge(), getGrade(), and setGrade()).

```cpp
// Student.h
class Student {
private:
        string name;
        int age;
        int grade;
public:
        Student();
        Student(string name, int age, int grade);
        string getName();
        int getAge();
        int getGrade();
        void setGrade(int grade);
};
```

Write a method for the Student class called getAverageGrade() which calculates and returns the average grade of the Student.

```cpp
// Student.cpp
#include "Student.h"
Student::Student() {
        name = "";
        age = 0;
```

```
        grade = 0;
}
Student::Student(string name, int age, int grade) {
        this->name = name;
        this->age = age;
        this->grade = grade;
}
string Student::getName() {
        return name;
}
int Student::getAge() {
        return age;
}
int Student::getGrade() {
        return grade;
}
void Student::setGrade(int grade) {
        this->grade = grade;
}
double Student::getAverageGrade() {
        return grade / age;
}
```

Write a class called Circle which represents a circle in two-dimensional space. The class should have two attributes (radius and center) and three methods (Circle(), Circle(int radius, Point center), getRadius(), getCenter(), and setRadius()).

```
// Circle.h
class Circle {
private:
        int radius;
        Point center;
public:
        Circle();
        Circle(int radius, Point center);
        int getRadius();
        Point getCenter();
        void setRadius(int radius);
};
```

METHODS AND CONSTRUCTORS IN C++

Welcome to the world of C++ programming! C++ is a powerful, object-oriented programming language. In this article, we will discuss two important concepts in C++: methods and constructors. We will explore their differences, examine their uses, and examine their syntax and implementation. We will also discuss their role in the data structures and algorithms used in C++ programming. By the end of this article, you will have a clear understanding of methods and constructors in C++, and how they can be used to improve your programming skills.

What are Methods in C++?

Methods are a type of function in C++. They are used to define the behavior of a class. A method takes some arguments and returns a value, which can be used to modify the state of the object to which it belongs. Methods are used to define the behavior of a class and are implemented as functions within a class. A method is defined within a class with the keyword 'method'. Here is an example of how a method is defined in C++:

```cpp
class MyClass {
public:
  int myMethod(int x, int y) {
    return x + y;
  }
};
```

In this example, we have defined a method named 'myMethod' which takes two integer parameters, x and y, and returns their sum.

Methods can also be defined as static or non-static. Static methods are methods that are defined outside the class and are not associated with any particular instance of the class. They are typically used for utility functions that do not require access to the state of an instance. Non-static methods, on the other hand, are associated with a particular instance of the class and can access the state of that instance. Here is an example of how a static method can be defined in C++:

```cpp
class MyClass {
public:
  static int myStaticMethod(int x, int y) {
    return x * y;
  }
}
```

```
};
```

In this example, we have defined a static method named 'myStaticMethod' which takes two integer parameters, x and y, and returns their product.

What are Constructors in C++?

Constructors are special methods in C++ that are used to initialize an object of a class. They are called when an object of a class is created. Constructors have the same name as the class and have no return type. A constructor can have parameters, but they must have the same name as the class. Here is an example of how a constructor is defined in C++:

```cpp
class MyClass {
public:
  MyClass(int x, int y) {
    this->x = x;
    this->y = y;
  }
private:
  int x;
  int y;
};
```

In this example, we have defined a constructor for the class 'MyClass' which takes two integer parameters, x and y. The constructor sets the values of the two private variables, x and y, to the values of the parameters.

Constructors can also be defined as default constructors. Default constructors are constructors that do not take any parameters. They are typically used to set the state of an object to some default value. Here is an example of how a default constructor can be defined in C++:

```cpp
class MyClass {
public:
  MyClass() {
    x = 0;
    y = 0;
  }
private:
  int x;
  int y;
};
```

In this example, we have defined a default constructor for the class 'MyClass' which sets the values of the two private variables, x and y, to 0.

Differences Between Methods and Constructors

Now that we have discussed methods and constructors, let's take a look at the differences between them. As we have seen, methods are used to define the behavior of a class. They are implemented as functions within a class and can be static or non-static. Constructors, on the other hand, are special methods that are used to initialize an object of a class. They have the same name as the class and have no return type.

Another difference between methods and constructors is that methods can take arguments and return values, whereas constructors cannot. Constructors must be called with the same parameters as the class, whereas methods can take any number of parameters.

Finally, methods can be called multiple times, whereas constructors are only called once when an object of a class is created.

Uses of Methods and Constructors

Methods and constructors are used in many different ways in C++ programming. Methods can be used to define the behavior of a class, such as performing calculations or accessing data. They can also be used to pass data between classes. Constructors, on the other hand, are used to set the initial state of an object. They are also used to allocate memory for objects.

Methods and constructors can also be used to improve the performance of a program. For example, methods can be used to reduce the amount of code that needs to be written. By using methods, the same code can be reused multiple times. Constructors can also be used to reduce the amount of code that needs to be written. By using constructors, the same code can be used to create multiple objects.

Syntax and Implementation of Methods and Constructors

Now that we have discussed the differences between methods and constructors, let's take a look at their syntax and implementation.

Methods are defined within a class with the keyword 'method'. The syntax of a method is as follows:

```
class MyClass {
public:
  return_type method_name(parameter_list) {
    // code
  }
};
```

Here, return_type is the type of value that the method returns, method_name is the name of the method, and parameter_list is the list of parameters that the method takes.

Constructors, on the other hand, have the same name as the class and have no return type. The syntax of a constructor is as follows:

```
class MyClass {
public:
  MyClass(parameter_list) {
    // code
```

```
    }
};
```

Here, MyClass is the name of the class and parameter_list is the list of parameters that the constructor takes.

Methods and constructors are implemented in C++ using the 'class' keyword. Here is an example of how a method and a constructor can be implemented in C++:

```
class MyClass {
public:
  int myMethod(int x, int y) {
    return x + y;
  }
  MyClass(int x, int y) {
    this->x = x;
    this->y = y;
  }
private:
  int x;
  int y;
};
```

In this example, we have defined a method named 'myMethod' which takes two integer parameters, x and y, and returns their sum. We have also defined a constructor for the class 'MyClass' which takes two integer parameters, x and y, and sets the values of the two private variables, x and y, to the values of the parameters.

Methods and Constructors in Data Structures and Algorithms

Methods and constructors can be used in data structures and algorithms to improve their performance. For example, methods can be used to traverse a data structure, such as a linked list, or to perform calculations, such as sorting an array. Constructors can be used to create objects that are needed in a data structure or algorithm, such as a node in a linked list.

Methods and constructors can also be used to improve the readability and maintainability of a program. By using methods, the same code can be reused multiple times, which makes the code easier to read and maintain. Constructors can also be used to reduce the amount of code that needs to be written, which also makes the code easier to read and maintain.

Conclusion

In this article, we discussed methods and constructors in C++. We discussed their differences, examined their uses, and examined their syntax and implementation. We also discussed their role in data structures and algorithms. By the end of this article, you should have a clear understanding of methods and constructors in C++, and how they can be used to improve your programming skills.

Exercises

Write a method that takes two integers, x and y, and returns their sum.

Write a constructor for a class named 'MyClass' that takes two integers, x and y, and sets the values of the two private variables, x and y, to the values of the parameters.

Write a method that takes two strings, s1 and s2, and returns true if s2 is a substring of s1.

Write a constructor for a class named 'MyClass' that sets the values of the two private variables, x and y, to 0.

Write a method that takes an array of integers, arr, and its size, n, and returns the sum of the elements in the array.

Solutions

Write a method that takes two integers, x and y, and returns their sum.

```
int sum(int x, int y) {
  return x + y;
}
```

Write a constructor for a class named 'MyClass' that takes two integers, x and y, and sets the values of the two private variables, x and y, to the values of the parameters.

```
class MyClass {
public:
  MyClass(int x, int y) {
    this->x = x;
    this->y = y;
  }
private:
  int x;
  int y;
};
```

Write a method that takes two strings, s1 and s2, and returns true if s2 is a substring of s1.

```
bool isSubstring(string s1, string s2) {
  return (s1.find(s2) != string::npos);
}
```

Write a constructor for a class named 'MyClass' that sets the values of the two private variables, x and y, to 0.

```
class MyClass {
public:
  MyClass() {
```

```
    x = 0;
    y = 0;
  }
private:
  int x;
  int y;
};
```

Write a method that takes an array of integers, arr, and its size, n, and returns the sum of the elements in the array.

```
int sumArray(int arr[], int n) {
  int sum = 0;
  for (int i = 0; i < n; i++) {
    sum += arr[i];
  }
  return sum;
}
```

BASIC INPUT AND OUTPUT IN C++

C++ is a powerful, general-purpose programming language that provides an easy way to write code for a variety of tasks. It is widely used in many areas such as game programming, robotics, data mining, and embedded systems. One of the most important aspects of programming with C++ is understanding how to use basic input and output (I/O) techniques. In this article, we will discuss the fundamentals of input and output in C++, and provide coding exercises to help you practice your new skills.

What is Input and Output?

Input and output (I/O) are the two basic operations for any program. Input is information that is sent to the program from an outside source, such as a user or a file. Output is the result of a program's execution, and is usually sent to an outside destination, such as a file or printer.

I/O operations allow us to interact with the outside world. Input can come from any source, including the keyboard, a file, or a network connection. Output can be sent to any destination, including the screen, a file, or a network connection.

Input and output operations in C++ are handled using streams, which are objects that allow programs to send and receive data. Streams can be connected to files, the keyboard, or other external devices.

Basic Input and Output in C++

In C++, I/O operations are accomplished using streams. A stream is an abstract object that provides an interface for reading and writing data. Streams can be connected to files, the keyboard, or other external devices.

Streams are classified as either input streams or output streams. An input stream is used for reading data from an external source, such as a file or the keyboard. An output stream is used for writing data to an external destination, such as a file or the screen.

C++ provides several predefined streams for performing I/O operations. The most commonly used streams are:

- cin: Standard input stream
- cout: Standard output stream
- cerr: Standard error stream
- clog: Standard log stream

The cin Stream

The cin stream is a predefined input stream that is connected to the keyboard. It can be used to read data from the keyboard and store it in a variable.

To use the cin stream, we must include the <iostream> header file in our program. This header file contains the declarations for the standard input/output functions.

Once we have included the header file, we can use the cin stream to read data from the keyboard. The syntax for using the cin stream is as follows:

```
cin >> variable_name;
```

The cin stream will read a value from the keyboard and store it in the specified variable. For example, to read an integer from the keyboard and store it in a variable named x, we could use the following code:

```
int x;
cin >> x;
```

The cout Stream

The cout stream is a predefined output stream that is connected to the screen. It can be used to write data to the screen.

To use the cout stream, we must include the <iostream> header file in our program. This header file contains the declarations for the standard input/output functions.

Once we have included the header file, we can use the cout stream to write data to the screen. The syntax for using the cout stream is as follows:

```
cout << expression;
```

The cout stream will evaluate the expression and print the result to the screen. For example, to print the value of the variable x to the screen, we could use the following code:

```
cout << x;
```

Formatting Output with the cout Stream

The cout stream can be used to format output. We can use the stream manipulators to control how the output is displayed. For example, we can use the setw() manipulator to set the width of the output field, and the setfill() manipulator to set the character used to pad the output field.

For example, to print the value of the variable x as a 5-digit number with leading zeros, we could use the following code:

```
cout << setw(5) << setfill('0') << x;
```

This code would print the value of x as a 5-digit number, with leading zeros if necessary.

The cerr and clog Streams

The cerr and clog streams are predefined output streams that are connected to the screen. They are used for printing error messages and logging information, respectively.

To use the cerr or clog streams, we must include the <iostream> header file in our program. This header file contains the declarations for the standard input/output functions.

Once we have included the header file, we can use the cerr or clog streams to write data to the screen. The syntax for using the cerr or clog streams is identical to that of the cout stream.

Conclusion

In this article, we have discussed the fundamentals of input and output in C++. We have seen how to use the cin, cout, cerr, and clog streams to read and write data. We have also seen how to use stream manipulators to format output.

Now that you have a basic understanding of input and output in C++, it's time to practice your new skills with the following coding exercises.

Exercises

Write a program that reads two integers from the keyboard and prints the sum of the numbers to the screen.

Write a program that reads five numbers from the keyboard and prints the average of the numbers to the screen.

Write a program that reads a number from the keyboard and prints it to the screen as a five-digit number with leading zeros.

Write a program that reads a string from the keyboard and prints it to the screen in uppercase.

Write a program that reads a number from the keyboard and prints it to the screen as a hexadecimal number.

Solutions

Write a program that reads two integers from the keyboard and prints the sum of the numbers to the screen.

```cpp
#include <iostream>
using namespace std;
int main()
{
    int x, y;
    cout << "Enter two integers: ";
    cin >> x >> y;
    cout << "The sum of the numbers is: " << x + y << endl;
    return 0;
}
```

Write a program that reads five numbers from the keyboard and prints the average of the numbers to the screen.

```cpp
#include <iostream>
```

```cpp
using namespace std;
int main()
{
  int x, y, z, a, b;
  cout << "Enter five numbers: ";
  cin >> x >> y >> z >> a >> b;
  cout << "The average of the numbers is: " << (x + y + z + a + b) / 5.0 << endl;
  return 0;
}
```

Write a program that reads a number from the keyboard and prints it to the screen as a five-digit number with leading zeros.

```cpp
#include <iostream>
#include <iomanip>
using namespace std;
int main()
{
  int x;
  cout << "Enter a number: ";
  cin >> x;
  cout << "The number as a five-digit number with leading zeros is: ";
  cout << setw(5) << setfill('0') << x << endl;
  return 0;
}
```

Write a program that reads a string from the keyboard and prints it to the screen in uppercase.

```cpp
#include <iostream>
#include <string>
#include <cctype>
using namespace std;
int main()
{
  string s;
  cout << "Enter a string: ";
  cin >> s;
  for (int i = 0; i < s.length(); i++)
  {
    s[i] = toupper(s[i]);
  }
  cout << "The string in uppercase is: " << s << endl;
  return 0;
}
```

Write a program that reads a number from the keyboard and prints it to the screen as

a hexadecimal number.

```cpp
#include <iostream>
#include <iomanip>
using namespace std;
int main()
{
   int x;
   cout << "Enter a number: ";
   cin >> x;
   cout << "The number in hexadecimal is: " << hex << x << endl;
   return 0;
}
```

DATA STRUCTURES

ARRAYS IN C++

Arrays are one of the most important data structures in C++ and are used to store collections of data. In this article, we will look at the basics of how to create and initialize arrays, access elements of arrays, modify elements of arrays, and use two-dimensional arrays. We will also look at some common array methods and provide several coding exercises to test your understanding of arrays in C++.

What is an Array?

An array is a data structure that stores a fixed-size sequential collection of elements of the same type. An array is used to store a collection of data, but it is often more useful to think of an array as a collection of variables of the same type. For example, if you want to store marks of 100 students, you can create an array for it. In C++, each element in an array is accessed by its index. The first element in an array has an index of 0, the second element has an index of 1, and so on.

Creating and Initializing Arrays

Arrays are declared in C++ using the following syntax:

```
type arrayName[size];
```

Here, type is the data type of the array elements and arrayName is the name of the array. The size parameter specifies the number of elements that can be stored in the array. The size of an array must be specified at the time it is declared. The following code declares an array of 10 integers:

```
int myArray[10];
```

Once the array is declared, we can initialize it with values. Arrays can be initialized using the same syntax as a normal variable:

```
int myArray[10] = {1, 2, 3, 4, 5, 6, 7, 8, 9, 10};
```

In this example, the first 10 elements of myArray are initialized to 1, 2, 3, 4, 5, 6, 7, 8, 9, and 10. Note that if the size of the array is not specified, the compiler will automatically determine the size of the array based on the number of elements in the initialization list.

Accessing Array Elements

Once we have an array initialized, we can access individual elements of the array using the array index. The index of an array is the position of an element in the array, starting from 0. For example, the first element of the array myArray is accessed using the index 0:

```
int firstElement = myArray[0]; // firstElement is equal to 1
```

We can also access elements of an array using a loop. The following code uses a for loop to print all elements of the array:

```
for(int i = 0; i < 10; i++) {
    std::cout << myArray[i] << std::endl;
}
```

Manipulating Array Elements

We can also modify elements of an array using the same syntax as accessing elements. The following code changes the value of the first element of the array:

```
myArray[0] = 100; // first element of myArray is now equal to 100
```

This will set the third element in the marks array to 100.

Dynamic Arrays in C++

Dynamic arrays in C++ are arrays that can change size at runtime. This is useful when you don't know the size of the array at compile time. The syntax for creating a dynamic array is similar to that of a regular array, except that instead of specifying the size of the array, you use a pointer:

```
type * arrayName;
```

For example, to create an array of integers that can change size at runtime, you would use the following code:

```
int * marks;
```

This will create a pointer to an array of integers. You can then use the new keyword to allocate memory for the array:

```
marks = new int[arraySize];
```

This will allocate memory for an array of the specified size. You can then use the [] operator to access and manipulate the elements of the array.

Common Array Methods

C++ offers several methods for manipulating arrays. The most commonly used methods are:

- push_back() – Adds an element to the end of an array.
- pop_back() – Removes the last element of an array.
- insert() – Inserts an element at a specified position in an array.
- erase() – Removes an element from a specified position in an array.
- sort() – Sorts the elements of an array in ascending or descending order.
-

Multidimensional Arrays in C++

Two-dimensional arrays are arrays that store multiple elements in a grid-like structure. To create a two-dimensional array, we use the following syntax:

```
type arrayName[size1][size2];
```

Here, size1 and size2 specify the number of rows and columns in the array, respectively.

We can also initialize a two-dimensional array with values:

```
int myArray[3][3] = {
  {1, 2, 3},
  {4, 5, 6},
  {7, 8, 9}
};
```

We can access elements of a two-dimensional array using two indices:

```
int element = myArray[0][2]; // element is equal to 3
```

Conclusion

In this article, we have looked at the basics of how to create and initialize arrays, access elements of arrays, modify elements of arrays, and use two-dimensional arrays in C++. We have also looked at some common array methods and provided several coding exercises to test your understanding of arrays in C++.

Exercises

Write a program to create an array of 10 integers and print its elements.

Write a program to create a dynamic array of 10 integers and print its elements.

Write a program to create a two-dimensional array of 10 rows and 5 columns and print its elements.

Write a program to create a two-dimensional array of 3 rows and 4 columns and print its elements in reverse order.

Write a program to create a two-dimensional array of 5 rows and 3 columns and print its elements in spiral order.

Solutions

Write a program to create an array of 10 integers and print its elements.

```
#include <iostream>
using namespace std;
int main()
{
  // Create an array of 10 elements
  int arr[10];
  // Store values in the array
  for (int i = 0; i < 10; i++)
    arr[i] = i;
  // Print the elements of the array
  for (int i = 0; i < 10; i++)
    cout << arr[i] << " ";
  return 0;
}
```

Write a program to create a dynamic array of 10 integers and print its elements.

```cpp
#include <iostream>
using namespace std;
int main()
{
  // Create a dynamic array of 10 elements
  int *arr = new int[10];
  // Store values in the array
  for (int i = 0; i < 10; i++)
    arr[i] = i;
  // Print the elements of the array
  for (int i = 0; i < 10; i++)
    cout << arr[i] << " ";
  // Deallocate the memory
  delete[] arr;
  return 0;
}
```

Write a program to create a two-dimensional array of 10 rows and 5 columns and print its elements.

```cpp
#include <iostream>
using namespace std;
int main()
{
  // Create a two-dimensional array of 10 rows and 5 columns
  int arr[10][5];
  // Store values in the array
  for (int i = 0; i < 10; i++)
  {
    for (int j = 0; j < 5; j++)
      arr[i][j] = (i + 1) * (j + 1);
  }
  // Print the elements of the array
  for (int i = 0; i < 10; i++)
  {
    for (int j = 0; j < 5; j++)
      cout << arr[i][j] << " ";
    cout << endl;
  }
  return 0;
}
```

Write a program to create a two-dimensional array of 3 rows and 4 columns and print its elements in reverse order.

```
#include <iostream>
using namespace std;
int main()
{
  // Create a two-dimensional array of 3 rows and 4 columns
  int arr[3][4];
  // Store values in the array
  for (int i = 0; i < 3; i++)
  {
    for (int j = 0; j < 4; j++)
      arr[i][j] = (i + 1) * (j + 1);
  }
  // Print the elements of the array in reverse order
  for (int i = 2; i >= 0; i--)
  {
    for (int j = 3; j >= 0; j--)
      cout << arr[i][j] << " ";
    cout << endl;
  }
  return 0;
}
```

Write a program to create a two-dimensional array of 5 rows and 3 columns and print its elements in spiral order.

```
#include <iostream>
using namespace std;
int main()
{
  // Create a two-dimensional array of 5 rows and 3 columns
  int arr[5][3];
  // Store values in the array
  for (int i = 0; i < 5; i++)
  {
    for (int j = 0; j < 3; j++)
      arr[i][j] = (i + 1) * (j + 1);
  }
  // Print the elements of the array in spiral order
  int rowStart = 0, rowEnd = 4, colStart = 0, colEnd = 2;
  while (rowStart <= rowEnd && colStart <= colEnd)
  {
    // Print first row from the remaining rows
    for (int i = colStart; i <= colEnd; i++)
      cout << arr[rowStart][i] << " ";
    rowStart++;
    // Print last column from the remaining columns
```

```cpp
        for (int i = rowStart; i <= rowEnd; i++)
            cout << arr[i][colEnd] << " ";
        colEnd--;
        // Print last row from the remaining rows
        if (rowStart <= rowEnd)
        {
            for (int i = colEnd; i >= colStart; i--)
                cout << arr[rowEnd][i] << " ";
            rowEnd--;
        }
        // Print first column from the remaining columns
        if (colStart <= colEnd)
        {
            for (int i = rowEnd; i >= rowStart; i--)
                cout << arr[i][colStart] << " ";
            colStart++;
        }
    }
    return 0;
}
```

STACKS AND QUEUES IN C++

Welcome to the world of data structures and algorithms with C++! This article will introduce you to the concepts of stacks and queues, and how you can use them to solve complex problems. We'll explore how to implement stacks and queues using arrays and classes, how to use the collections framework for stacks and queues, and the various applications of stacks and queues. By the end of this article, you should have a good understanding of how to use stacks and queues in C++.

What are Stacks and Queues?

Stacks and queues are two of the most basic data structures in computer science. They are linear data structures that store data in a certain order. A stack is a "last in, first out" (LIFO) data structure, meaning that the last item to be added to the stack will be the first item to be removed. A queue is a "first in, first out" (FIFO) data structure, meaning that the first item to be added to the queue will be the first item to be removed.

Implementing Stacks and Queues using Arrays

You can implement a stack or queue using an array. When implementing a stack using an array, you must keep track of the size of the stack. You can do this by using a variable to keep track of the number of elements in the stack. In addition, you must also keep track of the top element in the stack. To do this, you can use a variable to keep track of the index of the top element.

Here is an example of a simple stack implementation using an array in C++:

```cpp
#include <iostream>
using namespace std;
const int MAX_SIZE = 10;
class Stack {
private:
  int arr[MAX_SIZE];
  int top;
public:
  Stack() {
    top = -1;
  }
  void push(int data) {
    if (top == MAX_SIZE - 1) {
      cout << "Stack overflow" << endl;
      return;
```

```cpp
        }
        arr[++top] = data;
    }
    int pop() {
        if (top == -1) {
            cout << "Stack underflow" << endl;
            return -1;
        }
        return arr[top--];
    }
};
int main() {
    Stack s;
    s.push(1);
    s.push(2);
    s.push(3);
    cout << s.pop() << endl;
    cout << s.pop() << endl;
    cout << s.pop() << endl;
    return 0;
}
```

The code above creates a stack with a maximum size of 10. We create a Stack class with a private array arr, and a variable top to keep track of the top element of the stack. We also create two methods: push() and pop() to add and remove elements from the stack.

Similarly, you can implement a queue using an array. You must keep track of the size of the queue, as well as the front and rear elements. You can do this by keeping track of the indices of the front and rear elements. Here is an example of a simple queue implementation using an array in C++:

```cpp
#include <iostream>
using namespace std;
const int MAX_SIZE = 10;
class Queue {
private:
    int arr[MAX_SIZE];
    int front;
    int rear;
public:
    Queue() {
        front = 0;
        rear = MAX_SIZE - 1;
    }
    void enqueue(int data) {
        if (front == rear + 1) {
            cout << "Queue overflow" << endl;
```

```
      return;
    }
    rear = (rear + 1) % MAX_SIZE;
    arr[rear] = data;
  }
  int dequeue() {
    if (front == rear + 1) {
      cout << "Queue underflow" << endl;
      return -1;
    }
    int data = arr[front];
    front = (front + 1) % MAX_SIZE;
    return data;
  }
};
int main() {
  Queue q;
  q.enqueue(1);
  q.enqueue(2);
  q.enqueue(3);
  cout << q.dequeue() << endl;
  cout << q.dequeue() << endl;
  cout << q.dequeue() << endl;
  return 0;
}
```

The code above creates a queue with a maximum size of 10. We create a Queue class with a private array arr, and variables front and rear to keep track of the front and rear elements of the queue. We also create two methods: enqueue() and dequeue() to add and remove elements from the queue.

Implementing Stacks and Queues using Classes

You can also implement a stack or queue using a class. To do this, you must create a class that contains two methods: push() and pop() for stacks, or enqueue() and dequeue() for queues.

Here is an example of a simple stack implementation using a class in C++:

```
#include <iostream>
#include <list>
using namespace std;
class Stack {
private:
  list<int> data;
public:
  void push(int n) {
    data.push_back(n);
```

```cpp
    }
    int pop() {
        if (data.empty()) {
            cout << "Stack underflow" << endl;
            return -1;
        }
        int n = data.back();
        data.pop_back();
        return n;
    }
};
int main() {
    Stack s;
    s.push(1);
    s.push(2);
    s.push(3);
    cout << s.pop() << endl;
    cout << s.pop() << endl;
    cout << s.pop() << endl;
    return 0;
}
```

The code above creates a stack using a class. We create a Stack class with a private list data. We also create two methods: push() and pop() to add and remove elements from the stack.

Similarly, you can implement a queue using a class. Here is an example of a simple queue implementation using a class in C++:

```cpp
#include <iostream>
#include <list>
using namespace std;
class Queue {
private:
    list<int> data;
public:
    void enqueue(int n) {
        data.push_back(n);
    }
    int dequeue() {
        if (data.empty()) {
            cout << "Queue underflow" << endl;
            return -1;
        }
        int n = data.front();
        data.pop_front();
        return n;
```

```
    }
};
int main() {
    Queue q;
    q.enqueue(1);
    q.enqueue(2);
    q.enqueue(3);
    cout << q.dequeue() << endl;
    cout << q.dequeue() << endl;
    cout << q.dequeue() << endl;
    return 0;
}
```

The code above creates a queue using a class. We create a Queue class with a private list data. We also create two methods: enqueue() and dequeue() to add and remove elements from the queue.

Using the Collections Framework for Stacks and Queues

In C++, you can also use the collections framework to implement stacks and queues. The collections framework provides several classes for implementing stacks and queues, such as stack, queue, and priority_queue.

Here is an example of a simple stack implementation using the collections framework in C++:

```
#include <iostream>
#include <stack>
using namespace std;
int main() {
    stack<int> s;
    s.push(1);
    s.push(2);
    s.push(3);
    cout << s.top() << endl;
    s.pop();
    cout << s.top() << endl;
    s.pop();
    cout << s.top() << endl;
    s.pop();
    return 0;
}
```

The code above creates a stack using the collections framework. We create a stack of integers, and then use the push(), pop(), and top() methods to add, remove, and access the top element of the stack.

Similarly, you can use the collections framework to implement a queue. Here is an example of a simple queue implementation using the collections framework in C++:

```cpp
#include <iostream>
#include <queue>
using namespace std;
int main() {
  queue<int> q;
  q.push(1);
  q.push(2);
  q.push(3);
  cout << q.front() << endl;
  q.pop();
  cout << q.front() << endl;
  q.pop();
  cout << q.front() << endl;
  q.pop();
  return 0;
}
```

The code above creates a queue using the collections framework. We create a queue of integers, and then use the push(), pop(), and front() methods to add, remove, and access the front element of the queue.

Applications of Stacks and Queues

Stacks and queues are widely used in many different applications. Stacks are commonly used for keeping track of function calls in a program, for storing expression evaluation and syntax parsing, and for implementing backtracking algorithms. Queues are commonly used for scheduling tasks, for implementing breadth-first search algorithms, and for simulating communication channels.

Conclusion

In this article, we've explored how to use stacks and queues in C++. We've looked at how to implement stacks and queues using arrays and classes, and how to use the collections framework for stacks and queues. We've also discussed the various applications of stacks and queues. By the end of this article, you should have a good understanding of how to use stacks and queues in C++.

Exercises

Given the following stack: [1, 2, 3, 4], write a function that removes the top element from the stack.

Given the following queue: [1, 2, 3, 4], write a function that removes the front element from the queue.

Given the following stack: [1, 2, 3, 4], write a function that adds the element 5 to the top of the stack.

Given the following queue: [1, 2, 3, 4], write a function that adds the element 5 to the back of the queue.

Given an array of integers, write a function that uses a stack to reverse the order of the elements in the array.

Solutions

Given the following stack: [1, 2, 3, 4], write a function that removes the top element from the stack.

```cpp
#include <iostream>
#include <vector>
using namespace std;
void pop(vector<int>& s) {
  if (s.empty()) {
    cout << "Stack underflow" << endl;
    return;
  }
  s.pop_back();
}
int main() {
  vector<int> s = {1, 2, 3, 4};
  pop(s);
  return 0;
}
```

Given the following queue: [1, 2, 3, 4], write a function that removes the front element from the queue.

```cpp
#include <iostream>
#include <list>
using namespace std;
void dequeue(list<int>& q) {
  if (q.empty()) {
    cout << "Queue underflow" << endl;
    return;
  }
  q.pop_front();
}
int main() {
  list<int> q = {1, 2, 3, 4};
  dequeue(q);
  return 0;
}
```

Given the following stack: [1, 2, 3, 4], write a function that adds the element 5 to the top of the stack.

```cpp
#include <iostream>
#include <vector>
using namespace std;
void push(vector<int>& s, int data) {
  s.push_back(data);
}
int main() {
  vector<int> s = {1, 2, 3, 4};
  push(s, 5);
  return 0;
}
```

Given the following queue: [1, 2, 3, 4], write a function that adds the element 5 to the back of the queue.

```cpp
#include <iostream>
#include <list>
using namespace std;
void enqueue(list<int>& q, int data) {
  q.push_back(data);
}
int main() {
  list<int> q = {1, 2, 3, 4};
  enqueue(q, 5);
  return 0;
}
```

Given an array of integers, write a function that uses a stack to reverse the order of the elements in the array.

```cpp
#include <iostream>
#include <vector>
#include <stack>
using namespace std;
void reverse(int arr[], int n) {
  stack<int> s;
  for (int i = 0; i < n; i++) {
    s.push(arr[i]);
  }
  for (int i = 0; i < n; i++) {
    arr[i] = s.top();
    s.pop();
  }
}
int main() {
  int arr[] = {1, 2, 3, 4};
  int n = sizeof(arr) / sizeof(arr[0]);
```

```
    reverse(arr, n);
    return 0;
}
```

LINKED LISTS IN C++

Linked lists are a fundamental data structure and are used widely in programming. They are useful for storing and manipulating data, as well as creating complex algorithms. Linked lists are a type of linear data structure, in which each element is a separate object that contains both data (value) and a link (reference) to the next element in the sequence. In this article, we will discuss linked lists in C++, and we will learn how to implement them using classes, as well as how to traverse, insert and delete elements from linked lists. We will also cover singly linked lists, doubly linked lists, and skip lists.

Overview of Linked Lists

Linked lists are a type of data structure that is used to store and manipulate data in an organized manner. Each element in the list is a separate object, and each object contains both data and a link (reference) to the next element in the sequence. This type of data structure can be used to store and manipulate any type of data, such as numbers, strings, and objects.

Linked lists have several advantages over other types of data structures, such as arrays and trees. For example, they are more efficient in terms of both time and space. They can also grow and shrink dynamically, and can be easily modified by adding or deleting elements.

Implementing Linked Lists Using Classes

Linked lists can be implemented in C++ using classes. Each node in the list is defined as a separate object, and each object contains both data and a link (reference) to the next element in the sequence. The following code snippet shows how to create a simple linked list class in C++:

```cpp
class Node {
  public:
    int data;
    Node* next;
};
```

The Node class has two data members: data, which stores the value of the node, and next, which stores the address of the next node in the list.

Singly Linked Lists

A singly linked list is a type of linked list in which each node contains a link (reference) to the next node in the list, but not to the previous node. This type of linked list is often used in applications where data needs to be inserted or deleted from the beginning or end of the list.

The following code snippet shows how to create a singly linked list in C++:

```cpp
class SinglyLinkedList {
  private:
    Node* head;
    Node* tail;
  public:
    SinglyLinkedList() {
      head = nullptr;
      tail = nullptr;
    }
    void insertAtBeginning(int val) {
      Node* newNode = new Node;
      newNode->data = val;
      newNode->next = head;
      head = newNode;
    }
};
```

The SinglyLinkedList class has two data members: head, which stores a pointer to the first node in the list, and tail, which stores a pointer to the last node in the list. The insertAtBeginning() method inserts a new node at the beginning of the list.

Doubly Linked Lists

A doubly linked list is a type of linked list in which each node contains both a link (reference) to the next node in the list, and a link to the previous node in the list. This type of linked list is often used in applications where data needs to be inserted or deleted from any position in the list.

The following code snippet shows how to create a doubly linked list in C++:

```cpp
class DoublyLinkedList {
  private:
    Node* head;
    Node* tail;
  public:
    DoublyLinkedList() {
      head = nullptr;
      tail = nullptr;
    }
    void insertAtBeginning(int val) {
      Node* newNode = new Node;
      newNode->data = val;
      newNode->next = head;
      newNode->prev = nullptr;
      if (head != nullptr)
        head->prev = newNode;
```

```
      head = newNode;
   }
};
```

The DoublyLinkedList class has two data members: head, which stores a pointer to the first node in the list, and tail, which stores a pointer to the last node in the list. The insertAtBeginning() method inserts a new node at the beginning of the list.

Traversing Linked Lists

Traversing a linked list means visiting each node in the list, starting from the head node. This can be done in several ways, including iterative and recursive approaches. The following code snippet shows how to traverse a linked list in a recursive manner:

```cpp
void traverse(Node* head) {
  if (head == nullptr)
    return;
  std::cout << head->data << std::endl;
  traverse(head->next);
}
```

The traverse() method prints the data stored in each node of the list. It uses recursion to visit each node in the list.

Inserting and Deleting Elements From Linked Lists

Inserting and deleting elements from linked lists can be done in several ways. Inserting a new element can be done at the beginning, end, or any other position in the list. Likewise, deleting an element can be done from the beginning, end, or any other position in the list.

The following code snippet shows how to insert a new element at the beginning of a singly linked list:

```cpp
void insertAtBeginning(int val) {
  Node* newNode = new Node;
  newNode->data = val;
  newNode->next = head;
  head = newNode;
}
```

The insertAtBeginning() method inserts a new node at the beginning of the list. It sets the new node's next pointer to the current head node, and sets the head pointer to the new node.

The following code snippet shows how to delete an element from the end of a singly linked list:

```cpp
void deleteFromEnd() {
  if (head == nullptr)
    return;
  Node* current = head;
  Node* prev = nullptr;
```

```
while (current->next != nullptr) {
    prev = current;
    current = current->next;
}
if (prev != nullptr)
    prev->next = nullptr;
else
    head = nullptr;
delete current;
}
```

The deleteFromEnd() method deletes the last node in the list. It first finds the last node in the list, and then sets the next pointer of the previous node to nullptr. Finally, it deletes the last node.

Skip Lists

A skip list is a type of linked list in which each node has multiple levels of links that point to different elements in the list. This type of linked list is useful for searching and sorting data, as it allows for faster access to elements in the list.

The following code snippet shows how to create a skip list in C++:

```
class SkipList {
  private:
    Node* head;
    Node* tail;
  public:
    SkipList() {
      head = nullptr;
      tail = nullptr;
    }
    void insert(int val, int level) {
      Node* newNode = new Node;
      newNode->data = val;
      newNode->next = nullptr;
      newNode->level = level;
      if (head == nullptr) {
        head = newNode;
        tail = newNode;
      }
      else {
        tail->next = newNode;
        tail = newNode;
      }
    }
};
```

The SkipList class has two data members: head, which stores a pointer to the first node in the list, and tail, which stores a pointer to the last node in the list. The insert() method inserts a new node into the list. It sets the new node's level to the specified value, and then sets the next pointer of the previous node to the new node.

Conclusion

In this article, we have discussed linked lists in C++, and how to implement them using classes. We have also discussed singly linked lists, doubly linked lists, and skip lists. We have also seen how to traverse, insert and delete elements from linked lists.

Exercises

Write a function to delete an element from a singly linked list given the value of the element.

Write a function to search for an element in a doubly linked list given the value of the element.

Write a function to insert an element into a skip list at a given level.

Write a function to delete an element from a skip list given the value of the element.

Write a function to search for an element in a skip list given the value of the element.

Solutions

Write a function to delete an element from a singly linked list given the value of the element.

```cpp
void deleteElement(int val, Node* head) {
  Node* current = head;
  Node* prev = nullptr;
  while (current != nullptr && current->data != val) {
    prev = current;
    current = current->next;
  }
  if (current == nullptr)
    return;
  if (prev != nullptr)
    prev->next = current->next;
  else
    head = current->next;
  delete current;
}
```

Write a function to search for an element in a doubly linked list given the value of the element.

```cpp
Node* searchElement(int val, Node* head) {
  Node* current = head;
  while (current != nullptr && current->data != val)
```

```
    current = current->next;
  return current;
}
```

Write a function to insert an element into a skip list at a given level.

```
void insertAtLevel(int val, int level, Node* head) {
  Node* current = head;
  Node* prev = nullptr;
  while (current != nullptr && current->level > level) {
    prev = current;
    current = current->next;
  }
  if (current == nullptr || current->level < level)
    return;
  Node* newNode = new Node;
  newNode->data = val;
  newNode->level = level;
  newNode->next = current;
  if (prev != nullptr)
    prev->next = newNode;
  else
    head = newNode;
}
```

Write a function to delete an element from a skip list given the value of the element.

```
void deleteElement(int val, Node* head) {
  Node* current = head;
  Node* prev = nullptr;
  while (current != nullptr && current->data != val) {
    prev = current;
    current = current->next;
  }
  if (current == nullptr)
    return;
  if (prev != nullptr)
    prev->next = current->next;
  else
    head = current->next;
  delete current;
}
```

Write a function to search for an element in a skip list given the value of the element.

```
Node* searchElement(int val, Node* head) {
  Node* current = head;
  while (current != nullptr && current->data != val)
    current = current->next;
```

```
    return current;
}
```

HASH TABLES IN C++

Hash tables are a fundamental data structure used in computer science, and are essential in helping to define algorithms and solve problems. There are many different implementations of hash tables in different programming languages, but in this article, we will focus on how to implement hash tables in C++. We will discuss the overview of hash tables, how to implement them using arrays, different types of hash functions, strategies for handling collisions, and the various applications of hash tables.

Overview of Hash Tables

A hash table is a data structure which organizes data using a key-value pair. A key is a unique identifier of a data item, and the value is the data itself. The hash table allows us to quickly search for data items in a collection by using their key. Hash tables are also known as hash maps, dictionaries, or associative arrays.

In C++, a hash table can be implemented as a template class. The template class will contain two type parameters: the type of the key, and the type of the value. The class will also provide methods for inserting, retrieving, and removing elements from the hash table.

Implementing Hash Tables Using Arrays

To implement a hash table in C++, we will use an array data structure. The array will store the key-value pairs that make up the hash table. We will also use a hash function to determine the index of the array where the key-value pair should be stored.

```cpp
template<typename Key, typename Value>
class HashTable {
private:
    std::vector<std::pair<Key, Value>> table;
public:
    HashTable(int size);
    void insert(Key key, Value value);
    Value get(Key key);
    void remove(Key key);
};
```

The above template class provides a constructor to initialize the size of the array and three methods to insert, retrieve, and remove elements from the hash table.

Hash Functions

A hash function is a function that takes a key as an input and returns an index into the array as an output. The index is used to store the key-value pair in the array.

There are a few different types of hash functions. The most common type is a modulo hash function, which takes the modulus of the key with the size of the array. This type of hash function is simple to implement and is suitable for small datasets.

The following is an example of a modulo hash function implemented in C++:

```cpp
int hash(int key, int arraySize) {
    return key % arraySize;
}
```

The modulo hash function takes an integer key and the size of the array as parameters, and returns the index of the array where the key-value pair should be stored.

Collision Handling

A collision occurs when two different keys are hashed to the same index. When this happens, we must find a way to store both keys at the same index. There are a few different strategies for handling collisions. The most common strategies are chaining and open addressing.

Chaining is a strategy where a linked list is used to store multiple key-value pairs at the same index. This is a simple strategy to implement, but it can be inefficient if the hash table is too small or if the hash function is not evenly distributed.

Open addressing is a strategy where the hash table is searched for an empty slot to store the key-value pair. If an empty slot is found, the key-value pair is stored in the empty slot. If no empty slot is found, then the hash table is rehashed and the search is repeated.

The following is an example of a collision handling strategy implemented in C++ using open addressing:

```cpp
void handleCollision(Key key, Value value, int arraySize) {
    int index = hash(key, arraySize);
    while (table[index].first != NULL) {
        index = (index + 1) % arraySize;
    }
    table[index] = std::make_pair(key, value);
}
```

The above code takes a key and a value as parameters, and a hash table size. It first computes the index of the array where the key-value pair should be stored. If the slot is already occupied, it searches for the next empty slot. If an empty slot is found, the key-value pair is stored in the empty slot.

Applications of Hash Tables

Hash tables are a very versatile data structure and are used in many different applications. They are often used for data storage and retrieval, caching, and for efficiently solving problems.

Hash tables are often used for data storage and retrieval. They allow us to quickly insert, retrieve, and delete data items by using their key. This makes them an ideal data structure for databases and other storage systems.

Hash tables are also used for caching. Caching is a technique used to store data in a faster storage system in order to improve the performance of a program. Hash tables are often used to cache data because they allow us to quickly retrieve data items by their key.

Finally, hash tables are often used to efficiently solve problems. Many algorithms can be implemented using hash tables, such as searching, sorting, and graph traversal algorithms. Hash tables can also be used to solve problems such as finding the shortest path or the maximum value in a collection.

Conclusion

In this article, we discussed how to implement hash tables in C++. We discussed the overview of hash tables, how to implement them using arrays, different types of hash functions, strategies for handling collisions, and the various applications of hash tables. Hash tables are an essential data structure for computer science and are used in many different applications.

Exercises

Write a C++ program that implements a hash table using an array data structure. The hash table should contain integers as keys and strings as values.

Write a C++ program that implements a hash table using open addressing for collision handling. The hash table should contain strings as keys and integers as values.

Write a C++ program to find the maximum value in a hash table. The hash table should contain strings as keys and integers as values.

Write a C++ program to sort a hash table. The hash table should contain integers as keys and strings as values.

Write a C++ program to search for a key in a hash table. The hash table should contain strings as keys and integers as values.

Solutions

Write a C++ program that implements a hash table using an array data structure. The hash table should contain integers as keys and strings as values.

```cpp
#include <iostream>
#include <vector>
#include <utility>
template<typename Key, typename Value>
class HashTable {
private:
  std::vector<std::pair<Key, Value>> table;
public:
  HashTable(int size);
  void insert(Key key, Value value);
```

```
  Value get(Key key);
  void remove(Key key);
};
template<typename Key, typename Value>
HashTable<Key, Value>::HashTable(int size) {
  table.resize(size);
}
template<typename Key, typename Value>
void HashTable<Key, Value>::insert(Key key, Value value) {
  int index = key % table.size();
  table[index] = std::make_pair(key, value);
}
template<typename Key, typename Value>
Value HashTable<Key, Value>::get(Key key) {
  int index = key % table.size();
  return table[index].second;
}
template<typename Key, typename Value>
void HashTable<Key, Value>::remove(Key key) {
  int index = key % table.size();
  table[index] = std::make_pair(NULL, NULL);
}
int main() {
  HashTable<int, std::string> hashTable(10);
  hashTable.insert(1, "one");
  hashTable.insert(2, "two");
  hashTable.insert(3, "three");
  std::cout << hashTable.get(1) << std::endl;
  std::cout << hashTable.get(2) << std::endl;
  std::cout << hashTable.get(3) << std::endl;
  hashTable.remove(2);
  std::cout << hashTable.get(2) << std::endl;
  return 0;
}
```

Write a C++ program that implements a hash table using open addressing for collision handling. The hash table should contain strings as keys and integers as values.

```
#include <iostream>
#include <vector>
#include <utility>
#include <string>
template<typename Key, typename Value>
class HashTable {
private:
  std::vector<std::pair<Key, Value>> table;
```

```cpp
public:
  HashTable(int size);
  int hash(Key key);
  void insert(Key key, Value value);
  Value get(Key key);
  void remove(Key key);
};
template<typename Key, typename Value>
HashTable<Key, Value>::HashTable(int size) {
  table.resize(size);
}
template<typename Key, typename Value>
int HashTable<Key, Value>::hash(Key key) {
  int hash = 0;
  for (int i = 0; i < key.length(); i++) {
    hash += (int)key[i];
  }
  return hash % table.size();
}
template<typename Key, typename Value>
void HashTable<Key, Value>::insert(Key key, Value value) {
  int index = hash(key);
  while (table[index].first != NULL) {
    index = (index + 1) % table.size();
  }
  table[index] = std::make_pair(key, value);
}
template<typename Key, typename Value>
Value HashTable<Key, Value>::get(Key key) {
  int index = hash(key);
  return table[index].second;
}
template<typename Key, typename Value>
void HashTable<Key, Value>::remove(Key key) {
  int index = hash(key);
  table[index] = std::make_pair(NULL, NULL);
}
int main() {
  HashTable<std::string, int> hashTable(10);
  hashTable.insert("one", 1);
  hashTable.insert("two", 2);
  hashTable.insert("three", 3);
  std::cout << hashTable.get("one") << std::endl;
  std::cout << hashTable.get("two") << std::endl;
  std::cout << hashTable.get("three") << std::endl;
```

```
  hashTable.remove("two");
  std::cout << hashTable.get("two") << std::endl;
  return 0;
}
```

Write a C++ program to find the maximum value in a hash table. The hash table should contain strings as keys and integers as values.

```cpp
#include <iostream>
#include <vector>
#include <utility>
#include <string>
template<typename Key, typename Value>
class HashTable {
private:
  std::vector<std::pair<Key, Value>> table;
public:
  HashTable(int size);
  int hash(Key key);
  void insert(Key key, Value value);
  Value get(Key key);
  void remove(Key key);
};
template<typename Key, typename Value>
HashTable<Key, Value>::HashTable(int size) {
  table.resize(size);
}
template<typename Key, typename Value>
int HashTable<Key, Value>::hash(Key key) {
  int hash = 0;
  for (int i = 0; i < key.length(); i++) {
    hash += (int)key[i];
  }
  return hash % table.size();
}
template<typename Key, typename Value>
void HashTable<Key, Value>::insert(Key key, Value value) {
  int index = hash(key);
  while (table[index].first != NULL) {
    index = (index + 1) % table.size();
  }
  table[index] = std::make_pair(key, value);
}
template<typename Key, typename Value>
Value HashTable<Key, Value>::get(Key key) {
  int index = hash(key);
```

```cpp
  return table[index].second;
}
template<typename Key, typename Value>
void HashTable<Key, Value>::remove(Key key) {
  int index = hash(key);
  table[index] = std::make_pair(NULL, NULL);
}
int findMaxValue(HashTable<std::string, int> &hashTable) {
  int maxValue = 0;
  for (int i = 0; i < hashTable.table.size(); i++) {
    if (hashTable.table[i].second > maxValue) {
      maxValue = hashTable.table[i].second;
    }
  }
  return maxValue;
}
int main() {
  HashTable<std::string, int> hashTable(10);
  hashTable.insert("one", 1);
  hashTable.insert("two", 2);
  hashTable.insert("three", 3);
  std::cout << findMaxValue(hashTable) << std::endl;
  return 0;
}
```

Write a C++ program to sort a hash table. The hash table should contain integers as keys and strings as values.

```cpp
#include <iostream>
#include <vector>
#include <utility>
#include <algorithm>
template<typename Key, typename Value>
class HashTable {
private:
  std::vector<std::pair<Key, Value>> table;
public:
  HashTable(int size);
  void insert(Key key, Value value);
  Value get(Key key);
  void remove(Key key);
  void sort();
};
template<typename Key, typename Value>
HashTable<Key, Value>::HashTable(int size) {
  table.resize(size);
```

```
}
template<typename Key, typename Value>
void HashTable<Key, Value>::insert(Key key, Value value) {
  int index = key % table.size();
  table[index] = std::make_pair(key, value);
}
template<typename Key, typename Value>
Value HashTable<Key, Value>::get(Key key) {
  int index = key % table.size();
  return table[index].second;
}
template<typename Key, typename Value>
void HashTable<Key, Value>::remove(Key key) {
  int index = key % table.size();
  table[index] = std::make_pair(NULL, NULL);
}
template<typename Key, typename Value>
void HashTable<Key, Value>::sort() {
  std::sort(table.begin(), table.end());
}
int main() {
  HashTable<int, std::string> hashTable(10);
  hashTable.insert(1, "one");
  hashTable.insert(2, "two");
  hashTable.insert(3, "three");
  hashTable.sort();
  std::cout << hashTable.get(1) << std::endl;
  std::cout << hashTable.get(2) << std::endl;
  std::cout << hashTable.get(3) << std::endl;
  return 0;
}
```

Write a C++ program to search for a key in a hash table. The hash table should contain strings as keys and integers as values.

```
#include <iostream>
#include <vector>
#include <utility>
#include <string>
template<typename Key, typename Value>
class HashTable {
private:
  std::vector<std::pair<Key, Value>> table;
public:
  HashTable(int size);
  int hash(const Key &key);
```

```cpp
    void insert(const Key &key, const Value &value);
    Value search(const Key &key);
};
template<typename Key, typename Value>
HashTable<Key, Value>::HashTable(int size) {
    table.resize(size);
}
template<typename Key, typename Value>
int HashTable<Key, Value>::hash(const Key &key) {
    // Implement your own hash function here
    return 0;
}
template<typename Key, typename Value>
void HashTable<Key, Value>::insert(const Key &key, const Value &value) {
    int index = hash(key);
    table[index] = std::make_pair(key, value);
}
template<typename Key, typename Value>
Value HashTable<Key, Value>::search(const Key &key) {
    int index = hash(key);
    return table[index].second;
}
int main() {
    HashTable<std::string, int> table(10);
    table.insert("Hello", 5);
    table.insert("World", 10);
    std::cout << "Hello: " << table.search("Hello") << std::endl;
    std::cout << "World: " << table.search("World") << std::endl;
    return 0;
}
```

TREES IN C++

Data Structures and Algorithms with C++ is a course designed to help students understand the fundamentals of data structures and algorithms, such as stacks, queues, linked lists, and trees. In this article, we will focus on trees, exploring how to implement them in C++ and how to traverse, insert, and delete elements from them. By the end of this article, readers should have a full understanding of trees in C++, including how to traverse, insert, and delete elements from them.

Overview of Trees

A tree is a hierarchical data structure that consists of nodes that are connected by edges. Each node has a value and can have zero or more children. The topmost node is called the root of the tree. The nodes that are directly connected to the root are called the children of the root, and the nodes that are connected to the children are called the grandchildren of the root. This pattern continues down the tree.

The most common type of tree is a binary tree, which is a tree with a maximum of two children per node. A binary tree can be either a full binary tree, which means that every node has either zero or two children, or a complete binary tree, which means that all levels except the last are full and all nodes are as far left as possible in the last level.

Implementing Trees Using Classes

In order to create a binary tree in C++, we must first create a class that will represent the nodes in the tree. Each node will have a value and two pointers, one for the left child and one for the right child. The following is an example of how to create a Node class in C++:

```cpp
class Node
{
  public:
    int data;
    Node *left, *right;
    Node(int data)
    {
      this->data = data;
      left = right = NULL;
    }
};
```

Once we have created the Node class, we can create a Tree class that will create and manage the binary tree. The Tree class will have a root node and methods that can be used to traverse, insert, and delete elements from the tree. The following is an example of what a Tree class might look like in C++:

```cpp
class Tree
{
  public:
    Node *root;
    Tree()
    {
      root = NULL;
    }
    void insert(int data);
    void delete(int data);
    void traverse();
};
```

Traversing a Tree

In order to traverse a tree, we must visit each node and perform some action on it. There are three common ways to traverse a tree: pre-order, in-order, and post-order.

Pre-order traversal visits the root node first and then traverses the left subtree followed by the right subtree. We can implement pre-order traversal in C++ using the following code:

```cpp
void Tree::preOrder(Node *node)
{
  if (node == NULL)
    return;
  cout << node->data << " ";
  preOrder(node->left);
  preOrder(node->right);
}
```

In-order traversal visits the left subtree first, then the root node, and then the right subtree. We can implement in-order traversal in C++ using the following code:

```cpp
void Tree::inOrder(Node *node)
{
  if (node == NULL)
    return;
  inOrder(node->left);
  cout << node->data << " ";
  inOrder(node->right);
}
```

Post-order traversal visits the left subtree first, then the right subtree, and then the root node. We can implement post-order traversal in C++ using the following code:

```cpp
void Tree::postOrder(Node *node)
{
  if (node == NULL)
```

```
    return;
  postOrder(node->left);
  postOrder(node->right);
  cout << node->data << " ";
}
```

Inserting and Deleting Elements from a Tree

In order to insert an element into a tree, we first need to find the appropriate spot for the element. To do this, we start at the root node and compare the value of the node to the value of the element we want to insert. If the value of the node is greater than the value of the element, we move down the left subtree. If the value of the node is less than the value of the element, we move down the right subtree. We continue this process until we find a node that has no children, at which point we can insert the element.

We can implement this insertion algorithm in C++ using the following code:

```cpp
void Tree::insert(int data)
{
  Node *node = new Node(data);
  if (root == NULL)
    root = node;
  else
  {
    Node *temp = root;
    Node *parent;
    while (true)
    {
      parent = temp;
      if (data < temp->data)
      {
        temp = temp->left;
        if (temp == NULL)
        {
          parent->left = node;
          break;
        }
      }
      else
      {
        temp = temp->right;
        if (temp == NULL)
        {
          parent->right = node;
          break;
        }
      }
    }
```

```
      }
    }
}
```

In order to delete an element from a tree, we must first find the element in the tree. To do this, we start at the root node and compare the value of the node to the value of the element we want to delete. If the value of the node is greater than the value of the element, we move down the left subtree. If the value of the node is less than the value of the element, we move down the right subtree. Once we find the element, we must delete it while preserving the structure of the tree.

We can implement this deletion algorithm in C++ using the following code:

```cpp
void Tree::delete(int data)
{
  Node *temp;
  Node *parent;
  bool isLeft = true;
  // Find the node to delete
  temp = root;
  while (temp->data != data)
  {
    parent = temp;
    if (data < temp->data)
    {
      isLeft = true;
      temp = temp->left;
    }
    else
    {
      isLeft = false;
      temp = temp->right;
    }
    if (temp == NULL)
      return;
  }
  // Node to delete has no children
  if (temp->left == NULL && temp->right == NULL)
  {
    if (temp == root)
      root = NULL;
    else if (isLeft)
      parent->left = NULL;
    else
      parent->right = NULL;
  }
  // Node to delete has one child
```

```
else if (temp->right == NULL)
{
  if (temp == root)
    root = temp->left;
  else if (isLeft)
    parent->left = temp->left;
  else
    parent->right = temp->left;
}
else if (temp->left == NULL)
{
  if (temp == root)
    root = temp->right;
  else if (isLeft)
    parent->left = temp->right;
  else
    parent->right = temp->right;
}
// Node to delete has two children
else
{
  Node *successor = getSuccessor(temp);
  if (temp == root)
    root = successor;
  else if (isLeft)
    parent->left = successor;
  else
    parent->right = successor;
  successor->left = temp->left;
}
delete temp;
}
```

Conclusion

In this article, we covered trees in C++, including how to implement them using classes, how to traverse them, how to insert and delete elements from them, and how to delete elements from them. With this knowledge, you should have a good understanding of how to work with trees in C++ and be able to create your own binary trees.

Exercises

Write a function to calculate the height of a binary tree.

Write a function to count the number of leaves in a binary tree.

Write a function to count the number of nodes at a given level in a binary tree.

Write a function to find the maximum element in a binary tree.

Write a function to find the minimum element in a binary tree.

Solutions

Write a function to calculate the height of a binary tree.

```cpp
int Tree::height(Node *node)
{
  if (node == NULL)
    return 0;
  int leftHeight = height(node->left);
  int rightHeight = height(node->right);
  if (leftHeight > rightHeight)
    return leftHeight + 1;
  else
    return rightHeight + 1;
}
```

Write a function to count the number of leaves in a binary tree.

```cpp
int Tree::countLeaves(Node *node)
{
  if (node == NULL)
    return 0;
  if (node->left == NULL && node->right == NULL)
    return 1;
  else
    return countLeaves(node->left) + countLeaves(node->right);
}
```

Write a function to count the number of nodes at a given level in a binary tree.

```cpp
int Tree::countNodesAtLevel(Node *node, int level)
{
  if (node == NULL)
    return 0;
  if (level == 1)
    return 1;
  else
    return countNodesAtLevel(node->left, level-1) +
      countNodesAtLevel(node->right, level-1);
}
```

Write a function to find the maximum element in a binary tree.

```cpp
int Tree::maxElement(Node *node)
{
  if (node == NULL)
    return INT_MIN;
  int max = node->data;
```

```
  int leftMax = maxElement(node->left);
  int rightMax = maxElement(node->right);
  if (leftMax > max)
    max = leftMax;
  if (rightMax > max)
    max = rightMax;
  return max;
}
```

Write a function to find the minimum element in a binary tree.

```
int Tree::minElement(Node *node)
{
  if (node == NULL)
    return INT_MAX;
  int min = node->data;
  int leftMin = minElement(node->left);
  int rightMin = minElement(node->right);
  if (leftMin < min)
    min = leftMin;
  if (rightMin < min)
    min = rightMin;
  return min;
}
```

TYPES OF TREES

BINARY SEARCH TREES IN C++

Data Structures and Algorithms with C++ is a great course to learn about the various data structures and algorithms used in C++. In this article, we'll be focusing on Binary Search Trees (BSTs). We'll discuss how the tree structure works, as well as the time and space complexity associated with access, search, insertion, and deletion.

What Are Binary Search Trees?

Binary Search Trees are a type of tree data structure where each node has up to two children. The left child node always has a lower value than its parent node, while the right child node always has a higher value. The root node of the tree is the topmost node, and is usually the highest or lowest value node in the entire tree.

The structure of a Binary Search Tree makes it easy to quickly access, search, insert, and delete nodes. This makes it a great choice for applications where fast access and manipulation of data is needed.

Time Complexity in Binary Search Trees

Time complexity refers to the amount of time it takes to access, search, insert, or delete nodes in a tree. The time complexity of these operations in a Binary Search Tree depends on the size of the tree.

Access

Accessing a single node in a Binary Search Tree has a time complexity of O(log n). This means that the time it takes to access a node increases as the size of the tree increases.

Search

Searching for a node in a Binary Search Tree has a time complexity of O(log n). This means that the time it takes to search for a node increases as the size of the tree increases.

Insertion

Inserting a new node into a Binary Search Tree has an average time complexity of O(log n). This means that the time it takes to insert a new node increases as the size of the tree increases.

Deletion

Deleting a node from a Binary Search Tree has an average time complexity of O(log n). This means that the time it takes to delete a node increases as the size of the tree increases.

Space Complexity in Binary Search Trees

Space complexity refers to the amount of memory needed to store a tree. The space complexity of a Binary Search Tree is O(n), meaning that the memory needed to store a tree increases as the size of the tree increases.

C++ Code for Binary Search Trees

Now that we have an understanding of the time and space complexity of Binary Search Trees, let's look at some code in C++ to see how they work.

Creating a Binary Search Tree

The first step in creating a Binary Search Tree is to create a node class. This class will contain the data for each node in the tree.

```cpp
// Node class for Binary Search Tree
class Node {
 public:
   int data;
   Node *left;
   Node *right;
};
```

Now that we have a node class, we can create a Binary Search Tree class. This class will contain the root node, as well as functions to insert and delete nodes.

```cpp
// Binary Search Tree class
class BST {
 public:
   Node *root;
   // Functions to insert and delete nodes
   void insert(int data);
   void delete(int data);
};
```

Inserting a Node

To insert a new node into a Binary Search Tree, we must first find the right place for it. We do this by starting at the root node and comparing the data of the new node to the data of the current node. If the data is lower, we move to the left child node. If the data is higher, we move to the right child node. We continue this process until we reach a node with no children, at which point we can insert the new node.

```cpp
// Function to insert a new node into a Binary Search Tree
void BST::insert(int data) {
 Node *node = new Node();
 node->data = data;
 node->left = NULL;
 node->right = NULL;
 if (root == NULL) {
```

```cpp
  root = node;
} else {
 Node *currentNode = root;
 Node *parentNode;
 while (true) {
  parentNode = currentNode;
  if (data < currentNode->data) {
   currentNode = currentNode->left;
   if (currentNode == NULL) {
    parentNode->left = node;
    break;
   }
  }
  else {
   currentNode = currentNode->right;
   if (currentNode == NULL) {
    parentNode->right = node;
    break;
   }
  }
 }
}
}
```

Deleting a Node

To delete a node from a Binary Search Tree, we must first find the node. We do this by starting at the root node and comparing the data of the node to be deleted to the data of the current node. If the data is lower, we move to the left child node. If the data is higher, we move to the right child node. We continue this process until we reach the node to be deleted.

Once we have found the node to be deleted, we have three different scenarios:

- The node has no children. In this case, we can simply delete the node.
- The node has one child. In this case, we can delete the node and replace it with its child.
- The node has two children. In this case, we must find the minimum value in the right subtree and replace the node to be deleted with this value.

```cpp
// Function to delete a node from a Binary Search Tree
void BST::delete(int data) {
 if (root == NULL)
  return;
 Node *currentNode = root;
 Node *parentNode = NULL;
 // Find the node to be deleted
 while (currentNode->data != data) {
```

```
 parentNode = currentNode;
 if (data < currentNode->data) {
  currentNode = currentNode->left;
 }
 else {
  currentNode = currentNode->right;
 }
 // Node to be deleted was not found
 if (currentNode == NULL)
  return;
}
// Node has no children
if (currentNode->left == NULL && currentNode->right == NULL) {
 if (parentNode == NULL) {
  root = NULL;
 }
 else {
  if (parentNode->left == currentNode)
   parentNode->left = NULL;
  else
   parentNode->right = NULL;
 }
}
// Node has one child
else if (currentNode->right == NULL) {
 if (parentNode == NULL) {
  root = currentNode->left;
 }
 else {
  if (parentNode->left == currentNode)
   parentNode->left = currentNode->left;
  else
   parentNode->right = currentNode->left;
 }
}
else if (currentNode->left == NULL) {
 if (parentNode == NULL) {
  root = currentNode->right;
 }
 else {
  if (parentNode->left == currentNode)
   parentNode->left = currentNode->right;
  else
   parentNode->right = currentNode->right;
 }
```

```
}
// Node has two children
else {
 Node *successor = getSuccessor(currentNode);
 if (parentNode == NULL) {
  root = successor;
 }
 else {
  if (parentNode->left == currentNode)
   parentNode->left = successor;
  else
   parentNode->right = successor;
 }
 successor->left = currentNode->left;
}
}
```

Conclusion

In conclusion, Binary Search Trees are a type of tree data structure where each node has up to two children. The structure of a Binary Search Tree makes it easy to quickly access, search, insert, and delete nodes. The time complexity for these operations is O(log n), while the space complexity is O(n).

Exercises

Write a function to traverse a Binary Search Tree in-order.

Write a function to find the minimum value in a Binary Search Tree.

Write a function to find the maximum value in a Binary Search Tree.

Write a function to check if a value exists in a Binary Search Tree.

Write a function to calculate the height of a Binary Search Tree.

Solutions

Write a function to traverse a Binary Search Tree in-order.

```
// Function to traverse a Binary Search Tree in-order
void inOrder(Node* root) {
 if (root != NULL) {
  inOrder(root->left);
  cout << root->data << " ";
  inOrder(root->right);
 }
}
```

Write a function to find the minimum value in a Binary Search Tree.

```
// Function to find the minimum value in a Binary Search Tree
```

```
int minValue(Node* root) {
 Node* current = root;
 if (current == NULL)
  return -1;
 while (current->left != NULL)
  current = current->left;
 return current->data;
}
```

Write a function to find the maximum value in a Binary Search Tree.

```
// Function to find the maximum value in a Binary Search Tree
int maxValue(Node* root) {
 Node* current = root;
 if (current == NULL)
  return -1;
 while (current->right != NULL)
  current = current->right;
 return current->data;
}
```

Write a function to check if a value exists in a Binary Search Tree.

```
// Function to check if a value exists in a Binary Search Tree
bool search(Node* root, int data) {
 if (root == NULL)
  return false;
 if (root->data == data)
  return true;
 if (data < root->data)
  return search(root->left, data);
 else
  return search(root->right, data);
}
```

Write a function to calculate the height of a Binary Search Tree.

```
// Function to calculate the height of a Binary Search Tree
int height(Node* root) {
 if (root == NULL)
  return -1;
 int leftHeight = height(root->left);
 int rightHeight = height(root->right);
 return 1 + max(leftHeight, rightHeight);
}
```

CARTESIAN TREES IN C++

The Cartesian tree, also known as a treap, is a data structure that combines the properties of a binary search tree and a heap. It is a self-balancing tree that can be used to efficiently access, search, insert and delete data. In this article, we will discuss the structure of a Cartesian tree, its time complexity for the four operations mentioned above, its space complexity, and a few coding exercises for readers to test their understanding of the concepts.

What is a Cartesian Tree?

A Cartesian tree is a binary tree that satisfies two properties: a heap property and a search tree property. The heap property requires that each node in the tree must have a key, or value, and that the parent node's key must be greater than or equal to the key of its children. The search tree property requires that the left subtree of any node must contain keys that are less than or equal to the key of the node, and the right subtree must contain keys that are greater than or equal to the node's key.

The Cartesian tree structure is advantageous because it provides the same level of performance as a heap, while also providing the same searching capabilities as a binary search tree. This makes it an ideal data structure for applications that need to perform both operations.

Time Complexity

The time complexity for accessing, searching, inserting and deleting data in a Cartesian tree can be broken down into average and worst-case scenarios.

Accessing a node in a Cartesian tree has an average time complexity of O(log n), where n is the number of nodes in the tree. In the worst case, the time complexity is O(n).

Searching for a node in a Cartesian tree has an average time complexity of O(log n) and a worst-case time complexity of O(n).

Inserting a node into a Cartesian tree has an average time complexity of O(log n) and a worst-case time complexity of O(n).

Deleting a node from a Cartesian tree has an average time complexity of O(log n) and a worst-case time complexity of O(n).

Space Complexity

The space complexity of a Cartesian tree is O(n), where n is the number of nodes in the tree. This means that the tree will use up a constant amount of space in memory, regardless of the number of nodes.

C++ Code

Below is an example of a C++ program that implements a Cartesian tree. The program includes a Node class, which is used to represent a node in the tree. It also includes functions for searching, inserting, and deleting nodes from the tree.

```cpp
#include <iostream>
class Node {
public:
  int data;
  Node* left;
  Node* right;
  Node(int data);
};
Node::Node(int data) {
  this->data = data;
  left = NULL;
  right = NULL;
}
class CartesianTree {
private:
  Node* root;
public:
  CartesianTree();
  Node* search(int data);
  Node* insert(int data);
  void deleteNode(int data);
};
CartesianTree::CartesianTree() {
  root = NULL;
}
Node* CartesianTree::search(int data) {
  Node* current = root;
  while (current != NULL) {
    if (current->data == data) {
      return current;
    } else if (current->data > data) {
      current = current->left;
    } else {
      current = current->right;
    }
  }
  return NULL;
}
Node* CartesianTree::insert(int data) {
  Node* newNode = new Node(data);
```

```cpp
  if (root == NULL) {
    root = newNode;
    return root;
  }
  Node* current = root;
  Node* parent = NULL;
  while (current != NULL) {
    parent = current;
    if (current->data > data) {
      current = current->left;
    } else {
      current = current->right;
    }
  }
  if (parent->data > data) {
    parent->left = newNode;
  } else {
    parent->right = newNode;
  }
  return newNode;
}
void CartesianTree::deleteNode(int data) {
  Node* current = root;
  Node* parent = NULL;
  Node* nodeToDelete = NULL;
  while (current != NULL) {
    if (current->data == data) {
      nodeToDelete = current;
      break;
    } else if (current->data > data) {
      parent = current;
      current = current->left;
    } else {
      parent = current;
      current = current->right;
    }
  }
  if (nodeToDelete == NULL) {
    return;
  }
  if (nodeToDelete->left == NULL && nodeToDelete->right == NULL) {
    if (nodeToDelete == root) {
      root = NULL;
    } else {
      if (parent->left == nodeToDelete) {
```

```
        parent->left = NULL;
      } else {
        parent->right = NULL;
      }
    }
  } else if (nodeToDelete->left != NULL && nodeToDelete->right != NULL) {
    Node* maxNode = nodeToDelete->left;
    Node* maxNodeParent = nodeToDelete;
    while (maxNode->right != NULL) {
      maxNodeParent = maxNode;
      maxNode = maxNode->right;
    }
    nodeToDelete->data = maxNode->data;
    if (maxNodeParent->left == maxNode) {
      maxNodeParent->left = maxNode->left;
    } else {
      maxNodeParent->right = maxNode->left;
    }
  } else {
    Node* childNode;
    if (nodeToDelete->left != NULL) {
      childNode = nodeToDelete->left;
    } else {
      childNode = nodeToDelete->right;
    }
    if (nodeToDelete == root) {
      root = childNode;
    } else {
      if (parent->left == nodeToDelete) {
        parent->left = childNode;
      } else {
        parent->right = childNode;
      }
    }
  }
  delete nodeToDelete;
}
int main() {
  CartesianTree tree;
  tree.insert(10);
  tree.insert(20);
  tree.insert(5);
  tree.insert(15);
  tree.insert(25);
  tree.deleteNode(20);
```

```
  Node* node = tree.search(15);
  std::cout << node->data << std::endl;
  return 0;
}
```

Conclusion

The Cartesian tree is a self-balancing binary tree that combines the properties of a heap and a binary search tree. It provides efficient access, search, insertion and deletion operations, with an average time complexity of O(log n) and a worst-case time complexity of O(n). It also has a space complexity of O(n).

Exercises

Write a C++ program that implements a Cartesian tree and includes a function to traverse the tree in pre-order.

Write a C++ program that implements a Cartesian tree and includes a function to calculate the height of the tree.

Write a C++ program that implements a Cartesian tree and includes a function to delete all nodes from the tree.

Write a C++ program that implements a Cartesian tree and includes a function to check if the tree is a valid Cartesian tree.

Write a C++ program that implements a Cartesian tree and includes a function to find the minimum value in the tree.

Solutions

Write a C++ program that implements a Cartesian tree and includes a function to traverse the tree in pre-order.

```cpp
#include <iostream>
class Node {
public:
  int data;
  Node* left;
  Node* right;
  Node(int data);
};
Node::Node(int data) {
  this->data = data;
  left = NULL;
  right = NULL;
}
class CartesianTree {
private:
  Node* root;
```

YASIN CAKAL

```cpp
public:
  CartesianTree();
  void traversePreOrder(Node* node);
};
CartesianTree::CartesianTree() {
  root = NULL;
}
void CartesianTree::traversePreOrder(Node* node) {
  if (node == NULL) {
    return;
  }
  std::cout << node->data << std::endl;
  traversePreOrder(node->left);
  traversePreOrder(node->right);
}
int main() {
  CartesianTree tree;
  tree.insert(10);
  tree.insert(20);
  tree.insert(5);
  tree.insert(15);
  tree.insert(25);
  tree.deleteNode(20);
  Node* node = tree.search(15);
  tree.traversePreOrder(node);
  return 0;
}
```

Write a C++ program that implements a Cartesian tree and includes a function to calculate the height of the tree.

```cpp
#include <iostream>
class Node {
public:
  int data;
  Node* left;
  Node* right;
  Node(int data);
};
Node::Node(int data) {
  this->data = data;
  left = NULL;
  right = NULL;
}
class CartesianTree {
private:
```

88

```cpp
  Node* root;
public:
  CartesianTree();
  int getHeight(Node* node);
};
CartesianTree::CartesianTree() {
  root = NULL;
}
int CartesianTree::getHeight(Node* node) {
  if (node == NULL) {
    return 0;
  }
  int leftHeight = getHeight(node->left);
  int rightHeight = getHeight(node->right);
  return std::max(leftHeight, rightHeight) + 1;
}
int main() {
  CartesianTree tree;
  tree.insert(10);
  tree.insert(20);
  tree.insert(5);
  tree.insert(15);
  tree.insert(25);
  tree.deleteNode(20);
  Node* node = tree.search(15);
  int height = tree.getHeight(node);
  std::cout << height << std::endl;
  return 0;
}
```

Write a C++ program that implements a Cartesian tree and includes a function to delete all nodes from the tree.

```cpp
#include <iostream>
class Node {
public:
  int data;
  Node* left;
  Node* right;
  Node(int data);
};
Node::Node(int data) {
  this->data = data;
  left = NULL;
  right = NULL;
}
```

```cpp
class CartesianTree {
private:
  Node* root;
public:
  CartesianTree();
  void deleteTree(Node* node);
};
CartesianTree::CartesianTree() {
  root = NULL;
}
void CartesianTree::deleteTree(Node* node) {
  if (node == NULL) {
    return;
  }
  deleteTree(node->left);
  deleteTree(node->right);
  delete node;
}
int main() {
  CartesianTree tree;
  tree.insert(10);
  tree.insert(20);
  tree.insert(5);
  tree.insert(15);
  tree.insert(25);
  tree.deleteNode(20);
  Node* node = tree.search(15);
  tree.deleteTree(node);
  return 0;
}
```

Write a C++ program that implements a Cartesian tree and includes a function to check if the tree is a valid Cartesian tree.

```cpp
#include <iostream>
class Node {
public:
  int data;
  Node* left;
  Node* right;
  Node(int data);
};
Node::Node(int data) {
  this->data = data;
  left = NULL;
  right = NULL;
```

```cpp
}
class CartesianTree {
private:
  Node* root;
public:
  CartesianTree();
  bool isValid(Node* node);
};
CartesianTree::CartesianTree() {
  root = NULL;
}
bool CartesianTree::isValid(Node* node) {
  if (node == NULL) {
    return true;
  }
  if (node->left != NULL && node->data < node->left->data) {
    return false;
  }
  if (node->right != NULL && node->data > node->right->data) {
    return false;
  }
  return isValid(node->left) && isValid(node->right);
}
int main() {
  CartesianTree tree;
  tree.insert(10);
  tree.insert(20);
  tree.insert(5);
  tree.insert(15);
  tree.insert(25);
  tree.deleteNode(20);
  Node* node = tree.search(15);
  bool isValid = tree.isValid(node);
  std::cout << isValid << std::endl;
  return 0;
}
```

Write a C++ program that implements a Cartesian tree and includes a function to find the minimum value in the tree.

```cpp
#include <iostream>
class Node {
public:
  int data;
  Node* left;
  Node* right;
```

```cpp
  Node(int data);
};
Node::Node(int data) {
  this->data = data;
  left = NULL;
  right = NULL;
}
class CartesianTree {
private:
  Node* root;
public:
  CartesianTree();
  int findMin(Node* node);
};
CartesianTree::CartesianTree() {
  root = NULL;
}
int CartesianTree::findMin(Node* node) {
  if (node == NULL) {
    return -1;
  }
  int minValue = node->data;
  int leftMin = findMin(node->left);
  int rightMin = findMin(node->right);
  if (leftMin != -1 && leftMin < minValue) {
    minValue = leftMin;
  }
  if (rightMin != -1 && rightMin < minValue) {
    minValue = rightMin;
  }
  return minValue;
}
int main() {
  CartesianTree tree;
  tree.insert(10);
  tree.insert(20);
  tree.insert(5);
  tree.insert(15);
  tree.insert(25);
  tree.deleteNode(20);
  Node* node = tree.search(15);
  int minValue = tree.findMin(node);
  std::cout << minValue << std::endl;
  return 0;
}
```

B-TREES IN C++

B-Trees are a type of self-balancing tree data structure that can store large amounts of data and allow for efficient retrieval, insertion, and deletion. B-Trees are particularly useful for situations where access times for large amounts of data need to be kept to a minimum. In this article, we will explore how B-Trees work and the time and space complexities associated with their operations. We will also learn how to implement a B-Tree in C++ and provide some coding exercises to test the reader's understanding of the material.

What is a B-Tree?

A B-Tree is a self-balancing tree data structure that offers efficient retrieval, insertion, and deletion operations. It is characterized by the following properties:

1. All internal nodes have two or more children.
2. All leaf nodes are at the same depth.
3. All keys in the nodes are arranged in increasing order.

The root node of a B-Tree can have any number of children, while each other node must have a minimum number of children (typically two). This minimum number of children is known as the order of the B-Tree. The order of a B-Tree is usually denoted by the letter "m".

The number of keys that a node can contain is equal to the order of the tree minus one. For example, if the order of a B-Tree is 3, then each node can contain up to two keys. This is known as the node's capacity.

Time Complexity

When it comes to time complexity, B-Trees offer the following performance metrics:

- Access: O(log n)
- Search: O(log n)
- Insertion: O(log n)
- Deletion: O(log n)

These metrics are based on the average case, but in the worst case, the time complexity for all operations is O(n).

Space Complexity

The space complexity of a B-Tree is equal to O(n), which is the worst-case scenario. This means that the B-Tree will take up more space than a regular binary tree.

Implementing a B-Tree in C++

Now that we have a basic understanding of how a B-Tree works, let's look at how to implement one in C++. The most important aspect of a B-Tree is the node structure. Each node contains a list of keys and a list of pointers to other nodes.

```cpp
struct Node {
  int* keys; // Array of keys
  Node** pointers; // Array of pointers to other nodes
};
```

We can then create a B-Tree class that will contain the root node and any other necessary information.

```cpp
class B_Tree {
private:
  Node* root;
  int order; // The order of the B-Tree
public:
  B_Tree(int order);
  void insert(int key);
  void remove(int key);
  Node* search(int key);
};
```

The constructor for the B-Tree class will take the order of the B-Tree as a parameter and initialize the root node to null.

```cpp
B_Tree::B_Tree(int order) {
  this->order = order;
  this->root = nullptr;
}
```

The insert() method is used to add a new key to the B-Tree. We can implement this method by first checking if the root node is null. If it is, then we can create a new root node with the given key. Otherwise, we need to traverse the tree to find the appropriate place for the new key.

```cpp
void B_Tree::insert(int key) {
  // If the root is null, create a new root node
  if (this->root == nullptr) {
    this->root = new Node();
    this->root->keys = new int[this->order - 1];
    this->root->pointers = new Node*[this->order];
    this->root->keys[0] = key;
    this->root->pointers[0] = nullptr;
  }
  // Otherwise, traverse the tree to find the appropriate place for the new key
  else {
    // Traverse the tree
```

```
    }
}
```

The remove() method is used to remove a key from the B-Tree. This can be done by first searching for the key and then deleting it from the node.

```
void B_Tree::remove(int key) {
  // Search for the key in the tree
  Node* node = search(key);
  if (node == nullptr) {
    return;
  }
  // Delete the key from the node
  // Code omitted for brevity
}
```

The search() method is used to search for a key in the B-Tree. This can be done by traversing the tree and comparing the keys in each node to the searched key.

```
Node* B_Tree::search(int key) {
  // If the root is null, return null
  if (this->root == nullptr) {
    return nullptr;
  }
  // Otherwise, traverse the tree
  else {
    // Traverse the tree
  }
}
```

Conclusion

In this article, we have explored the B-Tree data structure and how to implement it in C++. We have learned about the time and space complexities associated with its operations and how to use them to efficiently store and retrieve large amounts of data. With this knowledge, we can now start using B-Trees in our data structures and algorithms with C++.

Exercises

Create a function that takes in a B-Tree and prints out all its elements in order.

Create a function that takes in a B-Tree and a key, and returns the node containing the key.

Create a function that takes in a B-Tree and a key, and returns the node containing the key or its closest ancestor.

Create a function that takes in a B-Tree and two keys, and returns the node containing the lowest common ancestor of the two keys.

Create a function that takes in a B-Tree and a key, and returns the node containing the predecessor of the key.

Solutions

Create a function that takes in a B-Tree and prints out all its elements in order.

```
void printTree(B_Tree* tree) {
  // If the root is null, return
  if (tree->root == nullptr) {
    return;
  }
  // Otherwise, traverse the tree and print out the elements
  else {
    traverseTree(tree->root);
  }
}
void traverseTree(Node* node) {
  int numKeys = node->order - 1;
  // Print out the keys
  for (int i = 0; i < numKeys; i++) {
    cout << node->keys[i] << " ";
  }
  // Traverse the subtrees
  for (int i = 0; i < node->order; i++) {
    if (node->pointers[i] != nullptr) {
      traverseTree(node->pointers[i]);
    }
  }
}
```

Create a function that takes in a B-Tree and a key, and returns the node containing the key.

```
Node* searchTree(B_Tree* tree, int key) {
  // If the root is null, return null
  if (tree->root == nullptr) {
    return nullptr;
  }
  // Otherwise, traverse the tree
  else {
    return traverseTree(tree->root, key);
  }
}
Node* traverseTree(Node* node, int key) {
  int numKeys = node->order - 1;
  // Check if the key is in the current node
  for (int i = 0; i < numKeys; i++) {
```

```cpp
    if (node->keys[i] == key) {
      return node;
    }
  }
  // Traverse the subtrees
  for (int i = 0; i < node->order; i++) {
    if (node->pointers[i] != nullptr) {
      Node* result = traverseTree(node->pointers[i], key);
      if (result != nullptr) {
        return result;
      }
    }
  }
  // Return null if the key is not found
  return nullptr;
}
```

Create a function that takes in a B-Tree and a key, and returns the node containing the key or its closest ancestor.

```cpp
Node* searchTree(B_Tree* tree, int key) {
  // If the root is null, return null
  if (tree->root == nullptr) {
    return nullptr;
  }
  // Otherwise, traverse the tree
  else {
    return traverseTree(tree->root, key);
  }
}
Node* traverseTree(Node* node, int key) {
  int numKeys = node->order - 1;
  Node* closestAncestor = node;
  // Check if the key is in the current node
  for (int i = 0; i < numKeys; i++) {
    if (node->keys[i] == key) {
      return node;
    }
    else if (node->keys[i] > key) {
      closestAncestor = node;
      break;
    }
  }
  // Traverse the subtrees
  for (int i = 0; i < node->order; i++) {
    if (node->pointers[i] != nullptr) {
```

```
      Node* result = traverseTree(node->pointers[i], key);
      if (result != nullptr) {
        return result;
      }
    }
  }
}
  // Return the closest ancestor if the key is not found
  return closestAncestor;
}
```

Create a function that takes in a B-Tree and two keys, and returns the node containing the lowest common ancestor of the two keys.

```
Node* commonAncestor(B_Tree* tree, int key1, int key2) {
  // If the root is null, return null
  if (tree->root == nullptr) {
    return nullptr;
  }
  // Otherwise, traverse the tree
  else {
    return traverseTree(tree->root, key1, key2);
  }
}
Node* traverseTree(Node* node, int key1, int key2) {
  int numKeys = node->order - 1;
  Node* ancestor = nullptr;
  // Check if the keys are in the current node
  for (int i = 0; i < numKeys; i++) {
    if (node->keys[i] == key1 || node->keys[i] == key2) {
      if (ancestor == nullptr) {
        ancestor = node;
      }
      else {
        return ancestor;
      }
    }
  }
  // Traverse the subtrees
  for (int i = 0; i < node->order; i++) {
    if (node->pointers[i] != nullptr) {
      Node* result = traverseTree(node->pointers[i], key1, key2);
      if (result != nullptr) {
        return result;
      }
    }
  }
}
```

```
  // Return the ancestor if it was found
  return ancestor;
}
```

Create a function that takes in a B-Tree and a key, and returns the node containing the predecessor of the key.

```cpp
Node* predecessor(B_Tree* tree, int key) {
  // If the root is null, return null
  if (tree->root == nullptr) {
    return nullptr;
  }
  // Otherwise, traverse the tree
  else {
    return traverseTree(tree->root, key);
  }
}
Node* traverseTree(Node* node, int key) {
  int numKeys = node->order - 1;
  Node* predecessor = nullptr;
  // Check if the key is in the current node
  for (int i = 0; i < numKeys; i++) {
    if (node->keys[i] == key) {
      // Check if there is a predecessor in the current node
      if (i > 0) {
        return node->pointers[i - 1];
      }
      // Otherwise, return the predecessor from the parent
      else {
        return predecessor;
      }
    }
    else if (node->keys[i] > key) {
      predecessor = node;
      break;
    }
  }
  // Traverse the subtrees
  for (int i = 0; i < node->order; i++) {
    if (node->pointers[i] != nullptr) {
      Node* result = traverseTree(node->pointers[i], key);
      if (result != nullptr) {
        return result;
      }
    }
  }
}
```

```
    // Return null if the key is not found
    return nullptr;
}
```

RED-BLACK TREES IN C++

Red-Black Trees are one of the most widely used data structures in computer science. These trees are a type of self-balancing binary search tree, which means the tree structure is able to maintain a balance between the left and right subtrees. This ensures that operations on the tree, such as insertion, search, and deletion, are performed quickly. Red-Black Trees are used in many applications, from databases to operating systems, and have become an essential tool for any programmer. In this article, we will discuss the fundamentals of Red-Black Trees in C++, including the tree structure, time complexity for operations, and space complexity.

Tree Structure of Red-Black Trees

A Red-Black Tree is a type of binary search tree that is self-balancing. This means that the tree is able to maintain a balance between the left and right subtrees, which ensures that operations on the tree are performed quickly. The tree structure of a Red-Black Tree is composed of nodes, which are connected by edges. Each node is labeled with either a red or black color, and the root node is always black.

Each node in a Red-Black Tree contains three pieces of information: a key, a color, and two pointers to left and right subtrees. The key is used to compare nodes and determine the order of the tree. The color of the node is either red or black, and is used to maintain a balance in the tree. The pointers are used to connect nodes to the left and right subtrees.

The following is a sample implementation of a Red-Black Tree in C++:

```cpp
struct Node {
 int data;
 bool color;
 Node *left, *right;
};
// Root node is always black
Node *root = new Node(data);
root->color = BLACK;
// Create new node
Node *newNode(int data) {
 Node *node = new Node(data);
 node->left = node->right = NULL;
 node->color = RED;
 return node;
}
```

Time Complexity of Red-Black Trees

The time complexity of Red-Black Trees is dependent on the type of operation being performed. Generally, the time complexity of operations on a Red-Black Tree is $O(\log n)$, where n is the number of nodes in the tree. This means that the time complexity of operations on a Red-Black Tree is much smaller than that of a regular binary search tree.

The average time complexity of operations on a Red-Black Tree is $O(\log n)$. This means that the time complexity of operations is small and consistent, regardless of the size of the tree.

The worst-case time complexity of operations on a Red-Black Tree is also $O(\log n)$. This means that the time complexity of an operation is not affected by the size of the tree, and will always be the same.

Space Complexity of Red-Black Trees

The space complexity of Red-Black Trees is $O(n)$, where n is the number of nodes in the tree. This means that the space complexity is dependent on the size of the tree and increases as the tree grows.

Insertion and Deletion in Red-Black Trees

Insertion and deletion in Red-Black Trees is similar to that of a regular binary search tree, but with the added complexity of maintaining the balance of the tree.

When inserting a new node into the tree, the node must be inserted in the correct position and the color of the node must be set to red. If the node's parent is red, then the tree must be rebalanced in order to maintain the balance of the tree. The process of rebalancing the tree is complex and beyond the scope of this article.

When deleting a node from the tree, the process is similar to that of insertion. The deleted node must be replaced with another node, and the color of the new node must be set to red. If the new node's parent is red, then the tree must be rebalanced in order to maintain the balance of the tree.

Conclusion

Red-Black Trees are a type of self-balancing binary search tree, which means the tree structure is able to maintain a balance between the left and right subtrees. This ensures that operations on the tree, such as insertion, search, and deletion, are performed quickly. The time complexity of operations on a Red-Black Tree is $O(\log n)$, and the space complexity is $O(n)$. Insertion and deletion in Red-Black Trees is similar to that of a regular binary search tree, but with the added complexity of maintaining the balance of the tree.

Exercises

Write a function to insert a node into a Red-Black Tree.

Write a function to search for a node in a Red-Black Tree.

Write a function to delete a node from a Red-Black Tree.

Write a function to find the successor of a node in a Red-Black Tree.

Write a function to rebalance a Red-Black Tree.

Solutions

Write a function to insert a node into a Red-Black Tree.

```cpp
void insertNode(Node *root, int data) {
 Node *newNode = new Node(data);
 if (root == NULL) {
  root = newNode;
  root->color = BLACK;
 }
 else {
  Node *current = root;
  while (current != NULL) {
   if (data < current->data) {
    if (current->left == NULL) {
     current->left = newNode;
     newNode->color = RED;
     break;
    }
    else {
     current = current->left;
    }
   }
   else {
    if (current->right == NULL) {
     current->right = newNode;
     newNode->color = RED;
     break;
    }
    else {
     current = current->right;
    }
   }
  }
 }
}
```

Write a function to search for a node in a Red-Black Tree.

```cpp
Node* searchNode(Node *root, int data) {
 if (root == NULL) {
  return NULL;
 }
 else {
```

```
  Node *current = root;
  while (current != NULL) {
   if (data == current->data) {
    return current;
   }
   else if (data < current->data) {
    current = current->left;
   }
   else {
    current = current->right;
   }
  }
  return NULL;
 }
}
```

Write a function to delete a node from a Red-Black Tree.

```
void deleteNode(Node* root, int data) {
 if (root == NULL) {
  return;
 }
 else {
  Node *current = root;
  Node *parent = NULL;
  while (current != NULL) {
   if (data == current->data) {
    // Node to be deleted is a leaf node
    if (current->left == NULL && current->right == NULL) {
     // If node is a left child of its parent
     if (parent->left == current)
      parent->left = NULL;
     // If node is a right child of its parent
     else
      parent->right = NULL;
     delete current;
     return;
    }
    // Node to be deleted has one child
    else if (current->left == NULL || current->right == NULL) {
     if (current->left == NULL) {
      // If node is a left child of its parent
      if (parent->left == current)
       parent->left = current->right;
      // If node is a right child of its parent
      else
```

```
      parent->right = current->right;
    }
    else {
      // If node is a left child of its parent
      if (parent->left == current)
        parent->left = current->left;
      // If node is a right child of its parent
      else
        parent->right = current->left;
    }
    delete current;
    return;
    }
    // Node to be deleted has two children
    else {
      Node *successor = findSuccessor(current);
      int successorData = successor->data;
      deleteNode(root, successorData);
      current->data = successorData;
      return;
    }
  }
  else if (data < current->data) {
    parent = current;
    current = current->left;
  }
  else {
    parent = current;
    current = current->right;
  }
}
cout << "Element not found." << endl;
}
}
```

Write a function to find the successor of a node in a Red-Black Tree.

```
Node* findSuccessor(Node *node) {
 if (node->right != NULL) {
  Node *current = node->right;
  while (current->left != NULL) {
   current = current->left;
  }
  return current;
 }
 else {
```

```
  Node *current = node->parent;
  while (current != NULL && node == current->right) {
    node = current;
    current = current->parent;
  }
  return current;
  }
}
```

Write a function to rebalance a Red-Black Tree.

```
void rebalanceTree(Node* root) {
 // Left-Left case
 if (root->left->left != NULL && root->left->color == RED) {
  root->color = RED;
  root->left->color = BLACK;
  rightRotate(root);
 }
 // Right-Right case
 if (root->right->right != NULL && root->right->color == RED) {
  root->color = RED;
  root->right->color = BLACK;
  leftRotate(root);
 }
 // Left-Right case
 if (root->left->right != NULL && root->left->color == RED) {
  root->left->right->color = BLACK;
  leftRotate(root->left);
  rightRotate(root);
 }
 // Right-Left case
 if (root->right->left != NULL && root->right->color == RED) {
  root->right->left->color = BLACK;
  rightRotate(root->right);
  leftRotate(root);
 }
}
```

SPLAY TREES IN C++

Data Structures and Algorithms are an essential part of programming. Understanding the different data structures and algorithms, and how to use them, is essential to becoming an effective programmer. In this article, we will be discussing Splay Trees, a type of self-balancing tree data structure, and how to implement them in C++. We will discuss the structure of the tree, its time and space complexities, and provide some code examples.

What is a Splay Tree?

A Splay Tree is a self-balancing binary search tree. It was first introduced by Daniel Sleator and Robert Tarjan in 1985 and is an efficient data structure for fast retrieval, insertion, and deletion. Splay Trees use the splay operation, which is a modification of the standard binary tree operations. The splay operation reorganizes the tree so that the recently accessed elements are faster to access again.

Splay Trees are a type of self-balancing tree, which means they keep the tree balanced after each operation. This helps to ensure the tree remains balanced and efficient.

How Does the Tree Structure Work?

A Splay Tree is a binary search tree, which means that each node in the tree has a left and right child. The root node of the tree is the entry point. Each node in the tree holds a data value. The tree is structured such that the left child of a node contains a data value that is smaller than or equal to the parent node, and the right child of a node contains a data value that is larger than or equal to the parent node.

The splay operation works by reorganizing the tree after each operation. When an element is accessed, the tree is modified such that the recently accessed element becomes the root of the tree. This makes it easier to access again.

Time Complexity

Splay Trees have an average time complexity of O(log n) for access, search, insertion, and deletion. This means that the time to complete an operation is proportional to the logarithm of the number of elements in the tree.

The worst-case time complexity of Splay Trees is also O(log n). This means that even in the worst case, the time to complete an operation is proportional to the logarithm of the number of elements in the tree.

Space Complexity

The space complexity of Splay Trees is O(n). This means that the amount of memory used by the tree is proportional to the number of elements in the tree.

Implementing Splay Trees in C++

Now that we have discussed the structure of Splay Trees and their time and space complexities, let's look at how to implement them in C++.

First, we must define the structure of the Splay Tree node. This will store the data value and the pointers to the left and right child nodes.

```cpp
struct Node {
  int data;
  Node *left;
  Node *right;
};
```

Next, we must define the structure of the Splay Tree. This will store the root node of the tree and the number of elements in the tree.

```cpp
struct SplayTree {
  Node *root;
  int size;
};
```

Now, we must define the operations that can be performed on the Splay Tree. These operations include insertion, search, deletion, and splay.

Insertion

The insertion operation adds a new element to the Splay Tree. It takes the data value to be inserted and the root node of the tree as parameters.

```cpp
// Function to insert a node in the Splay Tree
void insert(int data, Node *&root)
{
  // Create a new node
  Node *newNode = new Node;
  newNode->data = data;
  newNode->left = newNode->right = NULL;
  // If the tree is empty, make the new node the root
  if (root == NULL)
  {
    root = newNode;
    return;
  }
  // Start at the root node
  Node *curr = root;
  // Traverse the tree to find the correct position for the new node
  while (true)
  {
    if (data < curr->data)
    {
```

```cpp
        // Go left
        if (curr->left == NULL)
        {
          curr->left = newNode;
          break;
        }
        else
        {
          curr = curr->left;
        }
      }
      else
      {
        // Go right
        if (curr->right == NULL)
        {
          curr->right = newNode;
          break;
        }
        else
        {
          curr = curr->right;
        }
      }
    }
    // Perform the splay operation
    splay(data, root);
}
```

Search

The search operation searches the Splay Tree for a given data value. It takes the data value to be searched for and the root node of the tree as parameters.

```cpp
// Function to search for a node in the Splay Tree
Node *search(int data, Node *&root)
{
  // Start at the root node
  Node *curr = root;
  // Traverse the tree to find the node
  while (curr != NULL)
  {
    if (data == curr->data)
    {
      // Perform the splay operation
      splay(data, root);
      return curr;
```

```
    }
    else if (data < curr->data)
    {
      // Go left
      curr = curr->left;
    }
    else
    {
      // Go right
      curr = curr->right;
    }
  }
  // If the node is not found, return NULL
  return NULL;
}
```

Deletion

The deletion operation deletes a node from the Splay Tree. It takes the data value to be deleted and the root node of the tree as parameters.

```
// Function to delete a node from the Splay Tree
void deleteNode(int data, Node *&root)
{
  // If the tree is empty, there is nothing to delete
  if (root == NULL)
  {
    return;
  }
  // Search for the node to be deleted
  Node *nodeToDelete = search(data, root);
  if (nodeToDelete != NULL)
  {
    // If the node has no children, just delete it
    if (nodeToDelete->left == NULL && nodeToDelete->right == NULL)
    {
      delete nodeToDelete;
      nodeToDelete = NULL;
      root = NULL;
    }
    else
    {
      // Find the inorder successor of the node
      Node *inorderSuccessor = findInorderSuccessor(nodeToDelete);
      // Copy the data of the inorder successor to the node to be deleted
      nodeToDelete->data = inorderSuccessor->data;
      // Delete the inorder successor
```

```cpp
      delete inorderSuccessor;
      inorderSuccessor = NULL;
    }
  }
}
```

Splay

The splay operation reorganizes the tree after each operation. It takes the data value of the node to be splayed and the root node of the tree as parameters.

```cpp
// Function to perform the splay operation
void splay(int data, Node *&root)
{
  // If the tree is empty, there is nothing to splay
  if (root == NULL)
  {
    return;
  }
  // Create two auxiliary trees
  Node *leftTreeMax = NULL;
  Node *rightTreeMin = NULL;
  // Start at the root node
  Node *curr = root;
  while (true)
  {
    if (data < curr->data)
    {
      // Go left
      if (curr->left == NULL)
      {
        break;
      }
      if (data < curr->left->data)
      {
        // Zig-Zig (Left Left)
        rotateRight(curr);
        if (curr->left == NULL)
        {
          break;
        }
      }
      // Link Right
      if (rightTreeMin == NULL)
      {
        rightTreeMin = curr;
      }
```

```
      else
      {
        rightTreeMin->right = curr;
      }
      curr = curr->left;
    }
    else if (data > curr->data)
    {
      // Go right
      if (curr->right == NULL)
      {
        break;
      }
      if (data > curr->right->data)
      {
        // Zig-Zag (Right Left)
        rotateLeft(curr);
        if (curr->right == NULL)
        {
          break;
        }
      }
      // Link Left
      if (leftTreeMax == NULL)
      {
        leftTreeMax = curr;
      }
      else
      {
        leftTreeMax->left = curr;
      }
      curr = curr->right;
    }
    else
    {
      break;
    }
  }
  // Reassemble the tree
  if (leftTreeMax != NULL)
  {
    leftTreeMax->left = curr->right;
  }
  if (rightTreeMin != NULL)
  {
```

```
    rightTreeMin->right = curr->left;
  }
  curr->left = root;
  curr->right = root->right;
  root->right = NULL;
  root = curr;
}
```

Conclusion

In this article, we discussed Splay Trees, a type of self-balancing binary search tree. We discussed the structure of the tree, its time and space complexities, and how to implement it in C++. We also provided code examples for the operations of insertion, search, deletion, and splay.

Exercises

Write a function to count the number of nodes in a Splay Tree.

Write a function to find the maximum value stored in a Splay Tree.

Write a function to delete all nodes in a Splay Tree.

Write a function to check if a Splay Tree is a valid binary search tree.

Write a function to find the height of a Splay Tree.

Solutions

Write a function to count the number of nodes in a Splay Tree.

```
// Function to count the number of nodes in a Splay Tree
int countNodes(Node *root)
{
  // Base case
  if (root == NULL)
  {
    return 0;
  }
  // Recursive case
  return 1 + countNodes(root->left) + countNodes(root->right);
}
```

Write a function to find the maximum value stored in a Splay Tree.

```
// Function to find the maximum value stored in a Splay Tree
int maxValue(Node *root)
{
  // Base case
  if (root == NULL)
  {
    return INT_MIN;
```

```
  }
  // Recursive case
  int leftMax = maxValue(root->left);
  int rightMax = maxValue(root->right);
  return max(root->data, max(leftMax, rightMax));
}
```

Write a function to delete all nodes in a Splay Tree.

```
// Function to delete all nodes in a Splay Tree
void deleteAllNodes(Node *&root)
{
  // Base case
  if (root == NULL)
  {
    return;
  }
  // Recursive case
  deleteAllNodes(root->left);
  deleteAllNodes(root->right);
  delete root;
  root = NULL;
}
```

Write a function to check if a Splay Tree is a valid binary search tree.

```
// Function to check if a Splay Tree is a valid binary search tree
bool isBST(Node *root, int minValue, int maxValue)
{
  // Base case
  if (root == NULL)
  {
    return true;
  }
  // Recursive case
  if (root->data < minValue || root->data > maxValue)
  {
    return false;
  }
  return isBST(root->left, minValue, root->data) && isBST(root->right, root->data, maxValue);
}
```

Write a function to find the height of a Splay Tree.

```
// Function to find the height of a Splay Tree
int height(Node *root)
{
  // Base case
  if (root == NULL)
```

```
{
    return 0;
}
// Recursive case
int leftHeight = height(root->left);
int rightHeight = height(root->right);
return 1 + max(leftHeight, rightHeight);
}
```

AVL TREES IN C++

AVL Trees in C++ are one of the most efficient data structures for implementing a self-balancing binary search tree. AVL Trees are named after their inventors, Adelson-Velsky and Landis, who first published them in their 1962 paper titled "An Algorithm for the Organization of Information." This data structure is used to store and manage data in a way that is both efficient and easily accessible. AVL Trees are popular due to their ability to maintain balance, which allows for time-efficient operations such as search, insert and delete. In this article, we will discuss the structure of an AVL Tree, the time complexity of its operations, the space complexity of an AVL Tree, and some sample C++ code to help you understand how to implement an AVL Tree in your own projects.

What is an AVL Tree?

An AVL Tree is a type of self-balancing binary search tree. A binary search tree is a data structure that stores data in a way that allows for quick retrieval and management of data. Each node in the tree stores a data element, and each node has two children, a left child and a right child. The left child contains a data element that is less than the parent node, and the right child contains a data element that is greater than the parent node. This structure allows for efficient searching and sorting of data.

The AVL Tree is a type of binary search tree that uses the concept of self-balancing to maintain optimal performance. This means that the AVL Tree uses a set of rules to ensure that the height of the tree is minimized. The AVL Tree is considered to be one of the most efficient data structures for implementing a self-balancing binary search tree.

Time Complexity of AVL Trees in C++

The time complexity of an AVL Tree in C++ depends on the operation that is being performed. The average time complexity of search, insert and delete operations on an AVL Tree is O(log n). The worst case time complexity of search, insert and delete operations on an AVL Tree is O(n).

Space Complexity of AVL Trees in C++

The space complexity of an AVL Tree in C++ is O(n). This means that the amount of space required to store the data in an AVL Tree is proportional to the number of elements in the tree.

How to Implement an AVL Tree in C++

Now that we have discussed the structure, time complexity, and space complexity of an AVL Tree, let's take a look at some sample C++ code to help you understand how to implement an AVL Tree in your own projects.

The first step in implementing an AVL Tree in C++ is to create a node class. This class will be used to store the data for each node in the tree. The node class should include data members for the data element, the left child, and the right child. The node class should also include a constructor to initialize the data members.

```cpp
class Node {
public:
  int data;
  Node* left;
  Node* right;
  Node(int d){
    data = d;
    left = NULL;
    right = NULL;
  }
};
```

Next, we need to create a tree class to represent our AVL Tree. The tree class should include a root node, which will be used to point to the root node of the AVL Tree. The tree class should also include methods to perform operations on the tree, such as insert, search, and delete.

```cpp
class AVLTree {
private:
  Node* root;
public:
  AVLTree(){
    root = NULL;
  }
  void insert(int data);
  void search(int data);
  void delete(int data);
};
```

Finally, we need to write the implementations for the insert, search, and delete methods of the tree class. The insert method should take a data element and insert it into the AVL Tree. The search method should take a data element and search the tree for it. The delete method should take a data element and delete it from the tree.

```cpp
// Method to insert a data element into the AVL Tree
void AVLTree::insert(int data) {
  // Create a new node with the given data
  Node* n = new Node(data);
  // If the tree is empty, set the root node to the new node
  if(root == NULL) {
    root = n;
  }
```

```
    else {
      // Traverse the tree to find the correct place to insert the node
      Node* current = root;
      Node* parent = NULL;
      while(true) {
        parent = current;
        if(data < current->data) {
          // Go to the left
          current = current->left;
          if(current == NULL) {
            // Insert the node
            parent->left = n;
            break;
          }
        }
        else {
          // Go to the right
          current = current->right;
          if(current == NULL) {
            // Insert the node
            parent->right = n;
            break;
          }
        }
      }
    }
    // Balance the tree
    balance(n,root);
}
// Method to search for a data element in the AVL Tree
void AVLTree::search(int data) {
  // Start at the root of the tree
  Node* current = root;
  // Traverse the tree until the node is found
  while(current != NULL) {
    if(current->data == data) {
      // Node found
      return;
    }
    else if(data < current->data) {
      // Go to the left
      current = current->left;
    }
    else {
      // Go to the right
```

```cpp
        current = current->right;
    }
  }
  // Node not found
  return;
}
// Method to delete a data element from the AVL Tree
void AVLTree::delete(int data) {
  // Start at the root of the tree
  Node* current = root;
  Node* parent = NULL;
  // Traverse the tree until the node is found
  while(current != NULL) {
    if(current->data == data) {
      // Node found
      break;
    }
    else {
      parent = current;
      if(data < current->data) {
        // Go to the left
        current = current->left;
      }
      else {
        // Go to the right
        current = current->right;
      }
    }
  }
  // Check if the node is a leaf node
  if(current->left == NULL && current->right == NULL) {
    // Node is a leaf node
    if(parent->left == current) {
      parent->left = NULL;
    }
    else {
      parent->right = NULL;
    }
  }
  // Check if the node has one child
  else if(current->left == NULL || current->right == NULL) {
    // Node has one child
    if(current->left != NULL) {
      if(parent->left == current) {
        parent->left = current->left;
```

```
      }
    else {
        parent->right = current->left;
      }
    }
    else {
      if(parent->left == current) {
        parent->left = current->right;
      }
      else {
        parent->right = current->right;
      }
    }
  }
  // Node has two children
  else {
    // Find the successor node
    Node* successor = getSuccessor(current);
    if(current == root) {
      root = successor;
    }
    else if(current == parent->left) {
      parent->left = successor;
    }
    else {
      parent->right = successor;
    }
    successor->left = current->left;
  }
  // Balance the tree
  balance(parent, root);
}
```

Conclusion

In conclusion, AVL Trees in C++ are an efficient data structure for implementing a self-balancing binary search tree. AVL Trees use a set of rules to ensure that the height of the tree is minimized, which allows for time-efficient operations such as search, insert and delete. The time complexity of search, insert and delete operations on an AVL Tree is O(log n) on average, and O(n) in the worst case. The space complexity of an AVL Tree is O(n).

Exercises

Write a program to insert the following values into an AVL Tree: 25, 15, 50, 10, 22, 35, 70, 4, 12, 18, 24, 31, 44, 66, 90.

Write a program to delete the value 50 from an AVL Tree.

Write a program to search for the value 44 in an AVL Tree.

Write a program to insert the value 22 into an AVL Tree.

Write a program to delete the value 55 from an AVL Tree.

Write a program to insert the following values into an AVL Tree: 25, 15, 50, 10, 22, 35, 70, 4, 12, 18, 24, 31, 44, 66, 90.

```cpp
#include <iostream>
#include <stdlib.h>
// Node class for AVL Tree nodes
class Node {
public:
  int data;
  Node* left;
  Node* right;
  Node(int d){
    data = d;
    left = NULL;
    right = NULL;
  }
};
// AVL Tree class
class AVLTree {
private:
  Node* root;
public:
  AVLTree(){
    root = NULL;
  }
  void insert(int data);
  void balance(Node* n, Node* root);
};
// Method to insert a data element into the AVL Tree
void AVLTree::insert(int data) {
  // Create a new node with the given data
  Node* n = new Node(data);
  // If the tree is empty, set the root node to the new node
  if(root == NULL) {
    root = n;
  }
  else {
    // Traverse the tree to find the correct place to insert the node
    Node* current = root;
    Node* parent = NULL;
```

```
        while(true) {
          parent = current;
          if(data < current->data) {
            // Go to the left
            current = current->left;
            if(current == NULL) {
              // Insert the node
              parent->left = n;
              break;
            }
          }
          else {
            // Go to the right
            current = current->right;
            if(current == NULL) {
              // Insert the node
              parent->right = n;
              break;
            }
          }
        }
      }
      // Balance the tree
      balance(n,root);
}
// Balance the tree
void AVLTree::balance(Node* n, Node* root) {
    // TODO: Balance the tree
}
int main() {
    AVLTree tree;
    tree.insert(25);
    tree.insert(15);
    tree.insert(50);
    tree.insert(10);
    tree.insert(22);
    tree.insert(35);
    tree.insert(70);
    tree.insert(4);
    tree.insert(12);
    tree.insert(18);
    tree.insert(24);
    tree.insert(31);
    tree.insert(44);
    tree.insert(66);
```

```
  tree.insert(90);
  return 0;
}
```

Write a program to delete the value 50 from an AVL Tree.

```cpp
#include <iostream>
#include <stdlib.h>
// Node class for AVL Tree nodes
class Node {
public:
  int data;
  Node* left;
  Node* right;
  Node(int d){
    data = d;
    left = NULL;
    right = NULL;
  }
};
// AVL Tree class
class AVLTree {
private:
  Node* root;
public:
  AVLTree(){
    root = NULL;
  }
  void delete(int data);
  Node* getSuccessor(Node* n);
  void balance(Node* n, Node* root);
};
// Method to delete a data element from the AVL Tree
void AVLTree::delete(int data) {
  // Start at the root of the tree
  Node* current = root;
  Node* parent = NULL;
  // Traverse the tree until the node is found
  while(current != NULL) {
    if(current->data == data) {
      // Node found
      break;
    }
    else {
      parent = current;
      if(data < current->data) {
```

YASIN CAKAL

```cpp
      // Go to the left
      current = current->left;
    }
    else {
      // Go to the right
      current = current->right;
    }
  }
}
// Check if the node is a leaf node
if(current->left == NULL && current->right == NULL) {
  // Node is a leaf node
  if(parent->left == current) {
    parent->left = NULL;
  }
  else {
    parent->right = NULL;
  }
}
// Check if the node has one child
else if(current->left == NULL || current->right == NULL) {
  // Node has one child
  if(current->left != NULL) {
    if(parent->left == current) {
      parent->left = current->left;
    }
    else {
      parent->right = current->left;
    }
  }
  else {
    if(parent->left == current) {
      parent->left = current->right;
    }
    else {
      parent->right = current->right;
    }
  }
}
// Node has two children
else {
  // Find the successor node
  Node* successor = getSuccessor(current);
  if(current == root) {
    root = successor;
```

```
    }
    else if(current == parent->left) {
      parent->left = successor;
    }
    else {
      parent->right = successor;
    }
    successor->left = current->left;
  }
  // Balance the tree
  balance(parent, root);
}
// Balance the tree
void AVLTree::balance(Node* n, Node* root) {
  // TODO: Balance the tree
}
int main() {
  AVLTree tree;
  tree.delete(50);
  return 0;
}
```

Write a program to search for the value 44 in an AVL Tree.

```cpp
#include <iostream>
#include <stdlib.h>
// Node class for AVL Tree nodes
class Node {
public:
        int data;
        Node *left;
        Node *right;
        Node(int);
};
Node::Node(int data)
{
        this->data = data;
        left = NULL;
        right = NULL;
}
// AVLTree class
class AVLTree {
        Node *root;
        // Gets the height of an AVL Tree node
        int height(Node *node)
        {
```

```cpp
            if (node == NULL)
                    return 0;
            return node->data;
    }
    // Searches for a given key in an AVL Tree
    bool search(Node *node, int key)
    {
            if (node == NULL)
                    return false;
            if (node->data == key)
                    return true;
            if (node->data < key)
                    return search(node->right, key);
            // else
            return search(node->left, key);
    }
public:
    AVLTree();
    // Searches for a given key in an AVL Tree
    bool search(int key)
    {
            return search(root, key);
    }
};
AVLTree::AVLTree()
{
    root = NULL;
}
// Driver code
int main()
{
    AVLTree tree;
    // Searches for the value 44 in the AVL Tree
    if (tree.search(44))
            std::cout << "Present";
    else
            std::cout << "Not Present";
    return 0;
}
```

Write a program to insert the value 22 into an AVL Tree.

```cpp
#include <iostream>
#include <stdlib.h>
// Node class for AVL Tree nodes
class Node {
```

```cpp
public:
        int data;
        Node *left;
        Node *right;
        Node(int);
};
Node::Node(int data)
{
        this->data = data;
        left = NULL;
        right = NULL;
}
// AVLTree class
class AVLTree {
        Node *root;
        // Gets the height of an AVL Tree node
        int height(Node *node)
        {
                if (node == NULL)
                        return 0;
                return node->data;
        }
        // Inserts a new value into an AVL Tree
        Node* insert(Node* node, int key)
        {
                if (node == NULL)
                        return new Node(key);
                if (key < node->data)
                        node->left = insert(node->left, key);
                else if (key > node->data)
                        node->right = insert(node->right, key);
                else
                        return node;
                // Update height of this ancestor node
                node->data = 1 + max(height(node->left),
                                                height(node->right));
                return node;
        }
public:
        AVLTree();
        // Inserts a new value into an AVL Tree
        void insert(int key)
        {
                root = insert(root, key);
        }
```

```
};
AVLTree::AVLTree()
{
        root = NULL;
}
// Driver code
int main()
{
        AVLTree tree;
        // Inserts the value 22 into the AVL Tree
        tree.insert(22);
        return 0;
}
```

Write a program to delete the value 55 from an AVL Tree.

```
#include <iostream>
#include <stdlib.h>
// Node class for AVL Tree nodes
class Node {
public:
        int data;
        Node *left;
        Node *right;
        Node(int);
};
Node::Node(int data)
{
        this->data = data;
        left = NULL;
        right = NULL;
}
// AVLTree class
class AVLTree {
        Node *root;
        // Gets the height of an AVL Tree node
        int height(Node *node)
        {
                if (node == NULL)
                        return 0;
                return node->data;
        }
        // Searches for a node with the given key in an AVL Tree
        Node* search(Node* node, int key)
        {
                if (node == NULL)
```

```
                return NULL;
        if (node->data == key)
                return node;
        if (node->data < key)
                return search(node->right, key);
        // else
        return search(node->left, key);
}
// Deletes a node with the given key from an AVL Tree
Node* deleteNode(Node* node, int key)
{
        if (node == NULL)
                return NULL;
        // If the key to be deleted is smaller than
        // the root's key, then it lies in left subtree
        if (key < node->data)
                node->left = deleteNode(node->left, key);
        // If the key to be deleted is greater than the
        // root's key, then it lies in right subtree
        else if (key > node->data)
                node->right = deleteNode(node->right, key);
        // if key is same as root's key, then this is the node
        // to be deleted
        else
        {
                // node with only one child or no child
                if (node->left == NULL)
                {
                        Node *temp = node->right;
                        free(node);
                        return temp;
                }
                else if (node->right == NULL)
                {
                        Node *temp = node->left;
                        free(node);
                        return temp;
                }
                // node with two children: Get the inorder successor (smallest
                // in the right subtree)
                Node* temp = minValueNode(node->right);
                // Copy the inorder successor's content to this node
                node->data = temp->data;
                // Delete the inorder successor
                node->right = deleteNode(node->right, temp->data);
```

```
                }
                return node;
        }
public:
        AVLTree();
        // Deletes a node with the given key from an AVL Tree
        void deleteNode(int key)
        {
                root = deleteNode(root, key);
        }
};
AVLTree::AVLTree()
{
        root = NULL;
}
// Driver code
int main()
{
        AVLTree tree;
        // Deletes the value 55 from the AVL Tree
        tree.deleteNode(55);
        return 0;
}
```

KD TREES IN C++

KD Trees are one of the most popular data structures used in computer science and programming today. A KD Tree, or K-dimensional Tree, is a type of space-partitioning data structure that is used to organize data points in a k-dimensional space. KD Trees are very useful in a number of applications, such as search algorithms, nearest neighbor search, and compression. In this article, we'll be exploring how KD Trees work, as well as their time and space complexity. We'll also provide code examples to illustrate how to use KD Trees in C++.

What is a KD Tree?

A KD Tree is a type of binary tree that is used to organize points in a k-dimensional space. It is a space-partitioning data structure that splits a k-dimensional space into two halves at each level. For example, a 3D KD Tree will split a 3D space into two halves at each level. The tree is constructed by recursively splitting the space into two halves using a hyperplane. The hyperplane is determined by the position of the data points in the space.

The tree is constructed in a top-down fashion and each node of the tree holds a single data point. The root of the tree is the data point that is farthest from the origin. The two children of the root are the two data points that are closest to the origin. The two children of the root are then split into two halves and the process is repeated until all of the data points have been assigned to a node.

Time Complexity

The time complexity of access, search, insertion, and deletion in a KD Tree is O(log n), where n is the number of data points. This is because the tree is constructed in a top-down fashion and the data points are assigned to nodes in a recursive manner. Thus, the time complexity is proportional to the length of the tree, which is proportional to the logarithm of the number of data points.

The average time complexity for search, insertion, and deletion is O(log n). This is because the data points are organized in a way that allows for efficient searching, insertion, and deletion. The worst-case time complexity is O(n), which occurs when all of the data points are located at the same level of the tree.

Space Complexity

The space complexity of a KD Tree is O(n), where n is the number of data points. This is because each node of the tree holds a single data point. Thus, the space complexity is proportional to the number of data points.

Implementing a KD Tree in C++

Now that we've discussed the basics of KD Trees, let's take a look at how to implement one in C++. We'll start by defining a Node class that will store the data points in the tree. The Node class will have two members: a data point and two pointers to its children.

```cpp
class Node {
public:
  int data;
  Node *left;
  Node *right;
};
```

Next, we'll define a KDTree class that will be used to construct and manage the tree. The KDTree class will have two members: a root pointer and a function to construct the tree.

```cpp
class KDTree {
private:
  Node *root;
public:
  KDTree();
  void buildTree(vector<int> &points);
};
```

The buildTree() function will take in an array of data points and construct the tree. The function will take the data points and recursively split the space into two halves using a hyperplane. The hyperplane is determined by the position of the data points in the space.

```cpp
void KDTree::buildTree(vector<int> &points) {
  if (points.size() == 0) {
    root = nullptr;
    return;
  }
  root = new Node();
  root->data = points[0];
  // Split the points into two halves
  vector<int> leftPoints, rightPoints;
  for (int i = 1; i < points.size(); i++) {
    if (points[i] < root->data) {
      leftPoints.push_back(points[i]);
    } else {
      rightPoints.push_back(points[i]);
    }
  }
  // Recursively build the left and right subtrees
  buildTree(leftPoints, root->left);
  buildTree(rightPoints, root->right);
}
```

Now that we have the KDTree class defined, we can use it to construct a KD Tree in C++. The following code example shows how to create a 3D KD Tree with 10 data points.

```cpp
int main() {
  vector<int> points = {3, 7, 4, 9, 5, 2, 8, 1, 6, 0};
  KDTree tree;
  tree.buildTree(points);
  return 0;
}
```

Conclusion

KD Trees are a powerful data structure that can be used to organize data points in a k-dimensional space. The time complexity of accessing, searching, inserting, and deleting data points in a KD Tree is O(log n). The space complexity is O(n). In this article, we've explored how to implement a KD Tree in C++.

Exercises

Given an array of integers, write a function to construct a KD Tree.

Given a KD Tree and a target data point, write a function to search for the data point in the tree.

Given a KD Tree and a data point, write a function to insert the data point into the tree.

Given a KD Tree and a data point, write a function to delete the data point from the tree.

Given a KD Tree, write a function to traverse the tree in pre-order.

Solutions

Given an array of integers, write a function to construct a KD Tree.

```cpp
#include <vector>
class Node {
public:
  int data;
  Node *left;
  Node *right;
};
class KDTree {
private:
  Node *root;
public:
  KDTree();
  void buildTree(vector<int> &points);
};
void KDTree::buildTree(vector<int> &points) {
  if (points.size() == 0) {
```

```
    root = nullptr;
    return;
  }
  root = new Node();
  root->data = points[0];
  // Split the points into two halves
  vector<int> leftPoints, rightPoints;
  for (int i = 1; i < points.size(); i++) {
    if (points[i] < root->data) {
      leftPoints.push_back(points[i]);
    } else {
      rightPoints.push_back(points[i]);
    }
  }
  // Recursively build the left and right subtrees
  buildTree(leftPoints, root->left);
  buildTree(rightPoints, root->right);
}
```

Given a KD Tree and a target data point, write a function to search for the data point in the tree.

```
#include <vector>
bool searchTree(Node *root, int target) {
  if (root == nullptr) {
    return false;
  }
  if (root->data == target) {
    return true;
  }
  if (target < root->data) {
    return searchTree(root->left, target);
  } else {
    return searchTree(root->right, target);
  }
}
```

Given a KD Tree and a data point, write a function to insert the data point into the tree.

```
#include <vector>
void insertNode(Node *root, int data) {
  if (root == nullptr) {
    root = new Node();
    root->data = data;
    return;
  }
  if (data < root->data) {
```

```
    insertNode(root->left, data);
  } else {
    insertNode(root->right, data);
  }
}
```

Given a KD Tree and a data point, write a function to delete the data point from the tree.

```
#include <vector>
void deleteNode(Node *root, int data) {
  if (root == nullptr) {
    return;
  }
  if (root->data == data) {
    // Code to delete the node
  }
  if (data < root->data) {
    deleteNode(root->left, data);
  } else {
    deleteNode(root->right, data);
  }
}
```

Given a KD Tree, write a function to traverse the tree in pre-order.

```
#include <vector>
void preOrderTraversal(Node *root) {
  if (root == nullptr) {
    return;
  }
  cout << root->data << " ";
  preOrderTraversal(root->left);
  preOrderTraversal(root->right);
}
```

MIN HEAP IN C++

Min Heap is a special type of data structure, which is a complete binary tree that follows the following two properties:

1. All nodes in the Min Heap are greater than or equal to their children.
2. The root node of the Min Heap is the minimum of all nodes.

Min Heap is a common data structure used in many algorithms such as heapsort, priority queues, and graph algorithms. It is also used to implement efficient priority queues. This article will discuss the tree structure of Min Heap, time complexity of access, search, insertion, and deletion, as well as the space complexity of Min Heap in C++.

Tree Structure of Min Heap

A Min Heap is a complete binary tree, meaning it is a binary tree in which all levels are filled except for the last level and all nodes are as far left as possible. The root node of a Min Heap is the minimum of all nodes, and all nodes in the Min Heap are greater than or equal to their children. In the following example of a Min Heap, the root node is 4, and all of its children (2 and 6) are greater than or equal to it.

```
int MinHeap[7] = {4, 2, 6, 1, 3, 5, 7};
```

Time Complexity

The time complexity of access, search, insertion, and deletion in a Min Heap is as follows:

- Access: The time complexity of access in a Min Heap is O(1), as we can directly access the root node which is the minimum.

- Search: The time complexity of search in a Min Heap is O(n), as we need to traverse the tree to find the element we are searching for.

- Insertion: The time complexity of insertion in a Min Heap is O(log n), as we need to insert the new element in the correct position in the heap.

- Deletion: The time complexity of deletion in a Min Heap is O(log n), as we need to delete the element from the heap and rearrange the elements accordingly.

Space Complexity

The space complexity of a Min Heap is O(n), as we need to store all of the nodes in the heap.

C++ Implementation

We can implement a Min Heap in C++ using an array. We can use the following code to create a Min Heap of size 7.

```cpp
// create an array of size 7
int MinHeap[7];
// insert elements into the array
MinHeap[0] = 4;
MinHeap[1] = 2;
MinHeap[2] = 6;
MinHeap[3] = 1;
MinHeap[4] = 3;
MinHeap[5] = 5;
MinHeap[6] = 7;
// create a function to heapify the array
void heapify(int MinHeap[], int n, int i)
{
  int smallest = i; // root
  int l = 2*i + 1; // left child
  int r = 2*i + 2; // right child
  // if left child is smaller than root
  if (l < n && MinHeap[l] < MinHeap[smallest])
    smallest = l;
  // if right child is smaller than root
  if (r < n && MinHeap[r] < MinHeap[smallest])
    smallest = r;
  // if root is not smallest
  if (smallest != i)
  {
    swap(MinHeap[i], MinHeap[smallest]);
    // heapify the root
    heapify(MinHeap, n, smallest);
  }
}
// create a function to build the Min Heap
void buildMinHeap(int MinHeap[], int n)
{
  // build the heap from the bottom up
  for (int i = n / 2 - 1; i >= 0; i--)
    heapify(MinHeap, n, i);
}
```

Conclusion

In conclusion, Min Heap is a special type of data structure that is used in many algorithms. It is a complete binary tree in which all nodes are greater than or equal to their children, and the root node is the minimum of all nodes. The time complexity of access, search, insertion, and deletion in a Min Heap is O(1), O(n), O(log n), and O(log n) respectively. The space complexity of Min Heap is O(n). Min Heap can be implemented in C++ using an array.

Exercises

Create a function to insert an element into a Min Heap.

Create a function to delete an element from a Min Heap.

Create a function to sort a Min Heap.

Create a function to find the minimum element in a Min Heap.

Create a function to search for an element in a Min Heap.

Solutions

Create a function to insert an element into a Min Heap.

```cpp
// function to insert an element into a Min Heap
void insert(int MinHeap[], int n, int x)
{
    // insert the element at the end of the heap
    MinHeap[n] = x;
    // heapify the root node
    int i = n;
    while (i != 0 && MinHeap[(i - 1)/2] > MinHeap[i])
    {
        swap(MinHeap[(i - 1)/2], MinHeap[i]);
        i = (i - 1) / 2;
    }
}
```

Create a function to delete an element from a Min Heap.

```cpp
// function to delete an element from a Min Heap
void deleteElement(int MinHeap[], int n, int x)
{
    // find the element to be deleted
    int i;
    for (i = 0; i < n; i++)
        if (MinHeap[i] == x)
            break;
    // replace the element to be deleted with the last element in the heap
    swap(MinHeap[i], MinHeap[n - 1]);
    // heapify the root node
    i = 0;
    while (i < n - 1 && MinHeap[i] > MinHeap[2*i + 1])
    {
        swap(MinHeap[i], MinHeap[2*i + 1]);
        i = 2*i + 1;
```

```
    }
}
```

Create a function to sort a Min Heap.

```cpp
// function to sort a Min Heap
void heapSort(int MinHeap[], int n)
{
  // build the heap from the bottom up
  for (int i = n / 2 - 1; i >= 0; i--)
    heapify(MinHeap, n, i);
  // sort the heap
  for (int i = n - 1; i >= 0; i--)
  {
    // move the root node to the end
    swap(MinHeap[i], MinHeap[0]);
    // heapify the root node
    heapify(MinHeap, i, 0);
  }
}
```

Create a function to find the minimum element in a Min Heap.

```cpp
// function to find the minimum element in a Min Heap
int minElement(int MinHeap[], int n)
{
  // the root node is the minimum element
  return MinHeap[0];
}
```

Create a function to search for an element in a Min Heap.

```cpp
// function to search for an element in a Min Heap
bool searchElement(int MinHeap[], int n, int x)
{
  // traverse the heap to search for the element
  for (int i = 0; i < n; i++)
  {
    if (MinHeap[i] == x)
      return true;
  }
  return false;
}
```

MAX HEAP IN C++

Max Heap is one of the most important data structures that a C++ programmer should be aware of. It is a type of binary heap tree structure which has the highest node value at the top. It is commonly used in priority queues, and for sorting and searching algorithms. In this article, we will discuss in detail how the tree structure works, and the time and space complexity of insertion, access, search and deletion operations on a Max Heap. We will also discuss C++ code examples to help understand each concept better.

What is a Max Heap?

A Max Heap is a type of binary tree structure where the highest node value is at the top. It is a complete binary tree which means that all levels of the tree are filled, except for the last level, and all nodes are as far left as possible. The parent node of a max heap is always greater than or equal to its two children nodes. This property is called the heap property.

Max Heap Tree Structure

The max heap tree structure is implemented using an array. The root node is at the 0th index of the array, and the following two equations are used to calculate the left and right child nodes of the parent node at index i:

- Left child node: 2*i + 1
- Right child node: 2*i + 2

The following code shows a sample implementation of a Max Heap in C++.

```cpp
int main()
{
  // Array representation of Max Heap
  // 10
  //  / \
  // 5  3
  // / \
  // 2 4
  int heap[] = {10, 5, 3, 2, 4};
  //Calculate the size of the heap
  int size = sizeof(heap)/sizeof(heap[0]);
  //Print the Max Heap
  for (int i = 0; i < size; i++)
    cout << heap[i] << " ";
  // Calculating the left and right child of the root node
  int left = (2 * 0) + 1;
```

```
    int right = (2 * 0) + 2;
    cout << "\nLeft Child of root node : " << heap[left]
        << " Right Child of root node : " << heap[right];
    return 0;
}
// Output:
// 10 5 3 2 4
// Left Child of root node : 5 Right Child of root node : 3
```

Time Complexity of Max Heap

When it comes to the time complexity of insertion, access, search and deletion on a Max Heap, the average case time complexity is O(log n) while the worst-case time complexity is O(n).

Insertion

Insertion into a Max Heap is quite simple. The new node is inserted at the end of the array. This is done to maintain the complete binary tree structure of the Max Heap. Then, the new node is compared to its parent node, and if it is greater than its parent node, then it is swapped with the parent node. This process is repeated until the new node is less than or equal to its parent node.

The following code is an example of insertion in a Max Heap in C++.

```
// Function to insert a new node into the Max Heap
void insert(int heap[], int x, int& size)
{
    // Insert the element at the end
    int i = size;
    heap[i] = x;
    // Check if it breaks the heap property and fix it
    while (i != 0 && heap[(i - 1) / 2] < heap[i]) {
        // Swap the elements
        int temp = heap[(i - 1) / 2];
        heap[(i - 1) / 2] = heap[i];
        heap[i] = temp;
        i = (i - 1) / 2;
    }
    // Increase the size
    size++;
}
```

Search

Searching for a node in a Max Heap is an O(n) operation. This is because the max heap structure is implemented using an array, and the search operation must go through each element in the array to find the node.

The following code is an example of searching for a node in a Max Heap in C++.

```
// Function to search for a node in the Max Heap
int search(int heap[], int x, int size)
{
  // Traverse the heap
  for (int i = 0; i < size; i++) {
    if (heap[i] == x)
      return i;
  }
  return -1;
}
```

Access

Accessing an element in a Max Heap is an O(1) operation. This is because the max heap structure is implemented using an array, and the access operation can be done in constant time.

The following code is an example of accessing an element in a Max Heap in C++.

```
// Function to access an element in the Max Heap
int access(int heap[], int i)
{
  // Return the element at index 'i'
  return heap[i];
}
```

Deletion

Deletion in a Max Heap is a bit more complicated than insertion, since the complete binary tree structure must be maintained. The node to be deleted is first swapped with the last node in the array. Then, the swapped node is compared to its children nodes, and if it is smaller than any of its children nodes, it is swapped with the larger of the two children nodes. This process is repeated until the node is greater than or equal to its children nodes.

The following code is an example of deletion from a Max Heap in C++.

```
// Function to delete a node from the Max Heap
void deleteNode(int heap[], int i, int& size)
{
  // Swap the node with the last element
  int temp = heap[i];
  heap[i] = heap[size - 1];
  heap[size - 1] = temp;
  // Decrease the size
  size--;
  // Compare the new node with its children and swap
  // it with the largest of the two children
  while (i < size && heap[i] < heap[2 * i + 1]
      || heap[i] < heap[2 * i + 2]) {
```

```
    if (heap[2 * i + 1] > heap[2 * i + 2]) {
      int temp = heap[i];
      heap[i] = heap[2 * i + 1];
      heap[2 * i + 1] = temp;
      i = 2 * i + 1;
    }
    else {
      int temp = heap[i];
      heap[i] = heap[2 * i + 2];
      heap[2 * i + 2] = temp;
      i = 2 * i + 2;
    }
  }
}
}
```

Space Complexity of Max Heap

The space complexity of a Max Heap is O(n), where n is the number of nodes in the Max Heap. This is because the max heap structure is implemented using an array, and the array must store each node in the Max Heap.

Conclusion

In this article, we discussed in detail about the Max Heap data structure in C++. We discussed how the tree structure works, and the time and space complexity of insertion, access, search and deletion operations on a Max Heap. We also discussed C++ code examples to help understand each concept better.

Exercises

Implement a function to insert a new node into a Max Heap.

Implement a function to search for a node in a Max Heap.

Implement a function to access an element in a Max Heap.

Implement a function to delete a node from a Max Heap.

Given an array of integers, sort it using a Max Heap.

Solutions

Implement a function to insert a new node into a Max Heap.

```
// Function to insert a new node into the Max Heap
void insert(int heap[], int x, int& size)
{
  // Insert the element at the end
  int i = size;
  heap[i] = x;
  // Check if it breaks the heap property and fix it
  while (i != 0 && heap[(i - 1) / 2] < heap[i]) {
```

```
    // Swap the elements
    int temp = heap[(i - 1) / 2];
    heap[(i - 1) / 2] = heap[i];
    heap[i] = temp;
    i = (i - 1) / 2;
  }
  // Increase the size
  size++;
}
```

Implement a function to search for a node in a Max Heap.

```
// Function to search for a node in the Max Heap
int search(int heap[], int x, int size)
{
  // Traverse the heap
  for (int i = 0; i < size; i++) {
    if (heap[i] == x)
      return i;
  }
  return -1;
}
```

Implement a function to access an element in a Max Heap.

```
// Function to access an element in the Max Heap
int access(int heap[], int i)
{
  // Return the element at index 'i'
  return heap[i];
}
```

Implement a function to delete a node from a Max Heap.

```
// Function to delete a node from the Max Heap
void deleteNode(int heap[], int i, int& size)
{
  // Swap the node with the last element
  int temp = heap[i];
  heap[i] = heap[size - 1];
  heap[size - 1] = temp;
  // Decrease the size
  size--;
  // Compare the new node with its children and swap
  // it with the largest of the two children
  while (i < size && heap[i] < heap[2 * i + 1]
      || heap[i] < heap[2 * i + 2]) {
    if (heap[2 * i + 1] > heap[2 * i + 2]) {
      int temp = heap[i];
```

```
      heap[i] = heap[2 * i + 1];
      heap[2 * i + 1] = temp;
      i = 2 * i + 1;
    }
    else {
      int temp = heap[i];
      heap[i] = heap[2 * i + 2];
      heap[2 * i + 2] = temp;
      i = 2 * i + 2;
    }
  }
}
```

Given an array of integers, sort it using a Max Heap.

```
// Function to sort an array using Max Heap
void sort(int arr[], int n)
{
  // Build a heap from the array
  for (int i = n / 2 - 1; i >= 0; i--)
    heapify(arr, n, i);
  // Heap sort
  for (int i = n - 1; i >= 0; i--) {
    // Swap the root element with the last element
    int temp = arr[0];
    arr[0] = arr[i];
    arr[i] = temp;
    // Heapify the reduced heap
    heapify(arr, i, 0);
  }
}
// Function to heapify the array
void heapify(int arr[], int n, int i)
{
  // Find the largest among root, left child and right child
  int largest = i;
  int left = 2 * i + 1;
  int right = 2 * i + 2;
  if (left < n && arr[left] > arr[largest])
    largest = left;
  if (right < n && arr[right] > arr[largest])
    largest = right;
  // Swap and continue heapifying if root is not largest
  if (largest != i) {
    int temp = arr[i];
    arr[i] = arr[largest];
```

```
    arr[largest] = temp;
    heapify(arr, n, largest);
  }
}
```

TRIE TREES IN C++

Trie Trees in C++ are an efficient data structure that allow for the efficient storage and retrieval of data. A trie tree works by storing data in a hierarchical, tree-like structure. In this article, we will discuss the basics of trie trees, how they can be implemented in C++, their time and space complexity, and how they can be used to solve various problems. We will also cover several coding exercises to help you practice and test your understanding of this data structure.

What is a Trie Tree?

A trie tree, also known as a digital tree or prefix tree, is a type of search tree used for storing and retrieving strings. It is an ordered tree data structure that is used to store strings in a sorted way. In a trie tree, each node contains a character from the string. The root node is an empty node, which is the starting point for inserting or retrieving a string.

The trie tree is an efficient data structure for searching for strings, as each node stores a single character and the edges connecting the nodes contain the characters of the string. This allows for fast searching and retrieval of strings, as the characters need not be compared to check for equality.

Implementing a Trie Tree in C++

A trie tree can be implemented in C++ using a class. This class will be used to create nodes in the trie tree. Each node will store a character, a Boolean value indicating whether the node is a leaf node, and a pointer to an array of 26 pointers (one for each alphabetic character). The array of pointers will be used to store the nodes of the tree.

```
struct TrieNode {
  char ch;
  bool isLeaf;
  struct TrieNode *children[26];
};
The following code is an example of a trie tree implemented in C++:
struct TrieNode
{
  char ch;
  bool isLeaf;
  struct TrieNode *children[26];
};
struct Trie
```

```
{
  struct TrieNode *root;
};
struct TrieNode * getNode(void)
{
  struct TrieNode *pNode = new TrieNode;
  pNode->isLeaf = false;
  for (int i = 0; i < 26; i++)
    pNode->children[i] = NULL;
  return pNode;
}
void insert(struct TrieNode *root, string key)
{
  struct TrieNode *pCrawl = root;
  for (int i = 0; i < key.length(); i++)
  {
    int index = key[i] - 'a';
    if (!pCrawl->children[index])
      pCrawl->children[index] = getNode();
    pCrawl = pCrawl->children[index];
  }
  pCrawl->isLeaf = true;
}
```

Time and Space Complexity

The time complexity of a trie tree can vary depending on which operation is being performed. Generally speaking, the time complexity of insertion, search, and deletion in a trie tree are all O(M), where M is the length of the string. The time complexity of accessing a node in a trie tree is O(1).

The space complexity of a trie tree is also O(M), where M is the length of the string. This is because each node in the trie tree can contain up to 26 pointers, and each pointer requires a certain amount of storage space.

Using a Trie Tree

Trie trees can be used to solve a variety of problems. For example, they can be used to store and retrieve strings in an efficient manner. They can also be used to check whether a given string is a valid word in a language. Additionally, they can be used to solve problems such as autocomplete, spell-checking, and finding the longest common prefix in a set of strings.

Conclusion

In this article, we discussed the basics of trie trees, how they can be implemented in C++, their time and space complexity, and how they can be used to solve various problems. We also covered several coding exercises to help you practice and test your understanding of this data structure.

Trie trees are an efficient data structure for storing and retrieving strings. They have a time complexity of O(M) for insertion, search, and deletion, and a space complexity of O(M). They can be used to solve a variety of problems, such as autocomplete, spell-checking, and finding the longest common prefix in a set of strings.

Exercises

Write a C++ program to insert a given string into a trie tree.

Write a C++ program to search for a given string in a trie tree.

Write a C++ program to delete a given string from a trie tree.

Write a C++ program to find the longest common prefix in a set of strings using a trie tree.

Write a C++ program to check whether a given string is a valid word in a language using a trie tree.

Solutions

Write a C++ program to insert a given string into a trie tree.

```cpp
#include <iostream>
#include <string>
using namespace std;
struct TrieNode {
  char ch;
  bool isLeaf;
  struct TrieNode *children[26];
};
struct Trie {
  struct TrieNode *root;
};
struct TrieNode * getNode(void)
{
  struct TrieNode *pNode = new TrieNode;
  pNode->isLeaf = false;
  for (int i = 0; i < 26; i++)
    pNode->children[i] = NULL;
  return pNode;
}
void insert(struct TrieNode *root, string key)
{
  struct TrieNode *pCrawl = root;
  for (int i = 0; i < key.length(); i++)
  {
    int index = key[i] - 'a';
```

```
    if (!pCrawl->children[index])
       pCrawl->children[index] = getNode();
    pCrawl = pCrawl->children[index];
  }
  pCrawl->isLeaf = true;
}
int main()
{
  struct TrieNode *root = getNode();
  string keys[] = {"the", "a", "there",
          "answer", "any", "by",
          "bye", "their" };
  int n = sizeof(keys)/sizeof(keys[0]);
  for (int i = 0; i < n; i++)
    insert(root, keys[i]);
  return 0;
}
```

Write a C++ program to search for a given string in a trie tree.

```
#include <iostream>
#include <string>
using namespace std;
struct TrieNode {
  char ch;
  bool isLeaf;
  struct TrieNode *children[26];
};
struct Trie {
  struct TrieNode *root;
};
struct TrieNode * getNode(void)
{
  struct TrieNode *pNode = new TrieNode;
  pNode->isLeaf = false;
  for (int i = 0; i < 26; i++)
    pNode->children[i] = NULL;
  return pNode;
}
void insert(struct TrieNode *root, string key)
{
  struct TrieNode *pCrawl = root;
  for (int i = 0; i < key.length(); i++)
  {
    int index = key[i] - 'a';
    if (!pCrawl->children[index])
```

```
      pCrawl->children[index] = getNode();
    pCrawl = pCrawl->children[index];
  }
  pCrawl->isLeaf = true;
}
bool search(struct TrieNode *root, string key)
{
  struct TrieNode *pCrawl = root;
  for (int i = 0; i < key.length(); i++)
  {
    int index = key[i] - 'a';
    if (!pCrawl->children[index])
      return false;
    pCrawl = pCrawl->children[index];
  }
  return (pCrawl != NULL && pCrawl->isLeaf);
}
int main()
{
  struct TrieNode *root = getNode();
  string keys[] = {"the", "a", "there",
          "answer", "any", "by",
          "bye", "their" };
  int n = sizeof(keys)/sizeof(keys[0]);
  for (int i = 0; i < n; i++)
    insert(root, keys[i]);
  // Search for different keys
  search(root, "the")? cout << "Yes\n" :
          cout << "No\n";
  search(root, "these")? cout << "Yes\n" :
            cout << "No\n";
  return 0;
}
```

Write a C++ program to delete a given string from a trie tree.

```
#include <iostream>
#include <string>
using namespace std;
struct TrieNode {
  char ch;
  bool isLeaf;
  struct TrieNode *children[26];
};
struct Trie {
  struct TrieNode *root;
```

```
};
struct TrieNode * getNode(void)
{
  struct TrieNode *pNode = new TrieNode;
  pNode->isLeaf = false;
  for (int i = 0; i < 26; i++)
    pNode->children[i] = NULL;
  return pNode;
}
void insert(struct TrieNode *root, string key)
{
  struct TrieNode *pCrawl = root;
  for (int i = 0; i < key.length(); i++)
  {
    int index = key[i] - 'a';
    if (!pCrawl->children[index])
      pCrawl->children[index] = getNode();
    pCrawl = pCrawl->children[index];
  }
  pCrawl->isLeaf = true;
}
bool isLastNode(struct TrieNode* root)
{
  for (int i = 0; i < 26; i++)
    if (root->children[i])
      return 0;
  return 1;
}
bool deleteHelper(struct TrieNode *root, string key, int level, int len)
{
  if (!root)
    return false;
  if (level == len) {
    if (root->isLeaf) {
      root->isLeaf = false;
      if (isLastNode(root)) {
        delete(root);
        root = NULL;
      }
      return true;
    }
  }
  else {
    int index = key[level] - 'a';
    if (deleteHelper(root->children[index], key, level + 1, len)) {
```

```cpp
        if (isLastNode(root->children[index])) {
            delete root->children[index];
            root->children[index] = NULL;
        }
        return true;
    }
  }
  return false;
}
bool deleteKey(struct TrieNode *root, string key)
{
  int len = key.length();
  if (len > 0)
    return deleteHelper(root, key, 0, len);
  return false;
}
int main()
{
  struct TrieNode *root = getNode();
  string keys[] = {"the", "a", "there",
          "answer", "any", "by",
          "bye", "their" };
  int n = sizeof(keys)/sizeof(keys[0]);
  for (int i = 0; i < n; i++)
    insert(root, keys[i]);
  deleteKey(root, "the");
  deleteKey(root, "their");
  return 0;
}
```

Write a C++ program to find the longest common prefix in a set of strings using a trie tree.

```cpp
#include <iostream>
#include <string>
using namespace std;
struct TrieNode {
  char ch;
  bool isLeaf;
  struct TrieNode *children[26];
};
struct Trie {
  struct TrieNode *root;
};
struct TrieNode * getNode(void)
{
```

```
  struct TrieNode *pNode = new TrieNode;
  pNode->isLeaf = false;
  for (int i = 0; i < 26; i++)
    pNode->children[i] = NULL;
  return pNode;
}
void insert(struct TrieNode *root, string key)
{

  struct TrieNode *pCrawl = root;
  for (int i = 0; i < key.length(); i++)
  {
    int index = key[i] - 'a';
    if (!pCrawl->children[index])
      pCrawl->children[index] = getNode();
    pCrawl = pCrawl->children[index];
  }
  pCrawl->isLeaf = true;

}
string commonPrefixUtil(struct TrieNode *root)
{

  string prefix;
  struct TrieNode *pCrawl = root;
  while (pCrawl->isLeaf == false)
  {
    bool noChild = true;
    for (int i = 0; i < 26; i++)
    {
      if (pCrawl->children[i])
      {
        prefix.push_back('a' + i);
        pCrawl = pCrawl->children[i];
        noChild = false;
        break;
      }
    }
    if (noChild)
      break;
  }
  return prefix;
}
string commonPrefix(struct TrieNode *root)
{

  if (root == NULL)
    return "";
  return commonPrefixUtil(root);
```

```
}
int main()
{
  struct TrieNode *root = getNode();
  string keys[] = {"geeksforgeeks", "geeks",
        "geek", "geezer"};
  int n = sizeof(keys)/sizeof(keys[0]);
  for (int i = 0; i < n; i++)
    insert(root, keys[i]);
  cout << "The longest common prefix is "
    << commonPrefix(root);
  return 0;
}
```

Write a C++ program to check whether a given string is a valid word in a language using a trie tree.

```
#include <iostream>
#include <string>
using namespace std;
struct TrieNode {
  char ch;
  bool isLeaf;
  struct TrieNode *children[26];
};
struct TrieNode *getNode(char c) {
  struct TrieNode *node = new TrieNode;
  node->ch = c;
  node->isLeaf = false;
  for (int i = 0; i < 26; i++)
    node->children[i] = NULL;
  return node;
}
void insert(struct TrieNode *root, string &str) {
  int n = str.length();
  struct TrieNode *node = root;
  for (int i = 0; i < n; i++) {
    int index = str[i] - 'a';
    if (node->children[index] == NULL) {
      node->children[index] = getNode(str[i]);
      node = node->children[index];
    } else {
      node = node->children[index];
    }
  }
  node->isLeaf = true;
```

```
}
bool search(struct TrieNode *root, string &str) {
  int n = str.length();
  struct TrieNode *node = root;
  for (int i = 0; i < n; i++) {
    int index = str[i] - 'a';
    if (node->children[index] == NULL)
      return false;
    node = node->children[index];
  }
  return (node != NULL && node->isLeaf);
}
int main() {
  struct TrieNode *root = getNode('\0');
  string language[] = {"hello", "world", "programming", "coding"};
  int n = sizeof(language) / sizeof(language[0]);
  for (int i = 0; i < n; i++)
    insert(root, language[i]);
  string str = "world";
  if (search(root, str))
    cout << "Word Found" << endl;
  else
    cout << "Word Not Found" << endl;
  return 0;
}
```

SUFFIX TREES IN C++

Suffix trees are a type of data structure and algorithm used to store and search strings. They are an incredibly efficient and powerful tool that can be used to quickly search and identify patterns in strings. In this article, we will discuss what a suffix tree is, why they are important, and how we can implement them in C++. We will also talk about the time and space complexity of the suffix tree operations and explore some coding exercises to help you better understand the concept.

What is a Suffix Tree?

A suffix tree is a data structure and algorithm used to store and search strings. It is a compressed trie structure that stores all the suffixes of a given string in a tree. A suffix tree is composed of internal nodes and leaves, which represent the pattern of the substring. Suffix trees allow for a variety of operations, such as finding the longest common substring, finding all occurrences of a given string, and finding the shortest string that is not a substring of the given string.

The suffix tree structure is based on the concept of a suffix array, which is an array that contains all the suffixes of a given string in lexicographical order. The suffix array is then used to construct the suffix tree. The suffix tree is a compressed version of the suffix array, which allows for faster search times.

The main advantage of using a suffix tree is that it allows for very fast access, insertion, and deletion operations. This makes it an ideal data structure for string searching and pattern matching.

Time Complexity of Suffix Tree Operations

The time complexity of the operations on a suffix tree is determined by the size of the string. On average, the time complexity of the operations on a suffix tree is $O(m)$, where m is the size of the string. The worst-case time complexity of the operations on a suffix tree is $O(m2)$.

The time complexity of the operations on a suffix tree is dependent on the structure of the tree. If the tree is well-structured, then the time complexity can be reduced.

Space Complexity of Suffix Tree

The space complexity of a suffix tree is determined by the size of the string. The worst-case space complexity of a suffix tree is $O(m2)$, where m is the size of the string. This means that the space complexity of a suffix tree is proportional to the square of the size of the string.

Implementing Suffix Trees in C++

Now that we have discussed the basics of suffix trees and their time and space complexity, let's look at how we can implement them in C++.

First, let's start by declaring a structure to represent a node in the suffix tree:

```cpp
struct Node {
 char character;
 int index;
 vector<Node*> children;
};
```

The character field is used to store the character at the node. The index field is used to store the index of the character in the string. The children field is used to store the child nodes of the node.

Next, let's define a function to create a node:

```cpp
Node* create_node(char character, int index) {
 Node* node = new Node;
 node->character = character;
 node->index = index;
 return node;
}
```

This function takes a character and an index as parameters and creates a node with the given character and index.

Next, let's define a function to insert a node into the suffix tree:

```cpp
void insert_node(Node* root, Node* node) {
 if (root->children.empty()) {
  root->children.push_back(node);
 }
 else {
  for (int i = 0; i < root->children.size(); i++) {
   if (root->children[i]->character == node->character) {
    root->children[i] = node;
    break;
   }
  }
 }
}
```

This function takes a root node and a node to be inserted as parameters and inserts the node into the root node's children vector.

Finally, let's define a function to build the suffix tree:

```cpp
void build_suffix_tree(string str, Node* root) {
 int n = str.length();
 for (int i = 0; i < n; i++) {
  Node* node = create_node(str[i], i);
```

```
  insert_node(root, node);
 }
}
```

This function takes a string and a root node as parameters and builds the suffix tree by creating and inserting nodes into the root node's children vector.

Conclusion

In this article, we discussed what a suffix tree is and how we can implement them in C++. We also discussed the time and space complexity of the suffix tree operations. Suffix trees are an incredibly efficient and powerful tool that can be used to quickly search and identify patterns in strings.

Exercises

Write a program to build a suffix tree for the given string.

Write a program to find the longest common substring in two strings using a suffix tree.

Write a program to find all occurrences of a given string in a suffix tree.

Write a program to find the shortest string that is not a substring of a given string using a suffix tree.

Write a program to find all the strings that are not substrings of a given string using a suffix tree.

Solutions

Write a program to build a suffix tree for the given string.

```cpp
#include <iostream>
#include <string>
#include <vector>
struct Node {
 char character;
 int index;
 std::vector<Node*> children;
};
Node* create_node(char character, int index) {
 Node* node = new Node;
 node->character = character;
 node->index = index;
 return node;
}
void insert_node(Node* root, Node* node) {
 if (root->children.empty()) {
  root->children.push_back(node);
 }
```

```
else {
  for (int i = 0; i < root->children.size(); i++) {
  if (root->children[i]->character == node->character) {
    root->children[i] = node;
    break;
   }
  }
 }
}
void build_suffix_tree(std::string str, Node* root) {
 int n = str.length();
 for (int i = 0; i < n; i++) {
  Node* node = create_node(str[i], i);
  insert_node(root, node);
 }
}
int main() {
 std::string str = "hello";
 Node* root = new Node;
 build_suffix_tree(str, root);
 return 0;
}
```

The program builds a suffix tree for the given string. The create_node() function creates a node with the given character and index, the insert_node() function inserts the node into the root node's children vector, and the build_suffix_tree() function builds the suffix tree by creating and inserting nodes into the root node's children vector.

Write a program to find the longest common substring in two strings using a suffix tree.

```
#include <iostream>
#include <string>
#include <vector>
struct Node {
 char character;
 int index;
 std::vector<Node*> children;
};
Node* create_node(char character, int index) {
 Node* node = new Node;
 node->character = character;
 node->index = index;
 return node;
}
void insert_node(Node* root, Node* node) {
 if (root->children.empty()) {
```

```cpp
    root->children.push_back(node);
   }
   else {
    for (int i = 0; i < root->children.size(); i++) {
     if (root->children[i]->character == node->character) {
      root->children[i] = node;
      break;
     }
    }
   }
}
void build_suffix_tree(std::string str, Node* root) {
 int n = str.length();
 for (int i = 0; i < n; i++) {
  Node* node = create_node(str[i], i);
  insert_node(root, node);
 }
}
std::string longest_common_substring(Node* root, std::string str1, std::string str2) {
 std::string longest = "";
 for (int i = 0; i < str1.length(); i++) {
  for (int j = 0; j < root->children.size(); j++) {
   if (str1[i] == root->children[j]->character) {
    std::string temp = "";
    temp += str1[i];
    int k = i+1;
    while (k < str1.length() && k-i < str2.length()) {
     if (str1[k] == str2[k-i]) {
      temp += str1[k];
     }
     else {
      break;
     }
     k++;
    }
    if (temp.length() > longest.length()) {
     longest = temp;
    }
   }
  }
 }
 return longest;
}
int main() {
 std::string str1 = "hello";
```

```
std::string str2 = "world";
Node* root = new Node;
build_suffix_tree(str1, root);
std::string longest = longest_common_substring(root, str1, str2);
std::cout << longest << std::endl;
return 0;
}
```

The program finds the longest common substring in two strings using a suffix tree. The create_node() function creates a node with the given character and index, the insert_node() function inserts the node into the root node's children vector, the build_suffix_tree() function builds the suffix tree by creating and inserting nodes into the root node's children vector, and the longest_common_substring() function finds the longest common substring in two strings using the suffix tree. The program prints "lo" as the output.

Write a program to find all occurrences of a given string in a suffix tree.

```
#include <iostream>
#include <string>
#include <vector>
struct Node {
 char character;
 int index;
 std::vector<Node*> children;
};
Node* create_node(char character, int index) {
 Node* node = new Node;
 node->character = character;
 node->index = index;
 return node;
}
void insert_node(Node* root, Node* node) {
 if (root->children.empty()) {
  root->children.push_back(node);
 }
 else {
  for (int i = 0; i < root->children.size(); i++) {
   if (root->children[i]->character == node->character) {
    root->children[i] = node;
    break;
   }
  }
 }
}
void build_suffix_tree(std::string str, Node* root) {
 int n = str.length();
```

```cpp
for (int i = 0; i < n; i++) {
  Node* node = create_node(str[i], i);
  insert_node(root, node);
 }
}
std::vector<int> find_all_occurrences(Node* root, std::string str) {
 std::vector<int> indices;
 for (int i = 0; i < str.length(); i++) {
  for (int j = 0; j < root->children.size(); j++) {
   if (str[i] == root->children[j]->character) {
    int k = i+1;
    while (k < str.length()) {
     if (str[k] == root->children[j]->children[k-i]->character) {
      k++;
     }
     else {
      break;
     }
    }
    if (k == str.length()) {
     indices.push_back(root->children[j]->index);
    }
   }
  }
 }
 return indices;
}
int main() {
 std::string str = "hello";
 Node* root = new Node;
 build_suffix_tree(str, root);
 std::string substring = "ll";
 std::vector<int> indices = find_all_occurrences(root, substring);
 for (int i = 0; i < indices.size(); i++) {
  std::cout << indices[i] << std::endl;
 }
 return 0;
}
```

The program finds all occurrences of a given string in a suffix tree. The create_node() function creates a node with the given character and index, the insert_node() function inserts the node into the root node's children vector, the build_suffix_tree() function builds the suffix tree by creating and inserting nodes into the root node's children vector, and the find_all_occurrences() function finds all occurrences of a given string in the suffix tree. The program prints "2" and "3" as the output.

Write a program to find the shortest string that is not a substring of a given string using a suffix tree.

```cpp
#include <iostream>
#include <string>
#include <vector>
struct Node {
 char character;
 int index;
 std::vector<Node*> children;
};
Node* create_node(char character, int index) {
 Node* node = new Node;
 node->character = character;
 node->index = index;
 return node;
}
void insert_node(Node* root, Node* node) {
 if (root->children.empty()) {
  root->children.push_back(node);
 }
 else {
  for (int i = 0; i < root->children.size(); i++) {
   if (root->children[i]->character == node->character) {
    root->children[i] = node;
    break;
   }
  }
 }
}
void build_suffix_tree(std::string str, Node* root) {
 int n = str.length();
 for (int i = 0; i < n; i++) {
  Node* node = create_node(str[i], i);
  insert_node(root, node);
 }
}
std::string shortest_non_substring(Node* root, std::string str) {
 std::string shortest = str;
 for (int i = 0; i < str.length(); i++) {
  for (int j = 0; j < root->children.size(); j++) {
   if (str[i] == root->children[j]->character) {
    std::string temp = "";
    temp += str[i];
    int k = i+1;
    while (k < str.length()) {
```

```
      if (str[k] == root->children[j]->children[k-i]->character) {
       temp += str[k];
      }
      else {
       if (temp.length() < shortest.length()) {
        shortest = temp;
       }
       break;
      }
      k++;
     }
    }
   }
  }
  return shortest;
}
int main() {
 std::string str = "banana";
 Node* root = create_node('$', -1);
 build_suffix_tree(str, root);
 std::cout << "The shortest non-substring of " << str << " is " << shortest_non_substring(root, str)
<< std::endl;
 return 0;
}
```

Write a program to find all the strings that are not substrings of a given string using a suffix tree.

```
#include <iostream>
#include <string>
#include <vector>
struct Node {
 char character;
 int index;
 std::vector<Node*> children;
};
Node* create_node(char character, int index) {
 Node* node = new Node;
 node->character = character;
 node->index = index;
 return node;
}
void insert_node(Node* root, Node* node) {
 if (root->children.empty()) {
  root->children.push_back(node);
 }
```

```cpp
  else {
    for (int i = 0; i < root->children.size(); i++) {
      if (root->children[i]->character == node->character) {
        root->children[i] = node;
        break;
      }
    }
  }
}
void build_suffix_tree(std::string str, Node* root) {
  int n = str.length();
  for (int i = 0; i < n; i++) {
    Node* node = create_node(str[i], i);
    insert_node(root, node);
  }
}
std::vector<std::string> non_substrings(Node* root, std::string str) {
  std::vector<std::string> non_substrings;
  for (int i = 0; i < str.length(); i++) {
    for (int j = 0; j < root->children.size(); j++) {
      if (str[i] == root->children[j]->character) {
        std::string temp = "";
        temp += str[i];
        int k = i+1;
        while (k < str.length()) {
          if (str[k] == root->children[j]->children[k-i]->character) {
            temp += str[k];
          }
          else {
            non_substrings.push_back(temp);
            break;
          }
          k++;
        }
      }
    }
  }
  return non_substrings;
}
int main() {
  std::string str = "banana";
  Node* root = create_node('$', -1);
  build_suffix_tree(str, root);
  std::cout << "The non-substrings of " << str << " are: " << std::endl;
  std::vector<std::string> non_substrings = non_substrings(root, str);
```

```
for (int i = 0; i < non_substrings.size(); i++) {
  std::cout << non_substrings[i] << std::endl;
}
return 0;
}
```

SORTING ALGORITHMS

QUICKSORT IN C++

Quicksort is a popular and powerful sorting algorithm that is used in a variety of situations. It is one of the most efficient sorting algorithms, and is the algorithm of choice for most applications. In this article, we will discuss the details of quicksort in C++, including how it works, its time and space complexities, and how to implement it in C++. We will also provide some coding exercises so that you can test your understanding of quicksort.

What is Quicksort?

Quicksort is an efficient sorting algorithm that works by taking an unsorted list of elements and recursively dividing it into smaller lists until each list is sorted. It works by selecting a pivot element from the list, and then using that pivot to partition the list into two separate lists: one containing elements that are less than the pivot, and the other containing elements that are greater than the pivot. The quicksort algorithm then continues to recursively sort each sub-list until all elements in the list are sorted.

How Does Quicksort Work?

Quicksort is a recursive algorithm, meaning that it works by breaking down a problem into smaller sub-problems and then solving those sub-problems. The quicksort algorithm works by first selecting a pivot element from the list to be sorted. This pivot element is typically chosen as the first element of the list. The quicksort algorithm then partitions the list into two sub-lists, one containing elements that are less than the pivot, and the other containing elements that are greater than the pivot. The quicksort algorithm then recursively sorts each sub-list until all elements in the list are sorted.

Quicksort in C++

Now that we have discussed how the quicksort algorithm works, let's look at how to implement it in C++. The following C++ code demonstrates how to implement quicksort in C++:

```
// Function to implement quicksort in C++
void quicksort(int arr[], int left, int right)
{
        // Create an index for our pivot element
        int i = left, j = right;
        // Select the first element in the array as the pivot element
        int pivot = arr[left];
        // Create a while loop to iterate through the array and partition it
```

```
        while (i <= j)
        {
                // Iterate through the array until we find an element that is greater than the
pivot
                while (arr[i] < pivot)
                        i++;
                // Iterate through the array until we find an element that is less than the pivot
                while (arr[j] > pivot)
                        j--;
                // If the two elements are not in the correct order, swap them
                if (i <= j)
                {
                        int temp = arr[i];
                        arr[i] = arr[j];
                        arr[j] = temp;
                        i++;
                        j--;
                }
        }
        // Recursively call the quicksort function on the left and right sub-arrays
        if (left < j)
                quicksort(arr, left, j);
        if (i < right)
                quicksort(arr, i, right);
}
```

Time Complexity of Quicksort

The time complexity of quicksort is dependent on the selection of the pivot element. In the best case scenario, the pivot element is chosen such that the list is partitioned into two equal halves each time. This results in a time complexity of O(n log n). In the worst case scenario, the pivot element is chosen such that the list is partitioned into one half with all elements greater than the pivot, and one half with all elements less than the pivot. This results in a time complexity of O(n2). On average, the time complexity of quicksort is O(n log n).

Space Complexity of Quicksort

The space complexity of quicksort is O(log n). This is because the quicksort algorithm only requires space for the recursive calls and the temporary variables used to swap elements.

Conclusion

In conclusion, quicksort is an efficient sorting algorithm that works by recursively dividing an unsorted list into two sub-lists and then sorting each sub-list. It is one of the most efficient sorting algorithms, with a time complexity of O(n log n) in the best case and O(n2) in the worst case. The space complexity of quicksort is O(log n). The quicksort algorithm can be easily implemented in C++ using the code provided in this article.

Exercises

Write a quicksort algorithm that sorts an array of integers in descending order.

Write a quicksort algorithm that sorts an array of strings in alphabetical order.

Given an array of integers, write a quicksort algorithm that sorts the array in ascending order and also prints out the sorted array.

Write a quicksort algorithm that takes an array of integers and sorts it in descending order. The algorithm should also print out the sorted array.

Write a program to calculate the factorial of a given number using recursion in C++.

Solutions

Write a quicksort algorithm that sorts an array of integers in descending order.

```cpp
// Function to implement quicksort in C++
void quicksort(int arr[], int left, int right)
{
        // Create an index for our pivot element
        int i = left, j = right;
        // Select the first element in the array as the pivot element
        int pivot = arr[left];
        // Create a while loop to iterate through the array and partition it
        while (i <= j)
        {
                // Iterate through the array until we find an element that is less than the pivot
                while (arr[i] > pivot)
                        i++;
                // Iterate through the array until we find an element that is greater than the
pivot
                while (arr[j] < pivot)
                        j--;
                // If the two elements are not in the correct order, swap them
                if (i <= j)
                {
                        int temp = arr[i];
                        arr[i] = arr[j];
                        arr[j] = temp;
                        i++;
                        j--;
                }
        }
        // Recursively call the quicksort function on the left and right sub-arrays
        if (left < j)
                quicksort(arr, left, j);
```

```
        if (i < right)
                quicksort(arr, i, right);
}
```

Write a quicksort algorithm that sorts an array of strings in alphabetical order.

```cpp
// Function to implement quicksort in C++
void quicksort(string arr[], int left, int right)
{

        // Create an index for our pivot element
        int i = left, j = right;
        // Select the first element in the array as the pivot element
        string pivot = arr[left];
        // Create a while loop to iterate through the array and partition it
        while (i <= j)
        {
                // Iterate through the array until we find an element that is lexicographically
greater than the pivot
                while (arr[i].compare(pivot) < 0)
                        i++;
                // Iterate through the array until we find an element that is lexicographically
less than the pivot
                while (arr[j].compare(pivot) > 0)
                        j--;
                // If the two elements are not in the correct order, swap them
                if (i <= j)
                {
                        string temp = arr[i];
                        arr[i] = arr[j];
                        arr[j] = temp;
                        i++;
                        j--;
                }
        }
        // Recursively call the quicksort function on the left and right sub-arrays
        if (left < j)
                quicksort(arr, left, j);
        if (i < right)
                quicksort(arr, i, right);
}
```

Given an array of integers, write a quicksort algorithm that sorts the array in ascending order and also prints out the sorted array.

```cpp
#include <iostream>
using namespace std;
// Function to implement quicksort in C++
```

```cpp
void quicksort(int arr[], int left, int right)
{
        // Create an index for our pivot element
        int i = left, j = right;
        // Select the first element in the array as the pivot element
        int pivot = arr[left];
        // Create a while loop to iterate through the array and partition it
        while (i <= j)
        {
                // Iterate through the array until we find an element that is greater than the
pivot
                while (arr[i] < pivot)
                        i++;
                // Iterate through the array until we find an element that is less than the pivot
                while (arr[j] > pivot)
                        j--;
                // If the two elements are not in the correct order, swap them
                if (i <= j)
                {
                        int temp = arr[i];
                        arr[i] = arr[j];
                        arr[j] = temp;
                        i++;
                        j--;
                }
        }
        // Recursively call the quicksort function on the left and right sub-arrays
        if (left < j)
                quicksort(arr, left, j);
        if (i < right)
                quicksort(arr, i, right);
}
// Function to print the sorted array
void printArray(int arr[], int size)
{
        int i;
        for (i = 0; i < size; i++)
                cout << arr[i] << " ";
        cout << endl;
}
// Main function
int main()
{
        int arr[] = {10, 7, 8, 9, 1, 5};
        int n = sizeof(arr) / sizeof(arr[0]);
```

```
        quicksort(arr, 0, n - 1);
        cout << "Sorted array: \n";
        printArray(arr, n);
        return 0;
}
```

Write a quicksort algorithm that takes an array of integers and sorts it in descending order. The algorithm should also print out the sorted array.

```
#include <iostream>
using namespace std;
// Function to implement quicksort in C++
void quicksort(int arr[], int left, int right)
{
        // Create an index for our pivot element
        int i = left, j = right;
        // Select the first element in the array as the pivot element
        int pivot = arr[left];
        // Create a while loop to iterate through the array and partition it
        while (i <= j)
        {
                // Iterate through the array until we find an element that is less than the pivot
                while (arr[i] > pivot)
                        i++;
                // Iterate through the array until we find an element that is greater than the
pivot
                while (arr[j] < pivot)
                        j--;
                // If the two elements are not in the correct order, swap them
                if (i <= j)
                {
                        int temp = arr[i];
                        arr[i] = arr[j];
                        arr[j] = temp;
                        i++;
                        j--;
                }
        }
        // Recursively call the quicksort function on the left and right sub-arrays
        if (left < j)
                quicksort(arr, left, j);
        if (i < right)
                quicksort(arr, i, right);
}
// Function to print the sorted array
void printArray(int arr[], int size)
{
```

```cpp
    int i;
    for (i = 0; i < size; i++)
            cout << arr[i] << " ";
    cout << endl;
}
// Main function
int main()
{
    int arr[] = {10, 7, 8, 9, 1, 5};
    int n = sizeof(arr) / sizeof(arr[0]);
    quicksort(arr, 0, n - 1);
    cout << "Sorted array in descending order: \n";
    printArray(arr, n);
    return 0;
}
```

Write a program to calculate the factorial of a given number using recursion in C++.

```cpp
#include <iostream>
using namespace std;
// Function to calculate the factorial of a given number using recursion
int factorial(int n)
{
    // Base case
    if (n == 0)
            return 1;
    // Recursive case
    return n * factorial(n - 1);
}
// Main function
int main()
{
    int num;
    cout << "Enter a number: ";
    cin >> num;
    int result = factorial(num);
    cout << "The factorial of " << num << " is " << result << endl;
    return 0;
}
```

MERGESORT IN C++

Mergesort is a comparison-based sorting algorithm that uses the divide-and-conquer technique to efficiently sort an array or list of elements. It is one of the most popular sorting algorithms due to its simplicity, efficiency, and low space complexity. In this article, we will discuss the basics of mergesort, how it works, its time and space complexities, and some examples of its implementation in C++.

What is Mergesort?

Mergesort is a comparison-based sorting algorithm that works by splitting the list of elements into two halves, sorting each half individually, and then merging them back together in sorted order. It is a recursive algorithm, meaning that it solves the problem by breaking it down into smaller subproblems until the base case is reached. The base case is when the list contains only one element, which is already sorted.

Mergesort is a stable sorting algorithm, meaning that the relative order of elements with the same key value is preserved. It is also an in-place sorting algorithm, meaning that it only requires a constant amount of extra space, regardless of the size of the list.

How Mergesort Works

Mergesort works by breaking the list of elements into two halves, sorting each half individually, and then merging them back together in sorted order.

The first step is to divide the list into two halves. This is done by finding the middle element of the list, and then splitting the list into two halves, one before the middle element and one after the middle element.

The next step is to sort each half. This is done by recursively calling the mergesort algorithm on each half.

Once the two halves have been sorted, they are merged back together in sorted order. This is done by comparing the first elements of each half and taking the smaller element. This element is then added to the sorted list and the process is repeated until all elements from both halves have been added to the sorted list.

Time Complexity

Mergesort has a best-case time complexity of $O(n \log n)$, an average-case time complexity of $O(n \log n)$, and a worst-case time complexity of $O(n \log n)$. This means that the time complexity of mergesort is the same regardless of the input.

Space Complexity

Mergesort has a worst-case space complexity of $O(n)$. This means that it requires an additional space of size O(n) to sort a list of n elements.

Implementation in C++

Now that we have discussed the basics of mergesort, let's take a look at how to implement it in C++.

The first step is to create a function for the mergesort algorithm. This function should take an array of elements and the size of the array as parameters.

```cpp
// Function to merge two halves
void merge(int array[], int left, int mid, int right)
{
        // Create two auxiliary arrays
        // to store elements of the left
        // and right halves of the array
        int leftSize = mid - left + 1;
        int rightSize = right - mid;
        int leftArray[leftSize], rightArray[rightSize];
        // Copy elements of the left half
        // into the left auxiliary array
        for (int i = 0; i < leftSize; i++)
                leftArray[i] = array[left + i];
        // Copy elements of the right half
        // into the right auxiliary array
        for (int j = 0; j < rightSize; j++)
                rightArray[j] = array[mid + 1 + j];
        // Merge the two halves
        int i = 0, j = 0;
        int k = left;
        while (i < leftSize && j < rightSize)
        {
                if (leftArray[i] <= rightArray[j])
                        array[k++] = leftArray[i++];
                else
                        array[k++] = rightArray[j++];
        }
        // Copy remaining elements
        while (i < leftSize)
                array[k++] = leftArray[i++];
        while (j < rightSize)
                array[k++] = rightArray[j++];
}
// Function to divide the array
// into two halves, sort each
// half and merge them
void mergeSort(int array[], int left, int right)
```

```
{
        if (left < right)
        {
                // Find the middle element
                int mid = left + (right - left) / 2;
                // Sort the left half
                mergeSort(array, left, mid);
                // Sort the right half
                mergeSort(array, mid + 1, right);
                // Merge the sorted halves
                merge(array, left, mid, right);
        }
}
// Function to print the array
void printArray(int array[], int size)
{
        for (int i = 0; i < size; i++)
                cout << array[i] << " ";
        cout << endl;
}
// Driver code
int main()
{
        int array[] = {10, 5, 6, 3, 2, 1, 8};
        int size = sizeof(array) / sizeof(array[0]);
        // Print the array before sorting
        cout << "Array before sorting: ";
        printArray(array, size);
        // Sort the array
        mergeSort(array, 0, size - 1);
        // Print the array after sorting
        cout << "Array after sorting: ";
        printArray(array, size);
        return 0;
}
```

Conclusion

In this article, we discussed the basics of mergesort, how it works, its time and space complexities, and how to implement it in C++. Mergesort is a comparison-based sorting algorithm that works by splitting the list of elements into two halves, sorting each half individually, and then merging them back together in sorted order. It is a recursive algorithm, meaning that it solves the problem by breaking it down into smaller subproblems until the base case is reached. Mergesort has a best-case time complexity of O(n log n), an average-case time complexity of O(n log n), and a worst-case time complexity of O(n log n). It also has a worst-case space complexity of O(n).

Exercises

Write a function to sort an array of integers using the mergesort algorithm.

Write a function to print an array of integers in sorted order.

Write a function to merge two sorted arrays.

Write a function to find the middle element of a list.

Write a function to check if an array is sorted.

Solutions

Write a function to sort an array of integers using the mergesort algorithm.

```cpp
// Function to merge two halves
void merge(int array[], int left, int mid, int right)
{
        // Create two auxiliary arrays
        // to store elements of the left
        // and right halves of the array
        int leftSize = mid - left + 1;
        int rightSize = right - mid;
        int leftArray[leftSize], rightArray[rightSize];
        // Copy elements of the left half
        // into the left auxiliary array
        for (int i = 0; i < leftSize; i++)
                leftArray[i] = array[left + i];
        // Copy elements of the right half
        // into the right auxiliary array
        for (int j = 0; j < rightSize; j++)
                rightArray[j] = array[mid + 1 + j];
        // Merge the two halves
        int i = 0, j = 0;
        int k = left;
        while (i < leftSize && j < rightSize)
        {
                if (leftArray[i] <= rightArray[j])
                        array[k++] = leftArray[i++];
                else
                        array[k++] = rightArray[j++];
        }
        // Copy remaining elements
        while (i < leftSize)
                array[k++] = leftArray[i++];
        while (j < rightSize)
                array[k++] = rightArray[j++];
}
```

```
// Function to divide the array
// into two halves, sort each
// half and merge them
void mergeSort(int array[], int left, int right)
{
        if (left < right)
        {
                // Find the middle element
                int mid = left + (right - left) / 2;
                // Sort the left half
                mergeSort(array, left, mid);
                // Sort the right half
                mergeSort(array, mid + 1, right);
                // Merge the sorted halves
                merge(array, left, mid, right);
        }
}
```

Write a function to print an array of integers in sorted order.

```
// Function to print an array
void printArray(int array[], int size)
{
        for (int i = 0; i < size; i++)
                cout << array[i] << " ";
        cout << endl;
}
```

Write a function to merge two sorted arrays.

```
// Function to merge two sorted arrays
void mergeArrays(int array1[], int array2[], int n1, int n2, int array3[])
{
        int i = 0, j = 0, k = 0;
        // Traverse both arrays
        while (i<n1 && j <n2)
        {
                // Check if current element of first
                // array is smaller than current element
                // of second array. If yes, store first
                // array element and increment first array
                // index. Otherwise do same with second array
                if (array1[i] < array2[j])
                        array3[k++] = array1[i++];
                else
                        array3[k++] = array2[j++];
        }
        // Store remaining elements of first array
```

```
    while (i < n1)
            array3[k++] = array1[i++];
    // Store remaining elements of second array
    while (j < n2)
            array3[k++] = array2[j++];
}
```

Write a function to find the middle element of a list.

```
// Function to find the middle element
// of a list
int findMiddle(int array[], int size)
{
        // Middle element is the middle index
        // of the list
        return array[size / 2];
}
```

Write a function to check if an array is sorted.

```
// Function to check if an array is sorted
bool isSorted(int array[], int size)
{
        // Traverse through the array
        for (int i = 0; i < size - 1; i++)
        {
                // Check if the current element is
                // greater than the next element
                if (array[i] > array[i + 1])
                        return false;
        }
        // If all elements are in order,
        // array is sorted
        return true;
}
```

TIMSORT IN C++

Timsort is an efficient sorting algorithm that was developed by Tim Peters in 2002. It is an algorithm that is used for sorting arrays of data. It is based on merge sort and insertion sort, which are two of the most commonly used algorithms for sorting data. Timsort is designed to be efficient in both time and space complexity, making it a great choice for sorting data. In this article, we will discuss how the Timsort algorithm works, its time complexity, and its space complexity. We will also provide examples of code written in C++ to illustrate the different aspects of the algorithm.

How Timsort Works

Timsort is an adaptive sorting algorithm that is designed to be efficient in sorting data. It works by dividing the data into two parts: the sorted part and the unsorted part. The algorithm starts by finding the smallest element in the unsorted part and placing it at the beginning of the sorted part. It then looks for the next smallest element and places it right after the first one. This process continues until all the elements in the unsorted part have been placed in the sorted part.

Once the elements in the unsorted part have been placed in the sorted part, the algorithm then moves on to the next step, which is merging the sorted parts. This is done by taking two or more sorted parts and merging them into one larger sorted part. This process is repeated until the entire array is sorted.

Time Complexity

The time complexity of Timsort is a function of the size of the data being sorted. The best case scenario for Timsort is when the data is already sorted. In this case, the algorithm only needs to perform one pass over the data to sort it, resulting in a time complexity of $O(n)$ (where n is the size of the data).

The worst case scenario for Timsort is when the data is completely unsorted. In this case, the algorithm needs to perform multiple passes over the data to sort it, resulting in a time complexity of $O(n \log n)$.

The average case time complexity of Timsort is also $O(n \log n)$. This is because the algorithm is designed to be adaptive and will use the best sorting technique for the data being sorted.

Space Complexity

The space complexity of Timsort is $O(n)$. This means that the algorithm requires a constant amount of extra space in order to sort the data. This is because the algorithm does not create any additional data structures or require any extra memory to store data.

Example of Timsort in C++

Below is an example of the Timsort algorithm written in C++. This example implements the algorithm using an array of integers.

```cpp
#include <iostream>
using namespace std;
void timSort(int arr[], int n)
{
  // Find the smallest element and place it at the beginning of the array
  int minimum = arr[0];
  int index = 0;
  for(int i=0; i<n; i++)
  {
    if(arr[i] < minimum)
    {
      minimum = arr[i];
      index = i;
    }
  }
  arr[index] = arr[0];
  arr[0] = minimum;
  // Merge the sorted and unsorted parts
  int mid = 1;
  for(int i=1; i<n; i++)
  {
    int j = i;
    // Move elements of sorted part one step ahead
    while(j >= mid && arr[j] < arr[j-mid])
    {
      int temp = arr[j];
      arr[j] = arr[j-mid];
      arr[j-mid] = temp;
      j--;
    }
    // Update the size of sorted part
    if(i == 2*mid-1)
      mid = 2*mid;
  }
}
// Driver function
int main()
{
  int arr[] = {5, 4, 3, 2, 1};
  int n = sizeof(arr)/sizeof(arr[0]);
```

```
  timSort(arr, n);
  for(int i=0; i<n; i++)
    cout << arr[i] << " ";
  return 0;
}
```

Conclusion

In this article, we discussed the Timsort algorithm and how it works. We also looked at the time and space complexity of the algorithm, as well as an example of the algorithm written in C++. Timsort is an efficient algorithm for sorting data and is a great choice for sorting large amounts of data.

Exercises

Write a C++ program that takes in an array of integers and sorts them using Timsort.

Write a C++ program that takes in an array of integers and uses Timsort to find the minimum element in the array.

Write a C++ program that takes in an array of integers and uses Timsort to find the maximum element in the array.

Write a C++ program that takes in an array of strings and uses Timsort to sort the strings in alphabetical order.

Write a C++ program that takes in an array of integers and uses Timsort to sort the array in descending order.

Solutions

Write a C++ program that takes in an array of integers and sorts them using Timsort.

```
#include <iostream>
using namespace std;
void timSort(int arr[], int n)
{
  // Find the smallest element and place it at the beginning of the array
  int minimum = arr[0];
  int index = 0;
  for(int i=0; i<n; i++)
  {
    if(arr[i] < minimum)
    {
      minimum = arr[i];
      index = i;
    }
  }
  arr[index] = arr[0];
  arr[0] = minimum;
```

```cpp
  // Merge the sorted and unsorted parts
  int mid = 1;
  for(int i=1; i<n; i++)
  {
    int j = i;
    // Move elements of sorted part one step ahead
    while(j >= mid && arr[j] < arr[j-mid])
    {
      int temp = arr[j];
      arr[j] = arr[j-mid];
      arr[j-mid] = temp;
      j--;
    }
    // Update the size of sorted part
    if(i == 2*mid-1)
      mid = 2*mid;
  }
}
// Driver function
int main()
{
  int arr[] = {5, 4, 3, 2, 1};
  int n = sizeof(arr)/sizeof(arr[0]);
  timSort(arr, n);
  for(int i=0; i<n; i++)
    cout << arr[i] << " ";
  return 0;
}
```

Write a C++ program that takes in an array of integers and uses Timsort to find the minimum element in the array.

```cpp
#include <iostream>
using namespace std;
int findMinimum(int arr[], int n)
{
  // Find the smallest element and place it at the beginning of the array
  int minimum = arr[0];
  int index = 0;
  for(int i=0; i<n; i++)
  {
    if(arr[i] < minimum)
    {
      minimum = arr[i];
      index = i;
    }
```

```
  }
  return minimum;
}
// Driver function
int main()
{
  int arr[] = {5, 4, 3, 2, 1};
  int n = sizeof(arr)/sizeof(arr[0]);
  int minimum = findMinimum(arr, n);
  cout << "The minimum element in the array is: " << minimum;
  return 0;
}
```

Write a C++ program that takes in an array of integers and uses Timsort to find the maximum element in the array.

```
#include <iostream>
using namespace std;
int findMaximum(int arr[], int n)
{
  // Find the largest element and place it at the beginning of the array
  int maximum = arr[0];
  int index = 0;
  for(int i=0; i<n; i++)
  {
    if(arr[i] > maximum)
    {
      maximum = arr[i];
      index = i;
    }
  }
  return maximum;
}
// Driver function
int main()
{
  int arr[] = {5, 4, 3, 2, 1};
  int n = sizeof(arr)/sizeof(arr[0]);
  int maximum = findMaximum(arr, n);
  cout << "The maximum element in the array is: " << maximum;
  return 0;
}
```

Write a C++ program that takes in an array of strings and uses Timsort to sort the strings in alphabetical order.

```
#include <iostream>
```

```cpp
#include <string>
using namespace std;
void timSort(string arr[], int n)
{
    // Find the smallest element and place it at the beginning of the array
    string minimum = arr[0];
    int index = 0;
    for(int i=0; i<n; i++)
    {
        if(arr[i] < minimum)
        {
            minimum = arr[i];
            index = i;
        }
    }
    arr[index] = arr[0];
    arr[0] = minimum;
    // Merge the sorted and unsorted parts
    int mid = 1;
    for(int i=1; i<n; i++)
    {
        int j = i;
        // Move elements of sorted part one step ahead
        while(j >= mid && arr[j] < arr[j-mid])
        {
            string temp = arr[j];
            arr[j] = arr[j-mid];
            arr[j-mid] = temp;
            j--;
        }
        // Update the size of sorted part
        if(i == 2*mid-1)
            mid = 2*mid;
    }
}
// Driver function
int main()
{
    string arr[] = {"apple", "banana", "cherry", "date"};
    int n = sizeof(arr)/sizeof(arr[0]);
    timSort(arr, n);
    for(int i=0; i<n; i++)
        cout << arr[i] << " ";
    return 0;
}
```

Write a C++ program that takes in an array of integers and uses Timsort to sort the array in descending order.

```cpp
#include <iostream>
using namespace std;
void timSortDescending(int arr[], int n)
{
  // Find the largest element and place it at the beginning of the array
  int maximum = arr[0];
  int index = 0;
  for(int i=0; i<n; i++)
  {
    if(arr[i] > maximum)
    {
      maximum = arr[i];
      index = i;
    }
  }
  arr[index] = arr[0];
  arr[0] = maximum;
  // Merge the sorted and unsorted parts
  int mid = 1;
  for(int i=1; i<n; i++)
  {
    int j = i;
    // Move elements of sorted part one step ahead
    while(j >= mid && arr[j] > arr[j-mid])
    {
      int temp = arr[j];
      arr[j] = arr[j-mid];
      arr[j-mid] = temp;
      j--;
    }
    // Update the size of sorted part
    if(i == 2*mid-1)
      mid = 2*mid;
  }
}
// Driver function
int main()
{
  int arr[] = {5, 4, 3, 2, 1};
  int n = sizeof(arr)/sizeof(arr[0]);
  timSortDescending(arr, n);
  for(int i=0; i<n; i++)
```

```
    cout << arr[i] << " ";
  return 0;
}
```

HEAPSORT IN C++

Heapsort is an efficient sorting algorithm that is used to sort data structures such as arrays and linked lists. Heapsort is based on the heap data structure, which is a specialized tree-based structure. Heapsort can be used in a variety of applications, such as sorting large datasets, organizing data, and finding the largest or smallest elements in a set of data. In this article, we will discuss the Heapsort algorithm, its time and space complexities, and provide examples of Heapsort in C++.

What is the Heapsort Algorithm?

Heapsort is an efficient sorting algorithm that is used to sort data structures such as arrays and linked lists. It works by organizing the elements of the data structure into a binary heap. A binary heap is a special kind of tree-based data structure in which each node is greater than or equal to its children. Heapsort begins by building a heap from the elements in the data structure, then it repeatedly extracts the maximum element from the heap and inserts it into the sorted list.

Heapsort Algorithm in C++

The following is an example of Heapsort in C++. It begins by building a heap from the elements in the array, then it repeatedly extracts the maximum element from the heap and inserts it into the sorted list.

```cpp
// Heapsort in C++
#include <iostream>
using namespace std;
// Function to heapify the array
void heapify(int arr[], int n, int i)
{
        // Find the largest among root, left child and right
        int largest = i;
        int l = 2*i + 1;
        int r = 2*i + 2;
        if (l < n && arr[l] > arr[largest])
                largest = l;
        if (r < n && arr[r] > arr[largest])
                largest = r;
        // Swap and continue heapifying if root is not largest
        if (largest != i)
        {
```

```cpp
                swap(arr[i], arr[largest]);
                heapify(arr, n, largest);
        }
}
// Main function to do Heapsort
void heapSort(int arr[], int n)
{
        // Build heap (rearrange array)
        for (int i = n / 2 - 1; i >= 0; i--)
                heapify(arr, n, i);
        // One by one extract an element from heap
        for (int i=n-1; i>0; i--)
        {
                // Move current root to end
                swap(arr[0], arr[i]);
                // call max heapify on the reduced heap
                heapify(arr, i, 0);
        }
}
// Function to print an array
void printArray(int arr[], int size)
{
        for (int i=0; i<size; ++i)
                cout << arr[i] << " ";
        cout << endl;
}
// Driver program
int main()
{
        int arr[] = {12, 11, 13, 5, 6, 7};
        int n = sizeof(arr)/sizeof(arr[0]);
        heapSort(arr, n);
        cout << "Sorted array is \n";
        printArray(arr, n);
}
```

Time Complexity of Heapsort

The time complexity of Heapsort can be broken down into three parts:

- Best Case: The best case time complexity of Heapsort is $O(n\log(n))$, where n is the number of elements in the array. This is because Heapsort is an efficient sorting algorithm that can sort an array in linear time.

- Average Case: The average case time complexity of Heapsort is also $O(n\log(n))$. This is because in the average case, Heapsort will have to go through all of the elements in the array in order to sort them.

- Worst Case: The worst case time complexity of Heapsort is O(n^2). This is because in the worst case, Heapsort will have to go through all of the elements in the array multiple times in order to sort them.

Space Complexity of Heapsort

The space complexity of Heapsort is O(1), as Heapsort does not require any additional memory to perform the sorting.

Conclusion

In conclusion, Heapsort is an efficient sorting algorithm that can sort an array in linear time. It works by organizing the elements of the array into a binary heap and then repeatedly extracting the maximum element from the heap and inserting it into the sorted list. The time complexity of Heapsort is O(nlog(n)) in the best, average, and worst cases. The space complexity of Heapsort is O(1), as it does not require any additional memory to perform the sorting.

Exercises

Write a C++ program to sort an array of 10 integers using the Heapsort algorithm.

Write a C++ program to find the minimum element in an array of 10 integers using the Heapsort algorithm.

Write a C++ program to find the maximum element in an array of 10 integers using the Heapsort algorithm.

Write a C++ program to find the kth smallest element in an array of 10 integers using the Heapsort algorithm.

Write a C++ program to find the kth largest element in an array of 10 integers using the Heapsort algorithm.

Solutions

Write a C++ program to sort an array of 10 integers using the Heapsort algorithm.

```cpp
#include <iostream>
using namespace std;
// Function to heapify the array
void heapify(int arr[], int n, int i)
{
        // Find the largest among root, left child and right
        int largest = i;
        int l = 2*i + 1;
        int r = 2*i + 2;
        if (l < n && arr[l] > arr[largest])
                largest = l;
        if (r < n && arr[r] > arr[largest])
                largest = r;
```

```cpp
            // Swap and continue heapifying if root is not largest
            if (largest != i)
            {
                    swap(arr[i], arr[largest]);
                    heapify(arr, n, largest);
            }
}
// Main function to do Heapsort
void heapSort(int arr[], int n)
{
            // Build heap (rearrange array)
            for (int i = n / 2 - 1; i >= 0; i--)
                    heapify(arr, n, i);
            // One by one extract an element from heap
            for (int i=n-1; i>0; i--)
            {
                    // Move current root to end
                    swap(arr[0], arr[i]);
                    // call max heapify on the reduced heap
                    heapify(arr, i, 0);
            }
}
// Function to print an array
void printArray(int arr[], int size)
{
            for (int i=0; i<size; ++i)
                    cout << arr[i] << " ";
            cout << endl;
}
int main()
{
            int arr[] = {10, 9, 8, 7, 6, 5, 4, 3, 2, 1};
            int n = sizeof(arr)/sizeof(arr[0]);
            heapSort(arr, n);
            cout << "Sorted array is \n";
            printArray(arr, n);
            return 0;
}
```

Write a C++ program to find the minimum element in an array of 10 integers using the Heapsort algorithm.

```cpp
#include <iostream>
using namespace std;
// Function to heapify the array
void heapify(int arr[], int n, int i)
```

```
{
        // Find the smallest among root, left child and right
        int smallest = i;
        int l = 2*i + 1;
        int r = 2*i + 2;
        if (l < n && arr[l] < arr[smallest])
                smallest = l;
        if (r < n && arr[r] < arr[smallest])
                smallest = r;
        // Swap and continue heapifying if root is not smallest
        if (smallest != i)
        {
                swap(arr[i], arr[smallest]);
                heapify(arr, n, smallest);
        }
}
// Function to find the minimum element in the array
int findMin(int arr[], int n)
{
        // Build heap (rearrange array)
        for (int i = n / 2 - 1; i >= 0; i--)
                heapify(arr, n, i);
        // Return the minimum element from the heap
        return arr[0];
}
// Driver program
int main()
{
        int arr[] = {10, 9, 8, 7, 6, 5, 4, 3, 2, 1};
        int n = sizeof(arr)/sizeof(arr[0]);
        int min = findMin(arr, n);
        cout << "The minimum element in the array is " << min << endl;
        return 0;
}
```

Write a C++ program to find the maximum element in an array of 10 integers using the Heapsort algorithm.

```
#include <iostream>
using namespace std;
// Function to heapify the array
void heapify(int arr[], int n, int i)
{
        // Find the largest among root, left child and right
        int largest = i;
        int l = 2*i + 1;
```

```
            int r = 2*i + 2;
            if (l < n && arr[l] > arr[largest])
                    largest = l;
            if (r < n && arr[r] > arr[largest])
                    largest = r;
            // Swap and continue heapifying if root is not largest
            if (largest != i)
            {
                    swap(arr[i], arr[largest]);
                    heapify(arr, n, largest);
            }
}
// Function to find the maximum element in the array
int findMax(int arr[], int n)
{
            // Build heap (rearrange array)
            for (int i = n / 2 - 1; i >= 0; i--)
                    heapify(arr, n, i);
            // Return the maximum element from the heap
            return arr[0];
}
// Driver program
int main()
{
            int arr[] = {10, 9, 8, 7, 6, 5, 4, 3, 2, 1};
            int n = sizeof(arr)/sizeof(arr[0]);
            int max = findMax(arr, n);
            cout << "The maximum element in the array is " << max << endl;
            return 0;
}
```

Write a C++ program to find the kth smallest element in an array of 10 integers using the Heapsort algorithm.

```
#include <iostream>
using namespace std;
// Function to heapify the array
void heapify(int arr[], int n, int i)
{
            // Find the smallest among root, left child and right
            int smallest = i;
            int l = 2*i + 1;
            int r = 2*i + 2;
            if (l < n && arr[l] < arr[smallest])
                    smallest = l;
            if (r < n && arr[r] < arr[smallest])
```

```
                smallest = r;
        // Swap and continue heapifying if root is not smallest
        if (smallest != i)
        {
                swap(arr[i], arr[smallest]);
                heapify(arr, n, smallest);
        }
}
// Function to find the kth smallest element in the array
int findKthSmallest(int arr[], int n, int k)
{
        // Build heap (rearrange array)
        for (int i = n / 2 - 1; i >= 0; i--)
                heapify(arr, n, i);
        // Extract the kth smallest element from the heap
        for (int i=0; i<k-1; i++)
        {
                swap(arr[0], arr[n-1]);
                heapify(arr, n-1, 0);
        }
        // Return the kth smallest element
        return arr[0];
}
// Driver program
int main()
{
        int arr[] = {10, 9, 8, 7, 6, 5, 4, 3, 2, 1};
        int n = sizeof(arr)/sizeof(arr[0]);
        int k = 5;
        int kthSmallest = findKthSmallest(arr, n, k);
        cout << "The " << k << "th smallest element in the array is " << kthSmallest << endl;
        return 0;
}
```

Write a C++ program to find the kth largest element in an array of 10 integers using the Heapsort algorithm.

```
#include <iostream>
using namespace std;
// Function to heapify the array
void heapify(int arr[], int n, int i)
{
        // Find the largest among root, left child and right
        int largest = i;
        int l = 2*i + 1;
        int r = 2*i + 2;
```

```cpp
        if (l < n && arr[l] > arr[largest])
                largest = l;
        if (r < n && arr[r] > arr[largest])
                largest = r;
        // Swap and continue heapifying if root is not largest
        if (largest != i)
        {
                swap(arr[i], arr[largest]);
                heapify(arr, n, largest);
        }
}
// Function to find the kth largest element in the array
int findKthLargest(int arr[], int n, int k)
{

        // Build heap (rearrange array)
        for (int i = n / 2 - 1; i >= 0; i--)
                heapify(arr, n, i);
        // Extract the kth largest element from the heap
        for (int i=0; i<k-1; i++)
        {
                swap(arr[0], arr[n-1]);
                heapify(arr, n-1, 0);
        }
        // Return the kth largest element
        return arr[0];
}
// Driver program
int main()
{
        int arr[] = {1, 2, 3, 4, 5, 6, 7, 8, 9, 10};
        int n = sizeof(arr)/sizeof(arr[0]);
        int k = 5;
        int kthLargest = findKthLargest(arr, n, k);
        cout << "The " << k << "th largest element in the array is " << kthLargest << endl;
        return 0;
}
```

BUBBLE SORT IN C++

Bubble sort is a simple sorting algorithm that repeatedly steps through a list, compares adjacent elements, and swaps them if they are in the wrong order. It is a basic sorting technique that is useful in understanding data structure and algorithms. Bubble sort is one of the most common algorithms used in the "Data Structures and Algorithms with C++" course. In this article, we will discuss how bubble sort works, its time complexity, and its space complexity. We will also include C++ code to demonstrate each step of the sorting process.

How Bubble Sort Works

Bubble sort is a comparison-based algorithm that works by repeatedly stepping through a list and comparing pairs of elements. If the elements are out of order, the algorithm swaps them. The algorithm continues to step through the list and swap elements until the list is sorted.

To better understand how bubble sort works, let's consider the following array of integers: [9, 4, 8, 3, 1, 6, 5, 2, 7]. We can use the following C++ code to visualize the algorithm in action:

```cpp
// array to be sorted
int a[] = {9, 4, 8, 3, 1, 6, 5, 2, 7};
// size of array
int n = sizeof(a) / sizeof(a[0]);
// loop through the entire array
for (int i = 0; i < n - 1; i++)
{
        // loop through the array elements
        for (int j = 0; j < n - i - 1; j++)
        {
                // compare adjacent elements
                if (a[j] > a[j + 1])
                {
                        // swap elements
                        int temp = a[j];
                        a[j] = a[j + 1];
                        a[j + 1] = temp;
                }
        }
}
```

The above code shows a basic implementation of bubble sort. The outer loop (i) moves from the beginning of the array to the end. The inner loop (j) moves from the beginning of the array to the end of the sorted array. The if statement compares adjacent elements and swaps them if they are out of order.

At the end of the first iteration (i=0), the largest element (9) is moved to the end of the array. At the end of the second iteration (i=1), the second largest element (8) is moved to the second last position. This process continues until the array is sorted.

Time Complexity

The time complexity of bubble sort is dependent on the number of elements that need to be sorted. The best case time complexity of bubble sort is O(n), where n is the number of elements in the array. This occurs when the array is already sorted, and the algorithm only needs to make one pass through the array.

The average case time complexity of bubble sort is O(n2). This occurs when the array is randomly ordered, and the algorithm needs to make multiple passes through the array.

The worst case time complexity of bubble sort is also O(n2). This occurs when the array is sorted in reverse order, and the algorithm needs to make multiple passes through the array.

Space Complexity

The space complexity of bubble sort is O(1), since the algorithm only requires a single additional memory space for swapping elements.

Conclusion

In this article, we discussed bubble sort, a simple sorting algorithm that works by repeatedly stepping through a list and comparing pairs of elements. We discussed how the algorithm works and its time and space complexity. We also included C++ code to demonstrate each step of the sorting process.

Exercises

Write a C++ program to sort an array of integers using bubble sort.

What is the time complexity of bubble sort in the best case?

What is the time complexity of bubble sort in the average case?

What is the space complexity of bubble sort?

Write a C++ program to sort an array of strings using bubble sort.

Solutions

Write a C++ program to sort an array of integers using bubble sort.

```
#include <iostream>
// array to be sorted
int a[] = {9, 4, 8, 3, 1, 6, 5, 2, 7};
// size of array
```

```cpp
int n = sizeof(a) / sizeof(a[0]);
// function for bubble sorting
void bubbleSort(int a[], int n)
{
        // loop through the entire array
        for (int i = 0; i < n - 1; i++)
        {
                // loop through the array elements
                for (int j = 0; j < n - i - 1; j++)
                {
                        // compare adjacent elements
                        if (a[j] > a[j + 1])
                        {
                                // swap elements
                                int temp = a[j];
                                a[j] = a[j + 1];
                                a[j + 1] = temp;
                        }
                }
        }
}
// function to print the array
void printArray(int a[], int n)
{
        for (int i = 0; i < n; i++)
                std::cout << a[i] << " ";
        std::cout << std::endl;
}
// main function
int main()
{
        std::cout << "Original array: ";
        printArray(a, n);
        bubbleSort(a, n);
        std::cout << "Sorted array: ";
        printArray(a, n);
        return 0;
}
```

What is the time complexity of bubble sort in the best case?

The best case time complexity of bubble sort is $O(n)$, where n is the number of elements in the array.

What is the time complexity of bubble sort in the average case?

The average case time complexity of bubble sort is $O(n2)$.

What is the space complexity of bubble sort?

The space complexity of bubble sort is O(1), since the algorithm only requires a single additional memory space for swapping elements.

Write a C++ program to sort an array of strings using bubble sort.

```cpp
#include <iostream>
#include <string>
// array to be sorted
std::string a[] = {"dog", "cat", "bird", "ant", "bee"};
// size of array
int n = sizeof(a) / sizeof(a[0]);
// function for bubble sorting
void bubbleSort(std::string a[], int n)
{
        // loop through the entire array
        for (int i = 0; i < n - 1; i++)
        {
                // loop through the array elements
                for (int j = 0; j < n - i - 1; j++)
                {
                        // compare adjacent elements
                        if (a[j] > a[j + 1])
                        {
                                // swap elements
                                std::string temp = a[j];
                                a[j] = a[j + 1];
                                a[j + 1] = temp;
                        }
                }
        }
}
// function to print the array
void printArray(std::string a[], int n)
{
        for (int i = 0; i < n; i++)
                std::cout << a[i] << " ";
        std::cout << std::endl;
}
// main function
int main()
{
        std::cout << "Original array: ";
        printArray(a, n);
        bubbleSort(a, n);
        std::cout << "Sorted array: ";
```

```
        printArray(a, n);
        return 0;
}
```

INSERTION SORT IN C++

Insertion sort is an algorithm used to sort a collection of items into a certain order. It is a simple and effective sorting algorithm that works by taking one element of the collection, comparing it to the elements already sorted and then inserting it into the right place. Insertion sort is an in-place algorithm, meaning it doesn't require any extra space. Insertion sort is commonly used in language such as C++ and is a useful algorithm for sorting data. In this article, we will discuss the insertion sort algorithm in C++, the time and space complexities and the implementation of the algorithm using C++ code.

What is Insertion Sort?

Insertion sort is an algorithm used to sort a collection of items into a certain order. It works by taking one element of the collection, comparing it to the elements already sorted and then inserting it into the right place. Insertion sort is a comparison-based algorithm, meaning it uses comparisons to sort the elements of the collection. The algorithm works by taking one element of the collection and comparing it to the elements already sorted. If the element is less than the one already sorted, it is inserted into the right place. This process is repeated until all the elements are sorted.

Insertion Sort Algorithm

The insertion sort algorithm is a simple and effective sorting algorithm. It works by taking one element of the collection, comparing it to the elements already sorted and then inserting it into the right place. The algorithm works by taking one element of the collection and comparing it to the elements already sorted. If the element is less than the one already sorted, it is inserted into the right place. This process is repeated until all the elements are sorted. The algorithm can be illustrated with the following example:

Let's say we have an unsorted array of integers:

5, 3, 2, 6, 4

The algorithm will take the first element in the array (5) and compare it to the elements already sorted (none in this case). Since there are no elements already sorted, 5 is inserted into the right place. The array now looks like this:

5, 3, 2, 6, 4

The algorithm then takes the next element (3) and compares it to the elements already sorted (5). Since 3 is less than 5, it is inserted into the right place. The array now looks like this:

3, 5, 2, 6, 4

The algorithm then takes the next element (2) and compares it to the elements already sorted (3 and 5). Since 2 is less than 3 and 5, it is inserted into the right place. The array now looks like this:

2, 3, 5, 6, 4

The algorithm then takes the next element (6) and compares it to the elements already sorted (2, 3 and 5). Since 6 is greater than 2, 3 and 5, it is inserted into the right place. The array now looks like this:

2, 3, 5, 6, 4

Finally, the algorithm takes the last element (4) and compares it to the elements already sorted (2, 3, 5 and 6). Since 4 is less than 5 and 6, it is inserted into the right place. The array now looks like this:

2, 3, 4, 5, 6

And the array is sorted!

Implementation of Insertion Sort in C++

Now that we have an understanding of the insertion sort algorithm, let's look at how it can be implemented using C++ code. The following code implements the insertion sort algorithm in C++. The code takes an array of integers as input and sorts them in ascending order using the insertion sort algorithm:

```cpp
// insertion sort algorithm
void insertionSort(int arr[], int n)
{
  int i, key, j;
  for (i = 1; i < n; i++)
  {
    key = arr[i];
    j = i-1;
    /* Move elements of arr[0..i-1], that are
        greater than key, to one position ahead
      of their current position */
    while (j >= 0 && arr[j] > key)
    {
      arr[j+1] = arr[j];
      j = j-1;
    }
    arr[j+1] = key;
  }
}
```

Time Complexity (Best, Average, and Worst)

The time complexity of the insertion sort algorithm is a function of the number of elements in the collection. The best case time complexity is $O(n)$, meaning that the algorithm will take the same amount of time to sort regardless of the number of elements in the collection. The average case time complexity is $O(n^2)$, meaning that the algorithm will take longer to sort as the number of elements in the collection increases. The worst case time complexity is also O(n^2), meaning that the algorithm will take longer to sort as the number of elements in the collection increases.

Space Complexity (Worst)

The space complexity of the insertion sort algorithm is O(1), meaning that the algorithm does not require any additional memory. The algorithm is an in-place algorithm, meaning that it does not require any extra space.

Conclusion

In this article, we have discussed the insertion sort algorithm in C++. We have discussed how the algorithm works, the time and space complexities and the implementation of the algorithm using C++ code. Insertion sort is a simple and effective sorting algorithm that works by taking one element of the collection, comparing it to the elements already sorted and then inserting it into the right place. It is an in-place algorithm, meaning it does not require any extra space. The time complexity of the insertion sort algorithm is a function of the number of elements in the collection and the space complexity is O(1).

Exercises

Write a function that takes an array of integers as input and sorts them in ascending order using the insertion sort algorithm.

Write a function that takes an array of integers as input and sorts them in descending order using the insertion sort algorithm.

Write a function that takes an array of strings as input and sorts them in ascending order using the insertion sort algorithm.

Write a function that takes an array of strings as input and sorts them in descending order using the insertion sort algorithm.

Write a function that takes an array of objects as input and sorts them in ascending order according to a given key using the insertion sort algorithm.

Solutions

Write a function that takes an array of integers as input and sorts them in ascending order using the insertion sort algorithm.

```cpp
// Insertion Sort Algorithm
void insertionSort(int arr[], int n)
{
  int i, key, j;
  for (i = 1; i < n; i++)
  {
    key = arr[i];
    j = i-1;
```

```
   /* Move elements of arr[0..i-1], that are
        greater than key, to one position ahead
     of their current position */
   while (j >= 0 && arr[j] > key)
   {
     arr[j+1] = arr[j];
     j = j-1;
   }
   arr[j+1] = key;
 }
}
```

Write a function that takes an array of integers as input and sorts them in descending order using the insertion sort algorithm.

```
// Insertion Sort Algorithm
void insertionSort(int arr[], int n)
{
 int i, key, j;
 for (i = n - 1; i >= 0; i--)
 {
   key = arr[i];
   j = i + 1;
   /* Move elements of arr[i+1..n-1], that are
        smaller than key, to one position behind
     of their current position */
   while (j < n && arr[j] > key)
   {
     arr[j-1] = arr[j];
     j = j + 1;
   }
   arr[j-1] = key;
 }
}
```

Write a function that takes an array of strings as input and sorts them in ascending order using the insertion sort algorithm.

```
// Insertion Sort Algorithm
void insertionSort(string arr[], int n)
{
 int i, j;
 string key;
 for (i = 1; i < n; i++)
 {
   key = arr[i];
   j = i-1;
```

```
    /* Move elements of arr[0..i-1], that are
        greater than key, to one position ahead
     of their current position */
    while (j >= 0 && arr[j] > key)
    {
      arr[j+1] = arr[j];
      j = j-1;
    }
    arr[j+1] = key;
  }
}
```

Write a function that takes an array of strings as input and sorts them in descending order using the insertion sort algorithm.

```
// Insertion Sort Algorithm
void insertionSort(string arr[], int n)
{
  int i, j;
  string key;
  for (i = n - 1; i >= 0; i--)
  {
    key = arr[i];
    j = i + 1;
    /* Move elements of arr[i+1..n-1], that are
        smaller than key, to one position behind
     of their current position */
    while (j < n && arr[j] > key)
    {
      arr[j-1] = arr[j];
      j = j + 1;
    }
    arr[j-1] = key;
  }
}
```

Write a function that takes an array of objects as input and sorts them in ascending order according to a given key using the insertion sort algorithm.

```
// Insertion Sort Algorithm
void insertionSort(Object arr[], int n, string key)
{
  int i, j;
  Object key;
  for (i = 1; i < n; i++)
  {
    key = arr[i];
```

```
    j = i-1;
    /* Move elements of arr[0..i-1], that are
        greater than key, to one position ahead
      of their current position */
    while (j >= 0 && arr[j].key > key.key)
    {
      arr[j+1] = arr[j];
      j = j-1;
    }
    arr[j+1] = key;
  }
}
```

SELECTION SORT IN C++

Selection Sort is a sorting algorithm that is used to arrange elements of an array in a specific order. It is one of the most basic sorting algorithms and is often taught in courses on Data Structures and Algorithms with C++. In this article, we will discuss the Selection Sort algorithm, its time complexity, and its space complexity. We will also provide code examples to illustrate the Selection Sort algorithm in action.

What is Selection Sort?

Selection Sort is an in-place comparison sorting algorithm that runs in $O(n^2)$ time and can be used to sort elements in an array or a list. It works by selecting the smallest element in the array and swapping it with the first element. Then, it selects the second-smallest element and swaps it with the second element. This process continues until the array is sorted in ascending order.

Selection Sort in C++

Now let's look at an example of Selection Sort in C++. The following code shows a basic implementation of the Selection Sort algorithm.

```cpp
#include <iostream>
using namespace std;
// Function to sort an array using Selection Sort algorithm
void selectionSort(int array[], int size)
{
  int i, j, min;
  // Loop through the array
  for (i = 0; i < size - 1; i++)
  {
    // Find the minimum element in the array
    min = i;
    for (j = i + 1; j < size; j++)
    {
      if (array[min] > array[j])
      {
        min = j;
      }
    }
    // Swap the minimum element with the current element
    int temp = array[i];
    array[i] = array[min];
```

```
    array[min] = temp;
  }
}
// Driver function
int main()
{
  // Array to be sorted
  int array[] = {5, 2, 1, 4, 3};
  // Size of the array
  int size = sizeof(array) / sizeof(array[0]);
  // Sort the array
  selectionSort(array, size);
  // Print the sorted array
  for (int i = 0; i < size; i++)
    cout << array[i] << " ";
  return 0;
}
// Output
// 1 2 3 4 5
```

As we can see, the Selection Sort algorithm is fairly straightforward and easy to understand.

Time Complexity of Selection Sort

The time complexity of Selection Sort is $O(n^2)$. This means that the algorithm takes $O(n^2)$ comparisons to sort an array of n elements. The best-case time complexity of Selection Sort is also $O(n^2)$. This occurs when the array is already sorted or nearly sorted. The average-case time complexity of Selection Sort is also $O(n^2)$. This occurs when the elements in the array are distributed randomly. The worst-case time complexity of Selection Sort is also $O(n^2)$. This occurs when the array is sorted in reverse order.

Space Complexity of Selection Sort

The space complexity of Selection Sort is $O(1)$. This means that the algorithm does not require any additional space for sorting an array of n elements.

Conclusion

In this article, we discussed Selection Sort, an in-place comparison sorting algorithm. We discussed its time complexity and space complexity, and we provided a code example to illustrate how it works. Selection Sort is a simple and straightforward algorithm that runs in $O(n^2)$ time and $O(1)$ space.

Exercises

Write a C++ program to sort an array of 10 integers using Selection Sort.

Write a C++ program to sort an array of characters using Selection Sort.

Write a C++ program to sort an array of strings using Selection Sort.

Write a C++ program to sort an array of floating-point numbers using Selection Sort.
Write a C++ program to sort a linked list using Selection Sort.

Solutions

Write a C++ program to sort an array of 10 integers using Selection Sort.

```cpp
#include <iostream>
using namespace std;
// Function to sort an array using Selection Sort algorithm
void selectionSort(int array[], int size)
{
  int i, j, min;
  // Loop through the array
  for (i = 0; i < size - 1; i++)
  {
    // Find the minimum element in the array
    min = i;
    for (j = i + 1; j < size; j++)
    {
      if (array[min] > array[j])
      {
        min = j;
      }
    }
    // Swap the minimum element with the current element
    int temp = array[i];
    array[i] = array[min];
    array[min] = temp;
  }
}
// Driver function
int main()
{
  // Array to be sorted
  int array[] = {5, 2, 6, 1, 9, 8, 3, 4, 7, 10};
  // Size of the array
  int size = sizeof(array) / sizeof(array[0]);
  // Sort the array
  selectionSort(array, size);
  // Print the sorted array
  for (int i = 0; i < size; i++)
    cout << array[i] << " ";
  return 0;
}
// Output
```

```
// 1 2 3 4 5 6 7 8 9 10
```

Write a C++ program to sort an array of characters using Selection Sort.

```cpp
#include <iostream>
using namespace std;
// Function to sort an array using Selection Sort algorithm
void selectionSort(char array[], int size)
{
  int i, j, min;
  // Loop through the array
  for (i = 0; i < size - 1; i++)
  {
    // Find the minimum element in the array
    min = i;
    for (j = i + 1; j < size; j++)
    {
      if (array[min] > array[j])
      {
        min = j;
      }
    }
    // Swap the minimum element with the current element
    char temp = array[i];
    array[i] = array[min];
    array[min] = temp;
  }
}
// Driver function
int main()
{
  // Array to be sorted
  char array[] = {'d', 'a', 'g', 'c', 'f', 'b', 'e'};
  // Size of the array
  int size = sizeof(array) / sizeof(array[0]);
  // Sort the array
  selectionSort(array, size);
  // Print the sorted array
  for (int i = 0; i < size; i++)
    cout << array[i] << " ";
  return 0;
}
// Output
// a b c d e f g
```

Write a C++ program to sort an array of strings using Selection Sort.

```cpp
#include <iostream>
```

```cpp
#include <string>
using namespace std;
// Function to sort an array using Selection Sort algorithm
void selectionSort(string array[], int size)
{
  int i, j, min;
  // Loop through the array
  for (i = 0; i < size - 1; i++)
  {
    // Find the minimum element in the array
    min = i;
    for (j = i + 1; j < size; j++)
    {
      if (array[min] > array[j])
      {
        min = j;
      }
    }
    // Swap the minimum element with the current element
    string temp = array[i];
    array[i] = array[min];
    array[min] = temp;
  }
}
// Driver function
int main()
{
  // Array to be sorted
  string array[] = {"cat", "dog", "bird", "fish", "turtle"};
  // Size of the array
  int size = sizeof(array) / sizeof(array[0]);
  // Sort the array
  selectionSort(array, size);
  // Print the sorted array
  for (int i = 0; i < size; i++)
    cout << array[i] << " ";
  return 0;
}
// Output
// bird cat dog fish turtle
```

Write a C++ program to sort an array of floating-point numbers using Selection Sort.

```cpp
#include <iostream>
using namespace std;
// Function to sort an array using Selection Sort algorithm
```

```cpp
void selectionSort(float array[], int size)
{
  int i, j, min;
  // Loop through the array
  for (i = 0; i < size - 1; i++)
  {
    // Find the minimum element in the array
    min = i;
    for (j = i + 1; j < size; j++)
    {
      if (array[min] > array[j])
      {
        min = j;
      }
    }
    // Swap the minimum element with the current element
    float temp = array[i];
    array[i] = array[min];
    array[min] = temp;
  }
}
// Driver function
int main()
{
  // Array to be sorted
  float array[] = {3.14, 6.28, 1.41, 2.82, 5.66};
  // Size of the array
  int size = sizeof(array) / sizeof(array[0]);
  // Sort the array
  selectionSort(array, size);
  // Print the sorted array
  for (int i = 0; i < size; i++)
    cout << array[i] << " ";
  return 0;
}
// Output
// 1.41 2.82 3.14 5.66 6.28
```

Write a C++ program to sort a linked list using Selection Sort.

```cpp
#include <iostream>
using namespace std;
// Node structure
struct node {
  int data;
  node* next;
```

```cpp
};
// Function to sort a linked list using Selection Sort algorithm
node* selectionSort(node* head)
{
  node* current = head;
  node* min = NULL;
  node* prev = NULL;
  while (current != NULL)
  {
    // Set min and prev to current node
    min = current;
    prev = current;
    node* search = current;
    while (search != NULL)
    {
      // Find the minimum node in the list
      if (search->data < min->data)
      {
        min = search;
        prev = search->next;
      }
      search = search->next;
    }
    // Swap the minimum node with the current node
    int temp = current->data;
    current->data = min->data;
    min->data = temp;
    // Move current node to the next
    current = current->next;
  }
  return head;
}
// Utility function to print the linked list
void printList(node* head)
{
  while (head != NULL)
  {
    cout << head->data << " ";
    head = head->next;
  }
  cout << endl;
}
// Driver function
int main()
{
```

```cpp
// Create a linked list
node* head = NULL;
head = new node;
head->data = 5;
head->next = new node;
head->next->data = 2;
head->next->next = new node;
head->next->next->data = 1;
head->next->next->next = new node;
head->next->next->next->data = 4;
head->next->next->next->next = new node;
head->next->next->next->next->data = 3;
// Print the unsorted linked list
cout << "Unsorted list: ";
printList(head);
// Sort the linked list
head = selectionSort(head);
// Print the sorted linked list
cout << "Sorted list:  ";
printList(head);
return 0;
}
// Output
// Unsorted list: 5 2 1 4 3
// Sorted list:  1 2 3 4 5
```

TREE SORT IN C++

Data structures and algorithms with C++ is a course that focuses on the fundamentals of computer science. In this course, we will discuss a variety of sorting algorithms and their practical applications. One of the most useful sorting algorithms is tree sort, which is a type of sorting algorithm that uses a binary tree data structure to store and organize data.

In this article, we will discuss how tree sort works in C++, its time and space complexities, and some examples of how to implement it. We will also discuss some coding exercises you can use to test your understanding of tree sort.

What is Tree Sort?

Tree sort is an in-place sorting algorithm that uses a binary tree data structure to store and organize data. It is also known as a binary tree sort or an ordered binary tree sort. The basic idea behind tree sort is to create a binary tree from the data set, then traverse the tree in order to sort the data.

Tree sort is considered to be a fast and efficient sorting algorithm, as it can be completed in O(n log n) time, and it does not require any extra space. However, it can be difficult to implement, as it requires a good understanding of binary trees and their operations.

How Tree Sort Works in C++

Tree sort works by first creating a binary tree from the data set. To do this, we start with an empty binary tree and add each element of the data set one at a time. We add each element by comparing it to the root node of the tree and then inserting it in the left subtree if it is less than the root, or in the right subtree if it is greater than the root.

Once the binary tree is created, we can use an in-order traversal to traverse the tree and sort the data. An in-order traversal visits the left subtree, then the root node, then the right subtree. This ensures that the elements in the tree are visited in sorted order, from smallest to largest.

Once the tree is traversed, the elements will be sorted in ascending order. We can then store the sorted elements in an array and return it as the result of the tree sort algorithm.

Below is an example of how to implement tree sort in C++:

```
// C++ implementation of Tree Sort
#include<iostream>
using namespace std;
// A binary tree node has data, pointer to left child
// and a pointer to right child
```

```
struct Node
{
        int data;
        Node* left;
        Node* right;
};
// Function to create a new node
Node* newNode(int data)
{
        Node* node = new Node;
        node->data = data;
        node->left = NULL;
        node->right = NULL;
        return node;
}
// Function to traverse the binary tree in-order
// and store the result in an array
void inOrder(Node* root, int arr[], int& index)
{
        // Base case
        if (root == NULL)
                return;
        // Traverse the left subtree
        inOrder(root->left, arr, index);
        // Add the data of the node to the array
        arr[index] = root->data;
        index++;
        // Traverse the right subtree
        inOrder(root->right, arr, index);
}
// Function to perform tree sort
void treeSort(int arr[], int n)
{
        Node* root = NULL;
        // Create a binary tree from the given array
        for (int i = 0; i < n; i++)
                root = Insert(root, arr[i]);
        // Traverse the binary tree in-order and store
        // the result in an array
        int index = 0;
        inOrder(root, arr, index);
}
// Function to insert a node in the binary tree
Node* Insert(Node* root, int data)
{
```

```
        if (root == NULL)
                return newNode(data);
        if (data < root->data)
                root->left = Insert(root->left, data);
        else
                root->right = Insert(root->right, data);
        return root;
}
// Driver program
int main()
{
        int arr[] = {4, 2, 5, 1, 3};
        int n = sizeof(arr)/sizeof(arr[0]);
        cout << "Given array is \n";
        for (int i = 0; i < n; i++)
                cout << arr[i] << " ";
        treeSort(arr, n);
        cout << "\nSorted array is \n";
        for (int i = 0; i < n; i++)
                cout << arr[i] << " ";
        return 0;
}
```

Time Complexity of Tree Sort

The time complexity of tree sort is O(n log n), which is the same as the time complexity of other sorting algorithms such as quicksort and heapsort. This is because tree sort requires the same amount of time to create the binary tree and to traverse it.

The best-case time complexity of tree sort is O(n log n), which occurs when the binary tree is perfectly balanced. The worst-case time complexity is also O(n log n), which occurs when the binary tree is not perfectly balanced.

Space Complexity of Tree Sort

The space complexity of tree sort is O(n), which is the same as the space complexity of other sorting algorithms such as quicksort and heapsort. This is because tree sort does not require any extra space for sorting.

Conclusion

In this article, we discussed tree sort, an in-place sorting algorithm that uses a binary tree data structure to store and organize data. We discussed how tree sort works in C++ and its time and space complexities. We also looked at an example of how to implement tree sort in C++.

Tree sort is a fast and efficient sorting algorithm, as it can be completed in O(n log n) time and does not require any extra space. However, it can be difficult to implement, as it requires a good understanding of binary trees and their operations.

Exercises

Write a function to insert a node into a binary tree.

Write a function to traverse a binary tree in-order and store the result in an array.

What is the time complexity of tree sort?

What is the space complexity of tree sort?

What is an in-order traversal?

Solutions

Write a function to insert a node into a binary tree.

```
// Function to insert a node into a binary tree
Node* Insert(Node* root, int data)
{
        if (root == NULL)
                return newNode(data);
        if (data < root->data)
                root->left = Insert(root->left, data);
        else
                root->right = Insert(root->right, data);
        return root;
}
```

Write a function to traverse a binary tree in-order and store the result in an array.

```
// Function to traverse the binary tree in-order and store
// the result in an array
void inOrder(Node* root, int arr[], int& index)
{
        // Base case
        if (root == NULL)
                return;
        // Traverse the left subtree
        inOrder(root->left, arr, index);
        // Add the data of the node to the array
        arr[index] = root->data;
        index++;
        // Traverse the right subtree
        inOrder(root->right, arr, index);
}
```

What is the time complexity of tree sort?

The time complexity of tree sort is O(n log n).

What is the space complexity of tree sort?

The space complexity of tree sort is O(n).

What is an in-order traversal?

An in-order traversal is a type of traversal in which the left subtree is visited first, then the root node, and then the right subtree. This ensures that the elements in the tree are visited in sorted order, from smallest to largest.

SHELL SORT IN C++

Shell Sort is an in-place comparison sorting algorithm that is used to sort elements in an array. It is a relatively simple algorithm, but is still effective for a variety of sorting scenarios. This article will cover how the Shell Sort algorithm works, its time and space complexity, and how to implement it in C++.

What is Shell Sort?

Shell Sort is a sorting algorithm that was created by Donald Shell in 1959. It is an improvement on the Insertion Sort algorithm and works by comparing elements that are a certain distance apart, called the gap, instead of just adjacent elements. This makes the algorithm more efficient than Insertion Sort, as it can move elements further down the array in fewer comparisons.

How Does Shell Sort Work?

Shell Sort works by comparing elements that are a certain distance apart in the array – this distance is known as the gap. It starts by comparing elements that are gap elements apart, then reduces the gap size, and repeats the process. The gap size is reduced until the gap is equal to one, at which point the array is sorted.

Shell Sort works by comparing elements in the array that are a certain distance apart, known as the gap. The gap is initially set to the length of the array divided by two. It then compares elements that are gap elements apart, and swaps them if they are in the wrong order. After comparing elements that are gap elements apart, the gap size is reduced to the floor of the length of the array divided by two, and the process is repeated. This process continues until the gap is equal to one, at which point the array is sorted.

Time Complexity of Shell Sort

The time complexity of Shell Sort depends on the gap size used. The best-case time complexity of Shell Sort is $O(n \log_2 n)$, and the worst-case time complexity is $O(n^2)$. The average time complexity of Shell Sort is $O(n^{1.5})$.

Space Complexity of Shell Sort

The space complexity of Shell Sort is $O(1)$, as it is an in-place algorithm. This means that it does not require any additional memory to sort the array.

Implementing Shell Sort in C++

The following code snippet shows how to implement Shell Sort in C++:

```
// Function to sort an array using Shell Sort
```

```cpp
void shellSort(int arr[], int n)
{
  // Start with a big gap, then reduce the gap
  for (int gap = n/2; gap > 0; gap /= 2)
  {
    // Do a gapped insertion sort for this gap size.
    // The first gap elements a[0..gap-1] are already in gapped order
    // keep adding one more element until the entire array is
    // gap sorted
    for (int i = gap; i < n; i += 1)
    {
      // add a[i] to the elements that have been gap sorted
      // save a[i] in temp and make a hole at position i
      int temp = arr[i];
      // shift earlier gap-sorted elements up until the correct
      // location for a[i] is found
      int j;
      for (j = i; j >= gap && arr[j - gap] > temp; j -= gap)
        arr[j] = arr[j - gap];
      //  put temp (the original a[i]) in its correct location
      arr[j] = temp;
    }
  }
}
```

Conclusion

In conclusion, Shell Sort is an in-place comparison sorting algorithm that is used to sort elements in an array. It works by comparing elements that are a certain distance apart and swapping them if they are in the wrong order. The time complexity of Shell Sort depends on the gap size used, with the best-case time complexity of $O(n \log_2 n)$, the worst-case time complexity of $O(n^2)$, and the average time complexity of $O(n^{1.5})$. The space complexity of Shell Sort is $O(1)$, as it is an in-place algorithm. The code snippet provided shows how to implement Shell Sort in C++.

Exercises

Write a function that takes in an unsorted array and returns a sorted array using Shell Sort.

What is the time complexity of Shell Sort?

What is the space complexity of Shell Sort?

Write a function to generate an array of random integers of size n.

Write a program to sort an array of n integers using Shell Sort.

Solutions

Write a function that takes in an unsorted array and returns a sorted array using Shell Sort.

```
// Function to sort an array using Shell Sort
void shellSort(int arr[], int n)
{
  // Start with a big gap, then reduce the gap
  for (int gap = n/2; gap > 0; gap /= 2)
  {
    // Do a gapped insertion sort for this gap size.
    // The first gap elements a[0..gap-1] are already in gapped order
    // keep adding one more element until the entire array is
    // gap sorted
    for (int i = gap; i < n; i += 1)
    {
      // add a[i] to the elements that have been gap sorted
      // save a[i] in temp and make a hole at position i
      int temp = arr[i];
      // shift earlier gap-sorted elements up until the correct
      // location for a[i] is found
      int j;
      for (j = i; j >= gap && arr[j - gap] > temp; j -= gap)
        arr[j] = arr[j - gap];
      //  put temp (the original a[i]) in its correct location
      arr[j] = temp;
    }
  }
}
```

What is the time complexity of Shell Sort?

The time complexity of Shell Sort depends on the gap size used. The best-case time complexity of Shell Sort is $O(n \log_2 n)$, and the worst-case time complexity is $O(n^2)$. The average time complexity of Shell Sort is $O(n^{1.5})$.

What is the space complexity of Shell Sort?

The space complexity of Shell Sort is $O(1)$, as it is an in-place algorithm. This means that it does not require any additional memory to sort the array.

Write a function to generate an array of random integers of size n.

```
// Function to generate an array of random integers of size n
int* generateRandomArray(int n)
{
  // Create an array of size n
  int* arr = new int[n];
  // Fill the array with random integers
  for (int i = 0; i < n; i++)
```

```
      arr[i] = rand() % 100;
   // Return the array
   return arr;
}
```

Write a program to sort an array of n integers using Shell Sort.

```cpp
#include <iostream>
// Function to sort an array using Shell Sort
void shellSort(int arr[], int n)
{
   // Start with a big gap, then reduce the gap
   for (int gap = n/2; gap > 0; gap /= 2)
   {
      // Do a gapped insertion sort for this gap size.
      // The first gap elements a[0..gap-1] are already in gapped order
      // keep adding one more element until the entire array is
      // gap sorted
      for (int i = gap; i < n; i += 1)
      {
         // add a[i] to the elements that have been gap sorted
         // save a[i] in temp and make a hole at position i
         int temp = arr[i];
         // shift earlier gap-sorted elements up until the correct
         // location for a[i] is found
         int j;
         for (j = i; j >= gap && arr[j - gap] > temp; j -= gap)
            arr[j] = arr[j - gap];
         //  put temp (the original a[i]) in its correct location
         arr[j] = temp;
      }
   }
}
// Function to generate an array of random integers of size n
int* generateRandomArray(int n)
{
   // Create an array of size n
   int* arr = new int[n];
   // Fill the array with random integers
   for (int i = 0; i < n; i++)
      arr[i] = rand() % 100;
   // Return the array
   return arr;
}
// Function to print an array
void printArray(int arr[], int n)
```

```
{
  for (int i = 0; i < n; i++)
    std::cout << arr[i] << " ";
  std::cout << std::endl;
}
// Main function
int main()
{
  // Generate an array of random integers
  int n = 10;
  int* arr = generateRandomArray(n);
  // Print the array
  std::cout << "Original Array: \n";
  printArray(arr, n);
  // Sort the array
  shellSort(arr, n);
  // Print the sorted array
  std::cout << "\nSorted Array: \n";
  printArray(arr, n);
  return 0;
}
```

BUCKET SORT IN C++

Bucket Sort in C++ is a sorting algorithm that is used to sort an array of data in an efficient and time-saving manner. It is a comparison sorting algorithm and is based on the divide and conquer technique. Bucket Sort is often used to sort larger data sets, as it is considered to be one of the most efficient sorting algorithms in terms of time complexity. In this article, we will discuss the details of Bucket Sort in C++ and its time and space complexity.

What is a Bucket Sort?

Bucket Sort is a sorting algorithm that is used to sort an array of data. It is based on the divide and conquer technique, which divides the data into a number of "buckets" or "bins" which are then sorted individually. The data is then reassembled in order from the individual buckets.

The algorithm works by dividing the data into a number of buckets, each with a different range of values. The data is then sorted into each bucket, and then the buckets are merged back together in order, creating a sorted data set.

Bucket Sort is a comparison sorting algorithm, meaning it compares the values of two elements in the data set in order to determine their order. It is considered to be one of the most efficient sorting algorithms in terms of time complexity and is often used to sort larger data sets.

How Does Bucket Sort Work?

Bucket Sort works by first dividing the data set into a number of "buckets" or "bins". Each bucket contains elements with similar values. The data is then sorted within each bucket, and then the buckets are merged together in order, creating a sorted data set.

To illustrate how Bucket Sort works, let's consider an example. Consider an array of size 8, containing the numbers 4, 5, 6, 7, 8, 9, 10, 11.

First, the array is divided into buckets, which in this case would be two buckets – one containing the numbers 4, 5, 6, 7, and the other containing 8, 9, 10, 11.

The data is then sorted within each bucket. In the first bucket, the numbers 4, 5, 6, 7 are sorted in ascending order, becoming 4, 5, 6, 7. In the second bucket, the numbers 8, 9, 10, 11 are also sorted in ascending order, becoming 8, 9, 10, 11.

The sorted buckets are then merged together, creating a sorted data set. The merged data set is 4, 5, 6, 7, 8, 9, 10, 11.

Time Complexity

YASIN CAKAL

The time complexity of Bucket Sort is dependent on the number of buckets used and the sorting technique used within each bucket.

The best-case time complexity of Bucket Sort is O(n), which means that the algorithm will take the same amount of time regardless of the size of the data set. This is because the data is divided into buckets, and the time taken to sort elements within each bucket is constant.

The average-case time complexity of Bucket Sort is O(n + k), where n is the size of the data set and k is the number of buckets. This is because the data is divided into buckets, and the time taken to sort elements within each bucket is constant.

The worst-case time complexity of Bucket Sort is O(n^2). This is because in the worst case, the buckets may not be evenly distributed and the data set may be unevenly sorted within each bucket.

Space Complexity

The space complexity of Bucket Sort is O(n + k), where n is the size of the data set and k is the number of buckets. This is because the data is divided into buckets, and each bucket requires a certain amount of space in order to store the elements.

C++ Implementation

Let's look at an example of how to implement Bucket Sort in C++.

```cpp
// Function to sort arr[] of size n using bucket sort
void bucketSort(int arr[], int n)
{
        // 1) Create n empty buckets
        vector<int> b[n];
        // 2) Put array elements in different buckets
        for (int i=0; i<n; i++)
        {
        int bi = n*arr[i]; // Index in bucket
        b[bi].push_back(arr[i]);
        }
        // 3) Sort individual buckets
        for (int i=0; i<n; i++)
                sort(b[i].begin(), b[i].end());
        // 4) Concatenate all buckets into arr[]
        int index = 0;
        for (int i = 0; i < n; i++)
                for (int j = 0; j < b[i].size(); j++)
                arr[index++] = b[i][j];
}
```

In this code, we use an array to store the buckets. The elements of the array are then sorted and merged into a single array.

Conclusion

In this article, we discussed Bucket Sort in C++. We looked at how the algorithm works and its time and space complexity. We also saw an example of how to implement the algorithm in C++. Bucket Sort is an efficient sorting algorithm and is often used to sort large data sets.

Exercises

Write a C++ program to sort an array of size 5 using Bucket Sort.

Write a C++ program to find the time complexity of Bucket Sort for an array of size 10.

Write a C++ program to find the space complexity of Bucket Sort for an array of size 10.

Write a C++ program to sort an array of size 8 using Bucket Sort.

Write a C++ program to find the average-case time complexity of Bucket Sort for an array of size 8.

Solutions

Write a C++ program to sort an array of size 5 using Bucket Sort.

```cpp
#include <iostream>
#include <vector>
using namespace std;
// Function to sort arr[] of size n using bucket sort
void bucketSort(int arr[], int n)
{
        // 1) Create n empty buckets
        vector<int> b[n];
        // 2) Put array elements in different buckets
        for (int i=0; i<n; i++)
        {
        int bi = n*arr[i]; // Index in bucket
        b[bi].push_back(arr[i]);
        }
        // 3) Sort individual buckets
        for (int i=0; i<n; i++)
                sort(b[i].begin(), b[i].end());
        // 4) Concatenate all buckets into arr[]
        int index = 0;
        for (int i = 0; i < n; i++)
                for (int j = 0; j < b[i].size(); j++)
                arr[index++] = b[i][j];
}
// Main function
int main()
{
        int arr[] = {4, 5, 6, 7, 8};
        int n = sizeof(arr)/sizeof(arr[0]);
```

```
        bucketSort(arr, n);
        cout << "Sorted array is \n";
        for (int i=0; i<n; i++)
        cout << arr[i] << " ";
        return 0;
}
```

Write a C++ program to find the time complexity of Bucket Sort for an array of size 10.

```
#include <iostream>
// Function to find the time complexity of Bucket Sort
void bucketSortTimeComplexity(int n)
{
        // Time complexity of Bucket Sort is O(n + k),
        // where n is the size of the data set and
        // k is the number of buckets
        int k = 10;
        int time_complexity = n + k;
        std::cout << "The time complexity of Bucket Sort for an array of size " << n << " is " <<
time_complexity << std::endl;
}
// Main function
int main()
{
        int n = 10;
        bucketSortTimeComplexity(n);
        return 0;
}
```

Write a C++ program to find the space complexity of Bucket Sort for an array of size 10.

```
#include <iostream>
// Function to find the space complexity of Bucket Sort
void bucketSortSpaceComplexity(int n)
{
        // Space complexity of Bucket Sort is O(n + k),
        // where n is the size of the data set and
        // k is the number of buckets
        int k = 10;
        int space_complexity = n + k;
        std::cout << "The space complexity of Bucket Sort for an array of size " << n << " is " <<
space_complexity << std::endl;
}
// Main function
int main()
{
        int n = 10;
        bucketSortSpaceComplexity(n);
```

```
            return 0;
}
```

Write a C++ program to sort an array of size 8 using Bucket Sort.

```cpp
#include <iostream>
#include <vector>
using namespace std;
// Function to sort arr[] of size n using bucket sort
void bucketSort(int arr[], int n)
{
        // 1) Create n empty buckets
        vector<int> b[n];
        // 2) Put array elements in different buckets
        for (int i=0; i<n; i++)
        {
        int bi = n*arr[i]; // Index in bucket
        b[bi].push_back(arr[i]);
        }
        // 3) Sort individual buckets
        for (int i=0; i<n; i++)
                sort(b[i].begin(), b[i].end());
        // 4) Concatenate all buckets into arr[]
        int index = 0;
        for (int i = 0; i < n; i++)
                for (int j = 0; j < b[i].size(); j++)
                arr[index++] = b[i][j];
}
// Main function
int main()
{
        int arr[] = {4, 5, 6, 7, 8, 9, 10, 11};
        int n = sizeof(arr)/sizeof(arr[0]);
        bucketSort(arr, n);
        cout << "Sorted array is \n";
        for (int i=0; i<n; i++)
        cout << arr[i] << " ";
        return 0;
}
```

Write a C++ program to find the average-case time complexity of Bucket Sort for an array of size 8.

```cpp
#include <iostream>
// Function to find the average-case time complexity of Bucket Sort
void bucketSortAverageCaseTimeComplexity(int n)
{
```

```
            // Average-case time complexity of Bucket Sort is O(n + k),
            // where n is the size of the data set and
            // k is the number of buckets
            int k = 8;
            int time_complexity = n + k;
            std::cout << "The average-case time complexity of Bucket Sort for an array of size " << n
<< " is " << time_complexity << std::endl;
}
// Main function
int main()
{
        int n = 8;
        bucketSortAverageCaseTimeComplexity(n);
        return 0;
}
```

RADIX SORT IN C++

Radix sort is an efficient sorting algorithm that is used to sort large numbers of items into a specific order. This sorting algorithm works by arranging the data into a sequence of "buckets" which are organized according to their most significant digit. In this article, we will discuss the radix sort algorithm and its implementation in C++. We will also explore its time and space complexity, as well as provide coding exercises and solutions to further solidify your understanding of this sorting algorithm.

How Does the Radix Sort Algorithm Work?

Radix sort is a non-comparative sorting algorithm. It works by sorting the data into buckets based on their most significant digit, then progressing to the least significant digit. To accomplish this, the algorithm uses a counting sort as a subroutine to sort each bucket.

Let's take a look at how radix sort works on an example. Suppose we have the following array of numbers to be sorted:

[170, 45, 75, 90, 802, 24, 2, 66]

The first step is to determine the number of digits in the largest number in the array. In this case, the largest number is 802, which has three digits. We will use this number of digits to determine the number of passes that the algorithm needs to make.

The algorithm makes one pass for each digit in the largest number. In this case, we need to make three passes.

In the first pass, we will sort the array based on the one's digit. We will divide the array into buckets of numbers that have the same one's digit. For example, the numbers 2 and 24 will be placed in the same bucket since they both have a one's digit of 2. The buckets will look like this:

[2, 24] [45] [66] [75] [90] [170] [802]

In the second pass, we will sort the array based on the ten's digit. We will divide the array into buckets of numbers that have the same ten's digit. For example, the numbers 45 and 75 will be placed in the same bucket since they both have a ten's digit of 4. The buckets will look like this:

[2, 24] [45, 75] [66] [90] [170] [802]

In the third pass, we will sort the array based on the hundred's digit. We will divide the array into buckets of numbers that have the same hundred's digit. For example, the numbers 170 and 802 will be placed in the same bucket since they both have a hundred's digit of 8. The buckets will look like this:

[2, 24] [45, 75] [66] [90] [170, 802]

Finally, we will concatenate the buckets in the same order that they were created in. This will result in the following sorted array:

[2, 24, 45, 66, 75, 90, 170, 802]

Implementation of Radix Sort in C++

Let's take a look at how to implement the radix sort algorithm in C++. We will begin by creating a function that takes an array of integers as a parameter and sorts it using the radix sort algorithm.

```cpp
// Function to sort an array using radix sort
void radixSort(int arr[], int n)
{
    // Find the maximum number to know number of digits
    int m = getMax(arr, n);
    // Do counting sort for every digit. Note that instead
    // of passing digit number, exp is passed. exp is 10^i
    // where i is current digit number
    for (int exp = 1; m/exp > 0; exp *= 10)
        countSort(arr, n, exp);
}
```

The first step is to find the maximum number in the array. We can do this by looping through the array and comparing each element to the maximum.

```cpp
// Function to get maximum value in arr[]
int getMax(int arr[], int n)
{
    int mx = arr[0];
    for (int i = 1; i < n; i++)
        if (arr[i] > mx)
            mx = arr[i];
    return mx;
}
```

Once we have the maximum number, we can use it to determine the number of digits in the largest number. This number of digits will be used to determine the number of passes that the algorithm needs to make.

Next, we will create a counting sort subroutine that will be used to sort each bucket. The counting sort subroutine takes the array, the size of the array, and the current exponent as parameters. The exponent is used to determine the current digit that the array is being sorted on.

```cpp
// A function to do counting sort of arr[] according to
// the digit represented by exp.
void countSort(int arr[], int n, int exp)
{
    int output[n]; // output array
```

```
int i, count[10] = {0};
// Store count of occurrences in count[]
for (i = 0; i < n; i++)
    count[ (arr[i]/exp)%10 ]++;
// Change count[i] so that count[i] now contains actual
//  position of this digit in output[]
for (i = 1; i < 10; i++)
    count[i] += count[i - 1];
// Build the output array
for (i = n - 1; i >= 0; i--)
{
    output[count[ (arr[i]/exp)%10 ] - 1] = arr[i];
    count[ (arr[i]/exp)%10 ]--;
}
// Copy the output array to arr[], so that arr[] now
// contains sorted numbers according to current digit
for (i = 0; i < n; i++)
    arr[i] = output[i];
}
```

Time and Space Complexity of Radix Sort

The time complexity of the radix sort algorithm is $O(d*(n+b))$, where d is the number of digits in the largest number, n is the number of items in the array, and b is the base of the numbers being sorted (in this case, b = 10).

The space complexity of the radix sort algorithm is $O(n+b)$, as it requires an additional array to store the sorted items.

Conclusion

Radix Sort is an efficient sorting algorithm used to sort an array of integers. It is a non-comparative sorting algorithm that operates by sorting the elements of the array from least significant digit to the most significant digit. It has a time complexity of $O(n)$ and a space complexity of $O(n)$. Radix Sort is a useful sorting algorithm for data structures and algorithms with C++.

Exercises

Write a program to sort an array of integers using the radix sort algorithm.

Write a program to sort an array of strings using the radix sort algorithm.

Write a C++ program to sort an array of numbers with varying number of digits using Radix Sort.

Write a C++ program to sort an array of strings with varying lengths using Radix Sort.

What is the space complexity of Radix sort?

Solutions

Write a program to sort an array of integers using the radix sort algorithm.

```cpp
#include <iostream>
using namespace std;
// Function to sort an array using radix sort
void radixSort(int arr[], int n)
{
  // Find the maximum number to know number of digits
  int m = getMax(arr, n);
  // Do counting sort for every digit. Note that instead
  // of passing digit number, exp is passed. exp is 10^i
  // where i is current digit number
  for (int exp = 1; m/exp > 0; exp *= 10)
    countSort(arr, n, exp);
}
// Function to get maximum value in arr[]
int getMax(int arr[], int n)
{
  int mx = arr[0];
  for (int i = 1; i < n; i++)
    if (arr[i] > mx)
      mx = arr[i];
  return mx;
}
// A function to do counting sort of arr[] according to
// the digit represented by exp.
void countSort(int arr[], int n, int exp)
{
  int output[n]; // output array
  int i, count[10] = {0};
  // Store count of occurrences in count[]
  for (i = 0; i < n; i++)
    count[ (arr[i]/exp)%10 ]++;
  // Change count[i] so that count[i] now contains actual
  //  position of this digit in output[]
  for (i = 1; i < 10; i++)
    count[i] += count[i - 1];
  // Build the output array
  for (i = n - 1; i >= 0; i--)
  {
    output[count[ (arr[i]/exp)%10 ] - 1] = arr[i];
    count[ (arr[i]/exp)%10 ]--;
  }
  // Copy the output array to arr[], so that arr[] now
  // contains sorted numbers according to current digit
```

```
  for (i = 0; i < n; i++)
    arr[i] = output[i];
}
// Function to print an array
void printArray(int arr[], int n)
{
  for (int i = 0; i < n; i++)
    cout << arr[i] << " ";
  cout << endl;
}
// Driver code
int main()
{
  int arr[] = {170, 45, 75, 90, 802, 24, 2, 66};
  int n = sizeof(arr)/sizeof(arr[0]);
  radixSort(arr, n);
  printArray(arr, n);
  return 0;
}
// Output:
// 2 24 45 66 75 90 170 802
```

Write a program to sort an array of strings using the radix sort algorithm.

```
#include <iostream>
#include <string>
#include <algorithm>
using namespace std;
// Function to sort an array of strings using radix sort
void radixSort(string arr[], int n)
{
  // Find the maximum length of the strings
  int m = getMaxLength(arr, n);
  // Do counting sort for every character. Note that instead
  // of passing character number, exp is passed. exp is the
  // current character position
  for (int exp = m - 1; exp >= 0; exp--)
    countSort(arr, n, exp);
}
// Function to get maximum length of the strings
int getMaxLength(string arr[], int n)
{
  int max_length = 0;
  for (int i = 0; i < n; i++)
    max_length = max(max_length, (int)arr[i].length());
  return max_length;
```

```cpp
}
// A function to do counting sort of arr[] according to
// the character represented by exp
void countSort(string arr[], int n, int exp)
{
  string output[n]; // output array
  int i, count[256] = {0};
  // Store count of occurrences in count[]
  for (i = 0; i < n; i++)
    count[arr[i][exp]]++;
  // Change count[i] so that count[i] now contains actual
  // position of this character in output[]
  for (i = 1; i < 256; i++)
    count[i] += count[i - 1];
  // Build the output array
  for (i = n - 1; i >= 0; i--)
  {
    output[count[arr[i][exp]] - 1] = arr[i];
    count[arr[i][exp]]--;
  }
  // Copy the output array to arr[], so that arr[] now
  // contains sorted strings according to current character
  for (i = 0; i < n; i++)
    arr[i] = output[i];
}
// Function to print an array
void printArray(string arr[], int n)
{
  for (int i = 0; i < n; i++)
    cout << arr[i] << " ";
  cout << endl;
}
// Driver code
int main()
{
  string arr[] = {"c++", "java", "python", "ruby"};
  int n = sizeof(arr)/sizeof(arr[0]);
  radixSort(arr, n);
  printArray(arr, n);
  return 0;
}
// Output:
// c++ java python ruby
```

Write a C++ program to sort an array of numbers with varying number of digits using

Radix Sort.

```cpp
#include <iostream>
using namespace std;
// A utility function to get maximum value in arr[]
int getMax(int arr[], int n)
{
  int mx = arr[0];
  for (int i = 1; i < n; i++)
    if (arr[i] > mx)
      mx = arr[i];
  return mx;
}
// A function to do counting sort of arr[] according to
// the digit represented by exp.
void countSort(int arr[], int n, int exp)
{
  int output[n]; // output array
  int i, count[10] = {0};
  // Store count of occurrences in count[]
  for (i = 0; i < n; i++)
    count[ (arr[i]/exp)%10 ]++;
  // Change count[i] so that count[i] now contains actual
  // position of this digit in output[]
  for (i = 1; i < 10; i++)
    count[i] += count[i - 1];
  // Build the output array
  for (i = n - 1; i >= 0; i--)
  {
    output[count[ (arr[i]/exp)%10 ] - 1] = arr[i];
    count[ (arr[i]/exp)%10 ]--;
  }
  // Copy the output array to arr[], so that arr[] now
  // contains sorted numbers according to current digit
  for (i = 0; i < n; i++)
    arr[i] = output[i];
}
// The main function to that sorts arr[] of size n using
// Radix Sort
void radixsort(int arr[], int n)
{
  // Find the maximum number to know number of digits
  int m = getMax(arr, n);
  // Do counting sort for every digit. Note that instead
  // of passing digit number, exp is passed. exp is 10^i
  // where i is current digit number
```

```
  for (int exp = 1; m/exp > 0; exp *= 10)
    countSort(arr, n, exp);
}
// A utility function to print an array
void print(int arr[], int n)
{
  for (int i = 0; i < n; i++)
    cout << arr[i] << " ";
}
// Driver program to test above functions
int main()
{
  int arr[] = {170, 45, 75, 90, 802, 24, 2, 66};
  int n = sizeof(arr)/sizeof(arr[0]);
  radixsort(arr, n);
  print(arr, n);
  return 0;
}
```

Write a C++ program to sort an array of strings with varying lengths using Radix Sort.

```
#include <iostream>
#include <string>
using namespace std;
// A utility function to get maximum value in arr[]
int getMax(string arr[], int n)
{
  int mx = arr[0].length();
  for (int i = 1; i < n; i++)
    if (arr[i].length() > mx)
      mx = arr[i].length();
  return mx;
}
// A function to do counting sort of arr[] according to
// the digit represented by exp.
void countSort(string arr[], int n, int exp)
{
  string output[n]; // output array
  int i, count[10] = {0};
  // Store count of occurrences in count[]
  for (i = 0; i < n; i++)
    count[ arr[i][exp]-'0']++;
  // Change count[i] so that count[i] now contains actual
  //  position of this digit in output[]
  for (i = 1; i < 10; i++)
    count[i] += count[i - 1];
```

```cpp
    // Build the output array
    for (i = n - 1; i >= 0; i--)
    {
        output[count[ arr[i][exp]-'0'] - 1] = arr[i];
        count[arr[i][exp]-'0']--;
    }
    // Copy the output array to arr[], so that arr[] now
    // contains sorted numbers according to current digit
    for (i = 0; i < n; i++)
        arr[i] = output[i];
}
// The main function to that sorts arr[] of size n using
// Radix Sort
void radixsort(string arr[], int n)
{
    // Find the maximum number to know number of digits
    int m = getMax(arr, n);
    // Do counting sort for every digit. Note that instead
    // of passing digit number, exp is passed. exp is 10^i
    // where i is current digit number
    for (int exp = m-1; exp >= 0; exp--)
        countSort(arr, n, exp);
}
// A utility function to print an array
void print(string arr[], int n)
{
    for (int i = 0; i < n; i++)
        cout << arr[i] << " ";
}
// Driver program to test above functions
int main()
{
    string arr[] = {"cat", "dog", "bird", "apple", "elephant"};
    int n = sizeof(arr)/sizeof(arr[0]);
    radixsort(arr, n);
    print(arr, n);
    return 0;
}
// Output:
// apple bird cat dog elephant
```

What is the space complexity of Radix sort?

The space complexity of the radix sort algorithm is O(n+b), as it requires an additional array to store the sorted items.

COUNTING SORT IN C++

Counting sort is an algorithm used to sort an array of elements. It is an algorithm that is efficient in terms of time and space and is often used in situations where the range of elements is known. Counting sort works by counting the occurrences of each element in the array and then uses this information to create a sorted output array. This article will cover how the algorithm works, its time complexity, and its space complexity. It will also provide examples of C++ code for each topic.

How the Algorithm Works

Counting sort is a non-comparative sorting algorithm which means that it does not compare the elements to each other. Instead, it uses the counts of each element to construct a sorted output array. The basic steps of the algorithm are as follows:

1. Calculate the frequency of each element in the input array.
2. Create an array (the output array) with the size equal to the number of unique elements in the input array.
3. Initialize the output array with all zeroes.
4. Use the frequency of each element to fill the output array.

The following example will illustrate how the algorithm works. Consider the following array of elements: [3, 4, 1, 5, 2].

First, we calculate the frequency of each element in the input array. The frequencies are as follows:

Element : Frequency

- 3 : 1
- 4 : 1
- 1 : 1
- 5 : 1
- 2 : 1

Next, we create an output array with the size equal to the number of unique elements in the input array, which in this case is 5. The output array is initialized with all zeroes.

Finally, we use the frequency of each element to fill the output array. We start by placing a 3 in the first position of the output array since its frequency is 1. We then place a 4 in the second position of the output array since its frequency is also 1. We continue in this manner until the output array is filled.

Output array: [3, 4, 1, 5, 2]

Time Complexity

The time complexity of counting sort is linear in the worst case, which means that the time taken to sort an array is directly proportional to its size. The best and average time complexities of counting sort are also linear.

The time complexity of the algorithm can be expressed as follows:

Time complexity: $O(n + k)$

Where n is the size of the input array and k is the number of unique elements in the array.

Space Complexity

The space complexity of counting sort is also linear, which means that the space taken to sort an array is directly proportional to its size. The space complexity of the algorithm can be expressed as follows:

Space complexity: $O(n + k)$

Where n is the size of the input array and k is the number of unique elements in the array.

C++ Code

The following C++ code implements the counting sort algorithm.

```cpp
//Function to sort an array using counting sort
void countingSort(int arr[], int n, int k)
{
  // Create an output array and initialize it with all zeroes
  int output[n];
  for(int i=0; i < n; i++)
    output[i] = 0;
  // Create an array to store the count of each element
  int count[k];
  for(int i=0; i < k; i++)
    count[i] = 0;
  // Store the count of each element
  for(int i=0; i < n; i++)
    count[arr[i]]++;
  // Store the cummulative count of each array
  for(int i=1; i < k; i++)
    count[i] += count[i-1];
  // Find the index of each element of the original array in count array
  // place the elements in output array
  for(int i=n-1; i >= 0; i--)
  {
    output[count[arr[i]]-1] = arr[i];
    count[arr[i]]--;
  }
}
```

```
// Copy the sorted elements into original array
for(int i=0; i < n; i++)
  arr[i] = output[i];
}
```

Conclusion

Counting sort is a non-comparative sorting algorithm which is efficient in terms of time and space. It is often used in situations where the range of elements is known. The basic steps of the algorithm are as follows: calculating the frequency of each element in the input array, creating an array with the size equal to the number of unique elements in the input array, initializing the output array with all zeroes, and using the frequency of each element to fill the output array. The time complexity of counting sort is linear in the worst case and its space complexity is also linear.

Exercises

Write a C++ program to implement counting sort.

Write a C++ program to find the time complexity of counting sort.

Write a C++ program to find the space complexity of counting sort.

Write a C++ program to demonstrate the working of counting sort.

Write a C++ program to find the frequency of each element in an array.

Solutions

Write a C++ program to implement counting sort.

```cpp
#include<iostream>
//Function to sort an array using counting sort
void countingSort(int arr[], int n, int k)
{
  // Create an output array and initialize it with all zeroes
  int output[n];
  for(int i=0; i < n; i++)
    output[i] = 0;
  // Create an array to store the count of each element
  int count[k];
  for(int i=0; i < k; i++)
    count[i] = 0;
  // Store the count of each element
  for(int i=0; i < n; i++)
    count[arr[i]]++;
  // Store the cummulative count of each array
  for(int i=1; i < k; i++)
    count[i] += count[i-1];
  // Find the index of each element of the original array in count array
  // place the elements in output array
```

```cpp
  for(int i=n-1; i >= 0; i--)
  {
    output[count[arr[i]]-1] = arr[i];
    count[arr[i]]--;
  }
  // Copy the sorted elements into original array
  for(int i=0; i < n; i++)
    arr[i] = output[i];
}
// Function to print the array
void printArray(int arr[], int n)
{
  for (int i=0; i<n; i++)
    std::cout << arr[i] << " ";
}
// Driver program to test above functions
int main()
{
  int arr[] = {3, 4, 1, 5, 2};
  int n = sizeof(arr)/sizeof(arr[0]);
  int k = 5;
  countingSort(arr, n, k);
  std::cout << "Sorted array is: ";
  printArray(arr, n);
  return 0;
}
```

Write a C++ program to find the time complexity of counting sort.

```cpp
#include<iostream>
#include<chrono>
//Function to sort an array using counting sort
void countingSort(int arr[], int n, int k)
{
  // Create an output array and initialize it with all zeroes
  int output[n];
  for(int i=0; i < n; i++)
    output[i] = 0;
  // Create an array to store the count of each element
  int count[k];
  for(int i=0; i < k; i++)
    count[i] = 0;
  // Store the count of each element
  for(int i=0; i < n; i++)
    count[arr[i]]++;
  // Store the cummulative count of each array
```

```cpp
  for(int i=1; i < k; i++)
    count[i] += count[i-1];
  // Find the index of each element of the original array in count array
  // place the elements in output array
  for(int i=n-1; i >= 0; i--)
  {
    output[count[arr[i]]-1] = arr[i];
    count[arr[i]]--;
  }
  // Copy the sorted elements into original array
  for(int i=0; i < n; i++)
    arr[i] = output[i];
}
// Function to calculate the time complexity of counting sort
void timeComplexity(int arr[], int n, int k)
{
  // Start the timer
  auto start = std::chrono::high_resolution_clock::now();
  // Call the sorting function
  countingSort(arr, n, k);
  // Stop the timer
  auto end = std::chrono::high_resolution_clock::now();
  // Calculate the time taken
  auto duration = std::chrono::duration_cast<std::chrono::microseconds>(end - start);
  // Print the time taken
  std::cout << "Time taken: " << duration.count() << " microseconds" << std::endl;
}
// Driver program to test above functions
int main()
{
  int arr[] = {3, 4, 1, 5, 2};
  int n = sizeof(arr)/sizeof(arr[0]);
  int k = 5;
  timeComplexity(arr, n, k);
  return 0;
}
```

Write a C++ program to find the space complexity of counting sort.

```cpp
#include<iostream>
//Function to sort an array using counting sort
void countingSort(int arr[], int n, int k)
{
  // Create an output array and initialize it with all zeroes
  int output[n];
  for(int i=0; i < n; i++)
```

```cpp
    output[i] = 0;
  // Create an array to store the count of each element
  int count[k];
  for(int i=0; i < k; i++)
    count[i] = 0;
  // Store the count of each element
  for(int i=0; i < n; i++)
    count[arr[i]]++;
  // Store the cummulative count of each array
  for(int i=1; i < k; i++)
    count[i] += count[i-1];
  // Find the index of each element of the original array in count array
  // place the elements in output array
  for(int i=n-1; i >= 0; i--)
  {
    output[count[arr[i]]-1] = arr[i];
    count[arr[i]]--;
  }
  // Copy the sorted elements into original array
  for(int i=0; i < n; i++)
    arr[i] = output[i];
}
// Function to calculate the space complexity of counting sort
void spaceComplexity(int arr[], int n, int k)
{
  // Calculate the space taken
  int space = (n + k) * sizeof(int);
  // Print the space taken
  std::cout << "Space taken: " << space << " bytes" << std::endl;
}
// Driver program to test above functions
int main()
{
  int arr[] = {3, 4, 1, 5, 2};
  int n = sizeof(arr)/sizeof(arr[0]);
  int k = 5;
  spaceComplexity(arr, n, k);
  return 0;
}
```

Write a C++ program to demonstrate the working of counting sort.

```cpp
#include<iostream>
//Function to sort an array using counting sort
void countingSort(int arr[], int n, int k)
{
```

```cpp
  // Create an output array and initialize it with all zeroes
  int output[n];
  for(int i=0; i < n; i++)
    output[i] = 0;
  // Create an array to store the count of each element
  int count[k];
  for(int i=0; i < k; i++)
    count[i] = 0;
  // Store the count of each element
  for(int i=0; i < n; i++)
    count[arr[i]]++;
  // Store the cummulative count of each array
  for(int i=1; i < k; i++)
    count[i] += count[i-1];
  // Find the index of each element of the original array in count array
  // place the elements in output array
  for(int i=n-1; i >= 0; i--)
  {
    output[count[arr[i]]-1] = arr[i];
    count[arr[i]]--;
  }
  // Copy the sorted elements into original array
  for(int i=0; i < n; i++)
    arr[i] = output[i];
}
// Function to print the array
void printArray(int arr[], int n)
{
  for (int i=0; i<n; i++)
    std::cout << arr[i] << " ";
}
// Driver program to test above functions
int main()
{
  int arr[] = {3, 4, 1, 5, 2};
  int n = sizeof(arr)/sizeof(arr[0]);
  int k = 5;
  std::cout << "Input array: ";
  printArray(arr, n);
  countingSort(arr, n, k);
  std::cout << "\nSorted array is: ";
  printArray(arr, n);
  return 0;
}
```

Write a C++ program to find the frequency of each element in an array.

```cpp
#include<iostream>
// Function to calculate the frequency of each element in an array
void frequency(int arr[], int n)
{

  // Create an array to store the count of each element
  int count[n];
  for(int i=0; i < n; i++)
    count[i] = 0;
  // Store the count of each element
  for(int i=0; i < n; i++)
    count[arr[i]]++;
  // Print the frequency of each element
  for (int i = 0; i < n; i++)
    std::cout << arr[i] << " " << count[arr[i]] << std::endl;
}
// Driver program to test above functions
int main()
{

  int arr[] = {3, 4, 1, 5, 2, 3, 4, 1, 5, 2, 1, 2};
  int n = sizeof(arr)/sizeof(arr[0]);
  frequency(arr, n);
  return 0;
}
```

CUBESORT IN C++

Cubesort is a sorting algorithm that works by recursively sorting the elements of an array into small cubes and then merging them back together. It is an efficient sorting algorithm that is particularly good at sorting small amounts of data. In this article, we will discuss how the algorithm works, its time and space complexities, and provide examples of Cubesort implemented in C++.

How Cubesort Works

Cubesort is a sorting algorithm that works by dividing an array into small cubes, sorting each cube, and then merging the cubes back together. The algorithm begins by dividing the array into small cubes of size N (where N is typically 8 or 16). The algorithm then sorts each cube using an internal sorting algorithm such as insertion sort or quicksort. Once each cube is sorted, the algorithm then merges the cubes back together using a merge sort algorithm. The result is an array that is sorted in ascending order.

Time Complexity

Cubesort has an average time complexity of O(n log n). This is because the algorithm performs an internal sorting algorithm on each cube, followed by a merge sort algorithm to merge the cubes together. The time complexity is dependent on the size of the array and the internal sorting algorithm used.

The best-case time complexity of Cubesort is O(n log n), which occurs when the array is already sorted. The worst-case time complexity of Cubesort is O(n^2), which occurs when the array is not in order.

Space Complexity

The space complexity of Cubesort is O(n), which is the same as the space complexity of the internal sorting algorithm used. This is because the algorithm does not require any additional space for the sorting process.

C++ Implementation

Now that we have an understanding of how the algorithm works and its time and space complexities, let's take a look at an example of Cubesort implemented in C++.

```cpp
#include <iostream>
#include <algorithm>
const int CUBE_SIZE = 8;
// function to sort the cube
void cubeSort(int arr[], int n)
```

```cpp
{
  // divide the array into cubes of size CUBE_SIZE
  for (int i = 0; i < n; i += CUBE_SIZE)
  {
    std::sort(arr + i, arr + std::min(i + CUBE_SIZE, n));
  }
  // merge the cubes
  int temp[n];
  for (int i = 0; i < n; i += CUBE_SIZE)
  {
    std::merge(arr + i, arr + std::min(i + CUBE_SIZE, n),
         arr + std::min(i + CUBE_SIZE, n),
         arr + std::min(i + 2*CUBE_SIZE, n),
         temp + i);
  }
  // copy the result from temp[] back to arr[]
  for (int i = 0; i < n; i++)
    arr[i] = temp[i];
}
// main function
int main()
{
  // input array
  int arr[] = {3, 6, 7, 1, 5, 2, 8, 4};
  int n = sizeof(arr) / sizeof(arr[0]);
  // call cubeSort
  cubeSort(arr, n);
  // print the sorted array
  for (int i = 0; i < n; i++)
    std::cout << arr[i] << " ";
  return 0;
}
```

Conclusion

Cubesort is an efficient sorting algorithm that works by recursively sorting elements of an array into small cubes and then merging them back together. The algorithm has an average time complexity of O(n log n) and a space complexity of O(n). The time complexity is dependent on the size of the array and the internal sorting algorithm used. The algorithm is particularly good at sorting small amounts of data. In this article, we discussed how Cubesort works, its time and space complexities, and provided an example of Cubesort implemented in C++.

Exercises

Write a C++ program to sort an array of integers using Cubesort.

Write a C++ program to find the time complexity of a Cubesort algorithm.

Write a C++ program to find the space complexity of a Cubesort algorithm.

Write a C++ program to implement Cubesort in an array of strings.

Write a C++ program to sort a two-dimensional array using Cubesort.

Solutions

Write a C++ program to sort an array of integers using Cubesort.

```cpp
#include <iostream>
#include <algorithm>
const int CUBE_SIZE = 8;
// function to sort the cube
void cubeSort(int arr[], int n)
{
  // divide the array into cubes of size CUBE_SIZE
  for (int i = 0; i < n; i += CUBE_SIZE)
  {
    std::sort(arr + i, arr + std::min(i + CUBE_SIZE, n));
  }
  // merge the cubes
  int temp[n];
  for (int i = 0; i < n; i += CUBE_SIZE)
  {
    std::merge(arr + i, arr + std::min(i + CUBE_SIZE, n),
        arr + std::min(i + CUBE_SIZE, n),
        arr + std::min(i + 2*CUBE_SIZE, n),
        temp + i);
  }
  // copy the result from temp[] back to arr[]
  for (int i = 0; i < n; i++)
    arr[i] = temp[i];
}
// main function
int main()
{
  // input array
  int arr[] = {3, 6, 7, 1, 5, 2, 8, 4};
  int n = sizeof(arr) / sizeof(arr[0]);
  // call cubeSort
  cubeSort(arr, n);
  // print the sorted array
  for (int i = 0; i < n; i++)
    std::cout << arr[i] << " ";
  return 0;
```

```
}
```

Write a C++ program to find the time complexity of a Cubesort algorithm.

```cpp
#include <iostream>
#include <algorithm>
const int CUBE_SIZE = 8;
// function to calculate the time complexity of Cubesort
int cubeSortTimeComplexity(int arr[], int n)
{
  int complexity = 0;
  // divide the array into cubes of size CUBE_SIZE
  for (int i = 0; i < n; i += CUBE_SIZE)
  {
    complexity += n * log(n);
  }
  // merge the cubes
  int temp[n];
  for (int i = 0; i < n; i += CUBE_SIZE)
  {
    complexity += n * log(n);
  }
  return complexity;
}
// main function
int main()
{
  // input array
  int arr[] = {3, 6, 7, 1, 5, 2, 8, 4};
  int n = sizeof(arr) / sizeof(arr[0]);
  // call cubeSortTimeComplexity
  int complexity = cubeSortTimeComplexity(arr, n);
  // print the time complexity
  std::cout << "Time complexity of Cubesort is: " << complexity << std::endl;
  return 0;
}
```

Write a C++ program to find the space complexity of a Cubesort algorithm.

```cpp
#include <iostream>
#include <algorithm>
const int CUBE_SIZE = 8;
// function to calculate the space complexity of Cubesort
int cubeSortSpaceComplexity(int n)
{
  int complexity = 0;
  // divide the array into cubes of size CUBE_SIZE
  complexity += n;
```

```
  // merge the cubes
  int temp[n];
  complexity += n;
  return complexity;
}
// main function
int main()
{
  // input array
  int arr[] = {3, 6, 7, 1, 5, 2, 8, 4};
  int n = sizeof(arr) / sizeof(arr[0]);
  // call cubeSortSpaceComplexity
  int complexity = cubeSortSpaceComplexity(n);
  // print the space complexity
  std::cout << "Space complexity of Cubesort is: " << complexity << std::endl;
  return 0;
}
```

Write a C++ program to implement Cubesort in an array of strings.

```
#include <iostream>
#include <algorithm>
#include <string>
const int CUBE_SIZE = 8;
// function to sort the cube
void cubeSort(std::string arr[], int n)
{
  // divide the array into cubes of size CUBE_SIZE
  for (int i = 0; i < n; i += CUBE_SIZE)
  {
    std::sort(arr + i, arr + std::min(i + CUBE_SIZE, n));
  }
  // merge the cubes
  std::string temp[n];
  for (int i = 0; i < n; i += CUBE_SIZE)
  {
    std::merge(arr + i, arr + std::min(i + CUBE_SIZE, n),
           arr + std::min(i + CUBE_SIZE, n),
           arr + std::min(i + 2*CUBE_SIZE, n),
           temp + i);
  }
  // copy the result from temp[] back to arr[]
  for (int i = 0; i < n; i++)
    arr[i] = temp[i];
}
// main function
```

```cpp
int main()
{
  // input array
  std::string arr[] = {"c", "a", "e", "b", "d"};
  int n = sizeof(arr) / sizeof(arr[0]);
  // call cubeSort
  cubeSort(arr, n);
  // print the sorted array
  for (int i = 0; i < n; i++)
    std::cout << arr[i] << " ";
  return 0;
}
```

Write a C++ program to sort a two-dimensional array using Cubesort.

```cpp
#include <iostream>
#include <algorithm>
const int CUBE_SIZE = 8;
// function to sort the cube
void cubeSort(int arr[][CUBE_SIZE], int n)
{
  // divide the array into cubes of size CUBE_SIZE
  for (int i = 0; i < n; i += CUBE_SIZE)
  {
    for (int j = 0; j < CUBE_SIZE; j++)
      std::sort(arr[i] + j, arr[i] + std::min(j + CUBE_SIZE, n));
  }
  // merge the cubes
  int temp[n][CUBE_SIZE];
  for (int i = 0; i < n; i += CUBE_SIZE)
  {
    for (int j = 0; j < CUBE_SIZE; j++)
      std::merge(arr[i] + j, arr[i] + std::min(j + CUBE_SIZE, n),
            arr[i] + std::min(j + CUBE_SIZE, n),
            arr[i] + std::min(j + 2*CUBE_SIZE, n),
            temp[i] + j);
  }
  // copy the result from temp[] back to arr[]
  for (int i = 0; i < n; i++)
  {
    for (int j = 0; j < CUBE_SIZE; j++)
      arr[i][j] = temp[i][j];
  }
}
// main function
int main()
```

```
{
  // input array
  int arr[][CUBE_SIZE] = {{3, 6, 7, 1, 5, 2, 8, 4},
                {3, 6, 7, 1, 5, 2, 8, 4},
                {3, 6, 7, 1, 5, 2, 8, 4}};
  int n = sizeof(arr) / sizeof(arr[0]);
  // call cubeSort
  cubeSort(arr, n);
  // print the sorted array
  for (int i = 0; i < n; i++)
  {
    for (int j = 0; j < CUBE_SIZE; j++)
      std::cout << arr[i][j] << " ";
    std::cout << std::endl;
  }
  return 0;
}
```

LINEAR SEARCH IN C++

Linear search is a simple yet effective algorithm used to search for a particular element or value in an array or list. It is one of the most fundamental algorithms used in data structures and algorithms with C++. In this article, we will discuss the basic concept of linear search, its time and space complexities, and a C++ implementation of the algorithm. We will also explore a few coding exercises at the end to test your understanding of linear search.

What is Linear Search?

Linear search is a technique of searching through a sequential set of elements or values until the desired element is found. It sequentially checks each element of the given array until a match is found or the end of the array is reached. As the name suggests, the elements are searched one by one in a linear fashion. The time required for a linear search depends on the size of the array and the location of the element.

Linear search is also known as a sequential search or brute-force search as it involves searching through every element until the desired element is found. This algorithm is simple to implement and does not require any pre-processing of the data. It is most suitable for smaller data sets as it has a time complexity of O(n).

Time Complexity of Linear Search

The time complexity of linear search is O(n), where n is the number of elements in the array. This means that the time required to search for an element increases linearly with the number of elements in the array.

The best-case time complexity of linear search is O(1) when the element is found at the beginning of the array. The worst-case time complexity is O(n) when the element is found at the end of the array. The average time complexity is also O(n).

Space Complexity of Linear Search

The space complexity of linear search is O(1). This means that the algorithm requires a constant amount of space irrespective of the size of the array.

C++ Implementation of Linear Search

Let's look at a simple implementation of linear search in C++. The following code searches for a given element in an array and returns its index if found; otherwise, it returns -1.

```
#include <iostream>
using namespace std;
```

```
int linearSearch(int arr[], int n, int x)
{
        int i;
        for (i = 0; i < n; i++)
                   if (arr[i] == x)
                               return i;
        return -1;
}
int main()
{
        int arr[] = { 1, 10, 30, 15 };
        int x = 30;
        int n = sizeof(arr) / sizeof(arr[0]);
        int result = linearSearch(arr, n, x);
        if (result == -1)
                   cout << "Element is not present in array" << endl;
        else
                   cout << "Element is present at index " << result << endl;
        return 0;
}
```

In the above code, we have declared a function linearSearch() which takes an array arr[], the size of the array n, and the element x to be searched. Then, we traverse the array from index 0 to n-1 and check if the element is equal to the desired element. If the element is found, the index is returned; otherwise, -1 is returned.

In the main() function, we have declared an array arr[] and an element x to be searched. Then, we call the linearSearch() function and pass the array, size, and element as parameters. This function returns the index at which the element is found, or -1 if it is not found.

Conclusion

In this article, we discussed linear search, its time and space complexities, and its C++ implementation. We also looked at a few coding exercises to test your understanding of linear search. Linear search is a simple algorithm and is best suited for small data sets. It has a time complexity of $O(n)$ and a space complexity of $O(1)$.

Linear search is one of the fundamental algorithms used in data structures and algorithms with C++. It is important to understand the basics of linear search, its implementation, and its complexities before moving on to more complex algorithms.

Exercises

Write a function to search for an element in a linked list using linear search.

Write a program to search for an element in a 2D array using linear search.

Write a program to search for an element in a BST using linear search.

Write a program to search for an element in a hash table using linear search.

Write a program to search for an element in a linked list using linear search in a recursive manner.

Solutions

Write a function to search for an element in a linked list using linear search.

```cpp
#include <iostream>
using namespace std;
struct Node
{
        int data;
        struct Node* next;
};
int linearSearch(struct Node* head, int x)
{
        struct Node* current = head;
        int index = 0;
        while (current != NULL)
        {
                if (current->data == x)
                        return index;
                current = current->next;
                index++;
        }
        return -1;
}
int main()
{
        struct Node* head = NULL;
        head = new Node;
        head->data = 10;
        head->next = new Node;
        head->next->data = 20;
        head->next->next = new Node;
        head->next->next->data = 30;
        head->next->next->next = NULL;
        int x = 20;
        int result = linearSearch(head, x);
        if (result == -1)
                cout << "Element is not present in the list" << endl;
        else
                cout << "Element is present at index " << result << endl;
        return 0;
}
```

YASIN CAKAL

Write a program to search for an element in a 2D array using linear search.

```cpp
#include <iostream>
using namespace std;
#define R 4
#define C 4
int linearSearch(int arr[R][C], int x)
{
        int i, j;
        for (i = 0; i < R; i++)
                for (j = 0; j < C; j++)
                        if (arr[i][j] == x)
                                return 1;
        return 0;
}
int main()
{
        int arr[R][C] = { { 10, 20, 30, 40 },
                          { 15, 25, 35, 45 },
                          { 27, 29, 37, 48 },
                          { 32, 33, 39, 50 } };
        int x = 29;
        int result = linearSearch(arr, x);
        if (result == 0)
                cout << "Element is not present in the array" << endl;
        else
                cout << "Element is present in the array" << endl;
        return 0;
}
```

Write a program to search for an element in a BST using linear search.

```cpp
#include <iostream>
using namespace std;
struct Node
{
        int data;
        struct Node* left, *right;
};
int linearSearch(struct Node* root, int x)
{
        if (root == NULL)
                return 0;
        if (root->data == x)
                return 1;
        if (root->data > x)
                return linearSearch(root->left, x);
```

```
            return linearSearch(root->right, x);
}
int main()
{
        struct Node* root = NULL;
        root = new Node;
        root->data = 20;
        root->left = new Node;
        root->left->data = 8;
        root->right = new Node;
        root->right->data = 22;
        root->left->left = new Node;
        root->left->left->data = 4;
        root->left->right = new Node;
        root->left->right->data = 12;
        int x = 22;
        int result = linearSearch(root, x);
        if (result == 0)
                cout << "Element is not present in the tree" << endl;
        else
                cout << "Element is present in the tree" << endl;
        return 0;
}
```

Write a program to search for an element in a hash table using linear search.

```
#include <iostream>
#include <list>
using namespace std;
class HashTable
{
        int size;
        list<int>* table;
public:
        HashTable(int size)
        {
                this->size = size;
                table = new list<int>[size];
        }
        void insertItem(int key)
        {
                int index = hashFunction(key);
                table[index].push_back(key);
        }
        int linearSearch(int key)
        {
```

```
                int index = hashFunction(key);
                list<int>::iterator i;
                for (i = table[index].begin(); i != table[index].end(); i++)
                        if (*i == key)
                                return 1;
                return 0;
        }
private:
        int hashFunction(int key)
        {
                return (key % size);
        }
};
int main()
{
        HashTable ht(7);
        ht.insertItem(18);
        ht.insertItem(25);
        ht.insertItem(42);
        ht.insertItem(17);
        int x = 18;
        int result = ht.linearSearch(x);
        if (result == 0)
                cout << "Element is not present in the hash table" << endl;
        else
                cout << "Element is present in the hash table" << endl;
        return 0;
}
```

Write a program to search for an element in a linked list using linear search in a recursive manner.

```
#include <iostream>
using namespace std;
struct Node
{
        int data;
        struct Node* next;
};
int linearSearchRecursive(struct Node* head, int x, int index)
{
        if (head == NULL)
                return -1;
        if (head->data == x)
                return index;
        return linearSearchRecursive(head->next, x, index+1);
```

```
}
int main()
{
        struct Node* head = NULL;
        head = new Node;
        head->data = 10;
        head->next = new Node;
        head->next->data = 20;
        head->next->next = new Node;
        head->next->next->data = 30;
        head->next->next->next = NULL;
        int x = 20;
        int result = linearSearchRecursive(head, x, 0);
        if (result == -1)
                cout << "Element is not present in the list" << endl;
        else
                cout << "Element is present at index " << result << endl;
        return 0;
}
```

BINARY SEARCH IN C++

Binary search is an efficient algorithm for searching large datasets. It is a divide-and-conquer method that works by repeatedly dividing the search interval in half until the desired value is found. It is one of the most used algorithms when it comes to searching for elements in an array, and it is also used in many sorting algorithms. In this article, we will discuss the basics of binary search in C++ and its time and space complexities.

What is Binary Search?

Binary search is a searching algorithm that works by repeatedly dividing the search interval in half until the desired value is found. This algorithm is used to search for an element in a sorted array. It works by comparing the element to be searched with the middle element in the array. If the element is equal to the middle element, then it is found. If not, the search continues in the left or right half of the array depending on the comparison. This process is repeated until the element is found or the search interval is empty.

Working of Binary Search in C++

Binary search in C++ works by repeatedly dividing the search interval in half until the desired value is found. The algorithm begins by setting the lower and upper bounds of the search interval to the first and last elements of the array. The algorithm then compares the element to be searched with the element at the middle of the search interval. If the element is equal to the middle element, then it is found. If not, the search continues in the left or right half of the interval depending on the comparison. This process is repeated until the element is found or the search interval is empty.

Here is an example of a binary search algorithm in C++:

```cpp
// Returns the index of the element if it is found in the array, else returns -1
int binarySearch(int arr[], int low, int high, int x)
{
  if (high >= low)
  {
    int mid = (low + high)/2;
    // If the element is present at the middle itself
    if (arr[mid] == x)
      return mid;
    // If element is smaller than mid, then it can only be present
    // in left subarray
    if (arr[mid] > x)
```

```
      return binarySearch(arr, low, mid-1, x);
   // Else the element can only be present in right subarray
   return binarySearch(arr, mid+1, high, x);
}
// We reach here when element is not present in array
return -1;
}
```

In the above code, the binarySearch() function takes four parameters: an array of integers, the lower bound of the search interval, the upper bound of the search interval, and the element to be searched. The function then checks if the element is present at the middle of the search interval. If it is, it returns the index of the element. If not, it continues the search in the left or right half of the interval depending on the comparison.

Time and Space Complexity of Binary Search in C++

The time complexity of binary search in C++ is O(log n). This means that the time taken to search for an element in an array increases logarithmically with the size of the array. This makes binary search an efficient algorithm for searching large datasets.

The space complexity of binary search in C++ is O(1). This means that the amount of memory needed to perform the search is fixed and does not depend on the size of the array.

Conclusion

In this article, we discussed binary search in C++ and its time and space complexities. We saw how the algorithm works and how it is used to search for an element in a sorted array. We also saw how the time and space complexities of binary search in C++ are O(log n) and O(1) respectively.

Exercises

Write a C++ program to find the index of a given element using binary search.

Write a C++ program to sort an array using binary search.

Write a C++ program to search for an element using binary search and return the number of comparisons.

Write a C++ program to search for an element in an array using binary search and return the number of comparisons.

Write a C++ program to find the number of comparisons needed to search for an element using binary search in an array of size n.

Solutions

Write a C++ program to find the index of a given element using binary search.

```
#include <iostream>
// Returns the index of the element if it is found in the array, else returns -1
```

```cpp
int binarySearch(int arr[], int low, int high, int x)
{
  if (high >= low)
  {
    int mid = (low + high)/2;
    // If the element is present at the middle itself
    if (arr[mid] == x)
      return mid;
    // If element is smaller than mid, then it can only be present
    // in left subarray
    if (arr[mid] > x)
      return binarySearch(arr, low, mid-1, x);
    // Else the element can only be present in right subarray
    return binarySearch(arr, mid+1, high, x);
  }
  // We reach here when element is not present in array
  return -1;
}
int main()
{
  int arr[] = {1, 2, 3, 4, 5, 6, 7, 8, 9};
  int n = sizeof(arr)/sizeof(arr[0]);
  int x = 8;
  int index = binarySearch(arr, 0, n-1, x);
  if (index != -1)
    std::cout << x << " is present at index: " << index << std::endl;
  else
    std::cout << x << " is not present in the array" << std::endl;
  return 0;
}
```

Write a C++ program to sort an array using binary search.

```cpp
#include <iostream>
// Function to perform binary search
int binarySearch(int arr[], int low, int high, int x)
{
  if (high >= low)
  {
    int mid = (low + high)/2;
    // If the element is present at middle itself
    if (arr[mid] == x)
      return mid;
    // If element is smaller than mid, then it can only be present
    // in left subarray
    if (arr[mid] > x)
```

```cpp
        return binarySearch(arr, low, mid-1, x);
    // Else the element can only be present in right subarray
    return binarySearch(arr, mid+1, high, x);
  }
  // We reach here when element is not present in array
  return -1;
}
// Function to sort an array using binary search
void sortArray(int arr[], int n)
{
  for (int i=0; i<n-1; i++)
  {
    int min_index = i;
    for (int j=i+1; j<n; j++)
    {
      // If the element at min_index is greater than the element at j
      if (arr[min_index] > arr[j])
      {
        // Update the min_index to j
        min_index = j;
      }
    }
    // Swap the elements at min_index and i
    int temp = arr[min_index];
    arr[min_index] = arr[i];
    arr[i] = temp;
  }
}
int main()
{
  int arr[] = {5, 4, 3, 2, 1};
  int n = sizeof(arr)/sizeof(arr[0]);
  // Sort the array
  sortArray(arr, n);
  // Find the index of the given element
  int x = 4;
  int index = binarySearch(arr, 0, n-1, x);
  if (index != -1)
    std::cout << x << " is present at index: " << index << std::endl;
  else
    std::cout << x << " is not present in the array" << std::endl;
  return 0;
}
```

Write a C++ program to search for an element using binary search and return the

number of comparisons.

```cpp
#include <iostream>
// Returns the index of the element if it is found in the array, else returns -1
int binarySearch(int arr[], int low, int high, int x, int &count)
{
  if (high >= low)
  {
    int mid = (low + high)/2;
    count++;
    // If the element is present at the middle itself
    if (arr[mid] == x)
      return mid;
    // If element is smaller than mid, then it can only be present
    // in left subarray
    if (arr[mid] > x)
      return binarySearch(arr, low, mid-1, x, count);
    // Else the element can only be present in right subarray
    return binarySearch(arr, mid+1, high, x, count);
  }
  // We reach here when element is not present in array
  return -1;
}
int main()
{
  int arr[] = {1, 2, 3, 4, 5, 6, 7, 8, 9};
  int n = sizeof(arr)/sizeof(arr[0]);
  int x = 8;
  int count = 0;
  int index = binarySearch(arr, 0, n-1, x, count);
  if (index != -1)
    std::cout << x << " is present at index: " << index << std::endl;
  else
    std::cout << x << " is not present in the array" << std::endl;
  std::cout << "Number of comparisons: " << count << std::endl;
  return 0;
}
```

Write a C++ program to search for an element in an array using binary search and return the number of comparisons.

```cpp
#include <iostream>
// Returns the index of the element if it is found in the array, else returns -1
int binarySearch(int arr[], int low, int high, int x, int &count)
{
  if (high >= low)
  {
```

```cpp
    int mid = (low + high)/2;
    count++;
    // If the element is present at the middle itself
    if (arr[mid] == x)
      return mid;
    // If element is smaller than mid, then it can only be present
    // in left subarray
    if (arr[mid] > x)
      return binarySearch(arr, low, mid-1, x, count);
    // Else the element can only be present in right subarray
    return binarySearch(arr, mid+1, high, x, count);
  }
  // We reach here when element is not present in array
  return -1;
}
int main()
{
  int arr[] = {1, 2, 3, 4, 5, 6, 7, 8, 9};
  int n = sizeof(arr)/sizeof(arr[0]);
  int x = 8;
  int count = 0;
  int index = binarySearch(arr, 0, n-1, x, count);
  if (index != -1)
    std::cout << x << " is present at index: " << index << std::endl;
  else
    std::cout << x << " is not present in the array" << std::endl;
  std::cout << "Number of comparisons: " << count << std::endl;
  return 0;
}
```

Write a C++ program to find the number of comparisons needed to search for an element using binary search in an array of size n.

```cpp
#include <iostream>
// Returns the number of comparisons needed to search for an element using binary search
int binarySearch(int n)
{
  if (n == 0)
    return 0;
  return 1 + binarySearch(n/2);
}
int main()
{
  int n = 8;
  int count = binarySearch(n);
  std::cout << "Number of comparisons: " << count << std::endl;
```

```
    return 0;
}
```

GRAPHING ALGORITHMS

BREADTH FIRST SEARCH (BFS) IN C++

Breadth-first search (BFS) is an algorithm used to traverse a graph or tree structure. It is often used in pathfinding and network traversal, and is also known as a level-order traversal. BFS is a popular choice for many graph-related problems, as it is often more efficient than depth-first search (DFS). In this article, we'll look at how the algorithm works, its time complexity, and its space complexity. We'll also provide some examples of BFS in C++ to help you understand the algorithm.

What is Breadth First Search (BFS)?

Breadth-first search is a graph traversal algorithm that starts at the root node and explores all the neighboring nodes before moving to the next level neighbors. As such, it traverses the graph level by level, and each level is explored completely before the next level is explored. The algorithm works by keeping track of the nodes in a queue, and it starts by adding the root node to the queue. Then, it explores the first node in the queue, adding its children to the queue, and then exploring the next node in the queue. This process continues until all nodes have been explored or until the desired node is found.

BFS in C++

To help you understand the BFS algorithm, let's look at an example in C++. The following code implements the BFS algorithm in C++. First, we declare an array to store the visited nodes. Then, we create a queue to store the nodes that need to be visited. In the main loop, we check if the queue is empty or not. If it's not empty, we remove the first element of the queue and add it to the visited array. Then, we check if the current node has any children and if it does, we add them to the queue. Finally, we repeat this process until all nodes have been visited.

```cpp
//BFS in C++
#include <iostream>
#include <queue>
#include <vector>
using namespace std;
// Array to store the visited nodes
bool visited[100];
// Function to perform the BFS
void bfs(vector<int> adj[], int source)
{
```

```cpp
        // Create a queue and add the source node
        queue<int> q;
        q.push(source);
        visited[source] = true;
        while (!q.empty())
        {
                // Take the front node from the queue
                int front = q.front();
                q.pop();
                // Visit all the nodes in the adjacency list of the node
                for (int i = 0; i < adj[front].size(); i++)
                {
                        if (!visited[adj[front][i]])
                        {
                                visited[adj[front][i]] = true;
                                q.push(adj[front][i]);
                        }
                }
        }
}
int main()
{
        // Adjacency list for the graph
        vector<int> adj[100];
        // Code for adding edges
        // ...
        // Perform BFS on the graph
        bfs(adj, 0);
        // Print the result
        // ...
        return 0;
}
```

Time and Space Complexity of Breadth First Search (BFS)

The time complexity of BFS depends on the number of nodes in the graph and the number of edges. In the worst case, the time complexity of BFS is O(V+E), where V is the number of nodes and E is the number of edges. In the best case, it is O(V).

The space complexity of BFS is O(V), as it requires an array to keep track of the visited nodes. Additionally, it requires a queue to store the nodes to be visited.

Conclusion

In this article, we looked at the Breadth First Search (BFS) algorithm and how it works. We also looked at its time and space complexity, and provided an example implementation in C++. BFS is a popular choice for many graph-related problems, as it is often more efficient than depth-first search (DFS).

Exercises

Write a C++ program to perform a Breadth First Search on a graph represented by an adjacency matrix.

Write a C++ program to perform a Breadth First Search on a binary tree.

Write a C++ program to find the shortest path between two nodes in a graph using Breadth First Search.

Write a C++ program to traverse a graph using Breadth First Search and check if a given node exists in the graph.

Write a C++ program to print the level order traversal of a binary tree using Breadth First Search.

Solutions

Write a C++ program to perform a Breadth First Search on a graph represented by an adjacency matrix.

```cpp
#include <iostream>
#include <queue>
#include <vector>
using namespace std;
// Array to store the visited nodes
bool visited[100];
// Function to perform the BFS
void bfs(int adj[][100], int source, int n)
{
        // Create a queue and add the source node
        queue<int> q;
        q.push(source);
        visited[source] = true;
        while (!q.empty())
        {
                // Take the front node from the queue
                int front = q.front();
                q.pop();
                // Visit all the nodes in the adjacency list of the node
                for (int i = 0; i < n; i++)
                {
                        if (adj[front][i] == 1 && !visited[i])
                        {
                                visited[i] = true;
```

```
                                    q.push(i);
                            }
                    }
            }
}
int main()
{
        // Adjacency matrix for the graph
        int adj[100][100];
        int n; // Number of nodes
        // Code for taking input
        // ...
        // Perform BFS on the graph
        bfs(adj, 0, n);
        // Print the result
        // ...
        return 0;
}
```

Write a C++ program to perform a Breadth First Search on a binary tree.

```
#include <iostream>
#include <queue>
using namespace std;
// Node structure for a binary tree
struct Node
{
        int data;
        Node *left, *right;
};
// Function to perform the BFS
void bfs(Node *root)
{
        // Create a queue and add the root node
        queue<Node *> q;
        q.push(root);
        while (!q.empty())
        {
                // Take the front node from the queue
                Node *front = q.front();
                q.pop();
                // Print the node data
                cout << front->data << " ";
                // Visit the left and right nodes
                if (front->left != NULL)
                        q.push(front->left);
```

```
                        if (front->right != NULL)
                                q.push(front->right);

        }
}
int main()
{
        // Binary tree
        Node *root;
        // Code for creating the binary tree
        // ...
        // Perform BFS on the binary tree
        bfs(root);
        return 0;
}
```

Write a C++ program to find the shortest path between two nodes in a graph using Breadth First Search.

```cpp
#include <iostream>
#include <queue>
#include <vector>
using namespace std;
// Array to store the visited nodes
bool visited[100];
// Array to store the distances of each node
int dist[100];
// Function to perform the BFS
void bfs(vector<int> adj[], int source, int destination)
{
        // Create a queue and add the source node
        queue<int> q;
        q.push(source);
        visited[source] = true;
        dist[source] = 0;
        while (!q.empty())
        {
                // Take the front node from the queue
                int front = q.front();
                q.pop();
                // Visit all the nodes in the adjacency list of the node
                for (int i = 0; i < adj[front].size(); i++)
                {
                        if (!visited[adj[front][i]])
                        {
                                visited[adj[front][i]] = true;
                                dist[adj[front][i]] = dist[front] + 1;
```

```
                    q.push(adj[front][i]);
                }
            }
        }
        // Print the shortest path
        cout << "The shortest path is: " << dist[destination] << endl;
}
int main()
{
        // Adjacency list for the graph
        vector<int> adj[100];
        int source, destination;
        // Code for adding edges
        // ...
        // Perform BFS on the graph
        bfs(adj, source, destination);
        return 0;
}
```

Write a C++ program to traverse a graph using Breadth First Search and check if a given node exists in the graph.

```
#include <iostream>
#include <queue>
#include <vector>
using namespace std;
// Array to store the visited nodes
bool visited[100];
// Function to perform the BFS
bool bfs(vector<int> adj[], int source, int dest)
{
        // Create a queue and add the source node
        queue<int> q;
        q.push(source);
        visited[source] = true;
        while (!q.empty())
        {
                // Take the front node from the queue
                int front = q.front();
                q.pop();
                // Visit all the nodes in the adjacency list of the node
                for (int i = 0; i < adj[front].size(); i++)
                {
                        if (!visited[adj[front][i]])
                        {
                                visited[adj[front][i]] = true;
```

```
                              q.push(adj[front][i]);

                              // Check if the node is the destination node
                              if (adj[front][i] == dest)
                                      return true;
                      }
              }
      }
      // Node does not exist in the graph
      return false;
}
int main()
{
      // Adjacency list for the graph
      vector<int> adj[100];
      int source, destination;
      // Code for adding edges
      // ...
      // Perform BFS on the graph
      if (bfs(adj, source, destination))
              cout << "Node exists in the graph" << endl;
      else
              cout << "Node does not exist in the graph" << endl;
      return 0;
}
```

Write a C++ program to print the level order traversal of a binary tree using Breadth First Search.

```
#include <iostream>
#include <queue>
using namespace std;
// Node structure for a binary tree
struct Node
{
      int data;
      Node *left, *right;
};
// Function to perform the BFS
void bfs(Node *root)
{
      // Create a queue and add the root node
      queue<Node *> q;
      q.push(root);
      while (!q.empty())
      {
```

```cpp
        // Take the front node from the queue
        Node *front = q.front();
        q.pop();
        // Print the node data
        cout << front->data << " ";
        // Visit the left and right nodes
        if (front->left != NULL)
                q.push(front->left);
        if (front->right != NULL)
                q.push(front->right);
    }
}
int main()
{
    // Binary tree
    Node *root;
    // Code for creating the binary tree
    // ...
    // Perform BFS on the binary tree
    bfs(root);
    return 0;
}
```

DEPTH FIRST SEARCH (DFS) IN C++

Depth First Search (DFS) is an algorithm used to traverse a graph or a tree. It is one of the most popular algorithms used to traverse a graph and is an important algorithm used in data structures and algorithms with C++. This article will cover the basics of Depth First Search, how it works, its time and space complexity, and have code examples of the algorithm implemented in C++.

What is Depth First Search?

Depth First Search (DFS) is a graph traversal algorithm that starts at the root node and explores as far as possible along each branch before backtracking. It is an algorithm for traversing or searching tree or graph data structures. The DFS algorithm traverses a graph in a depth-ward motion and uses a stack to remember to get the next vertex to start a search, when a dead end occurs in any iteration.

DFS Algorithm

The DFS algorithm consists of three main steps:

1. Initialize a stack to store the nodes to be visited.
2. Push the root node onto the stack.
3. While the stack is not empty:
    1. Pop the node from the stack.
    2. If the node has not been visited, mark it as visited and add all of its adjacent nodes to the stack.
    3. If the node has been visited, move on to the next node.

Time Complexity

The time complexity of the DFS algorithm is $O(V + E)$, where V is the number of vertices and E is the number of edges in the graph. The best case time complexity is $O(V)$ when all nodes are reachable from the source vertex, while the worst case time complexity is $O(V * E)$ when the graph is completely disconnected.

Space Complexity

The space complexity of the DFS algorithm is $O(V)$, where V is the number of vertices in the graph. This is because the algorithm uses a stack to store the nodes that need to be visited.

Implementing Depth First Search in C++

Now that we have an understanding of what Depth First Search is and how it works, let's look at how to implement the algorithm in C++.

Let's start by defining a Graph class. The Graph class will represent our graph data structure and will contain the following:

1. A vector of nodes
2. A function to add an edge between two nodes
3. A function to print the graph

The following code shows how we can define the Graph class in C++:

```cpp
class Graph
{
        vector<int> nodes;
        void addEdge(int u, int v);
        void printGraph();
};
```

Next, we will define a function to add an edge between two nodes in the graph. This function will take two integers as arguments, which represent the two nodes that the edge will connect. The following code shows how this can be done in C++:

```cpp
void Graph::addEdge(int u, int v)
{
        nodes.push_back(u);
        nodes.push_back(v);
}
```

Finally, we will define a function to print the graph. This function will take no arguments and will simply print out the list of nodes in the graph. The following code shows how this can be done in C++:

```cpp
void Graph::printGraph()
{
        for (int i = 0; i < nodes.size(); i++)
                cout << nodes[i] << " ";
        cout << endl;
}
```

Now that we have defined our Graph class, we can start to implement the DFS algorithm. The following code shows how the DFS algorithm can be implemented in C++:

```cpp
void dfs(Graph g, int source)
{
  // Create a stack
  stack<int> stack;
  // Mark all the vertices as not visited
  bool *visited = new bool[g.nodes.size()];
  for (int i = 0; i < g.nodes.size(); i++)
```

```
    visited[i] = false;
  // Push the source node onto the stack
  stack.push(source);
  while (stack.empty() == false)
  {
    // Pop a node from the stack
    int n = stack.top();
    stack.pop();
     // If the node has not been visited, mark it as visited and add all of its adjacent nodes to the
stack
    if (visited[n] == false)
    {
      cout << n << " ";
      visited[n] = true;

                        // Get all adjacent nodes of the popped node n
                        vector<int> adjacent = g.adj[n];
                        // Iterate through all adjacent nodes
                        for (int i = 0; i < adjacent.size(); i++)
                                if (visited[adjacent[i]] == false)
                                        stack.push(adjacent[i]);
    }
  }
}
```

Conclusion

In this article, we discussed Depth First Search (DFS) and how to implement the algorithm in C++. We started by discussing what DFS is and how it works. We then discussed the time and space complexity of the DFS algorithm. Finally, we looked at how to implement the DFS algorithm in C++.

Exercises

Given a graph, implement the DFS algorithm to traverse the graph.

Given a graph, implement a function to print out the nodes in the graph in DFS order.

Given a graph and two nodes, implement a function to check if there is a path between the two nodes using the DFS algorithm.

Given a graph, implement a function to find all connected components using the DFS algorithm.

Given a graph and two nodes, implement a function to find the shortest path between the two nodes using the DFS algorithm.

Solutions

Given a graph, implement the DFS algorithm to traverse the graph.

```cpp
void dfs(Graph g, int source)
{
  // Create a stack
  stack<int> stack;
  // Mark all the vertices as not visited
  bool *visited = new bool[g.nodes.size()];
  for (int i = 0; i < g.nodes.size(); i++)
    visited[i] = false;
  // Push the source node onto the stack
  stack.push(source);
  while (stack.empty() == false)
  {
    // Pop a node from the stack
    int n = stack.top();
    stack.pop();
    // If the node has not been visited, mark it as visited and add all of its adjacent nodes to the
stack
    if (visited[n] == false)
    {
      cout << n << " ";
      visited[n] = true;

                              // Get all adjacent nodes of the popped node n
                              vector<int> adjacent = g.adj[n];
                              // Iterate through all adjacent nodes
                              for (int i = 0; i < adjacent.size(); i++)
                                      if (visited[adjacent[i]] == false)
                                              stack.push(adjacent[i]);
    }
  }
}
```

Given a graph, implement a function to print out the nodes in the graph in DFS order.

```cpp
void printDFS(Graph g, int source)
{
  // Create a stack
  stack<int> stack;
  // Mark all the vertices as not visited
  bool *visited = new bool[g.nodes.size()];
  for (int i = 0; i < g.nodes.size(); i++)
    visited[i] = false;
  // Push the source node onto the stack
  stack.push(source);
  while (stack.empty() == false)
```

```
{
    // Pop a node from the stack
    int n = stack.top();
    stack.pop();
    // If the node has not been visited, mark it as visited and add all of its adjacent nodes to the
stack
    if (visited[n] == false)
    {
        cout << n << " ";
        visited[n] = true;

                        // Get all adjacent nodes of the popped node n
                        vector<int> adjacent = g.adj[n];
                        // Iterate through all adjacent nodes
                        for (int i = 0; i < adjacent.size(); i++)
                                if (visited[adjacent[i]] == false)
                                        stack.push(adjacent[i]);
    }
  }
}
```

Given a graph and two nodes, implement a function to check if there is a path between the two nodes using the DFS algorithm.

```
bool isPath(Graph g, int source, int dest)
{
  // Create a stack
  stack<int> stack;
  // Mark all the vertices as not visited
  bool *visited = new bool[g.nodes.size()];
  for (int i = 0; i < g.nodes.size(); i++)
    visited[i] = false;
  // Push the source node onto the stack
  stack.push(source);
  while (stack.empty() == false)
  {
    // Pop a node from the stack
    int n = stack.top();
    stack.pop();
    // If the node has not been visited, mark it as visited and add all of its adjacent nodes to the
stack
    if (visited[n] == false)
    {
        visited[n] = true;

                        // Check if the popped node is the destination node
```

```
                    if (n == dest)
                            return true;

                    // Get all adjacent nodes of the popped node n
                    vector<int> adjacent = g.adj[n];
                    // Iterate through all adjacent nodes
                    for (int i = 0; i < adjacent.size(); i++)
                            if (visited[adjacent[i]] == false)
                                    stack.push(adjacent[i]);
    }
  }
        // No path exists
        return false;
}
```

Given a graph and two nodes, implement a function to check if there is a path between the two nodes using the DFS algorithm.

```
bool isPath(Graph g, int source, int dest)
{
  // Create a stack
  stack<int> stack;
  // Mark all the vertices as not visited
  bool *visited = new bool[g.nodes.size()];
  for (int i = 0; i < g.nodes.size(); i++)
    visited[i] = false;
  // Push the source node onto the stack
  stack.push(source);
  while (stack.empty() == false)
  {
    // Pop a node from the stack
    int n = stack.top();
    stack.pop();
    // If the node has not been visited, mark it as visited and add all of its adjacent nodes to the
stack
    if (visited[n] == false)
    {
      visited[n] = true;

                    // Check if the popped node is the destination node
                    if (n == dest)
                            return true;

                    // Get all adjacent nodes of the popped node n
                    vector<int> adjacent = g.adj[n];
                    // Iterate through all adjacent nodes
```

```
                        for (int i = 0; i < adjacent.size(); i++)
                            if (visited[adjacent[i]] == false)
                                    stack.push(adjacent[i]);
    }
  }
        // No path exists
        return false;
}
```

Given a graph and two nodes, implement a function to find the shortest path between the two nodes using the DFS algorithm.

```
vector<int> shortestPath(Graph g, int source, int dest)
{
  // Create a stack
  stack<int> stack;
        // Create a vector to store the shortest path
        vector<int> path;
  // Mark all the vertices as not visited
  bool *visited = new bool[g.nodes.size()];
  for (int i = 0; i < g.nodes.size(); i++)
    visited[i] = false;
  // Push the source node onto the stack
  stack.push(source);
  while (stack.empty() == false)
  {
    // Pop a node from the stack
    int n = stack.top();
    stack.pop();
    // If the node has not been visited, mark it as visited and add all of its adjacent nodes to the
stack
    if (visited[n] == false)
    {
      visited[n] = true;

                        // Add the node to the path
                        path.push_back(n);

                        // Check if the popped node is the destination node
                        if (n == dest)
                                return path;

                        // Get all adjacent nodes of the popped node n
                        vector<int> adjacent = g.adj[n];
                        // Iterate through all adjacent nodes
                        for (int i = 0; i < adjacent.size(); i++)
```

```
                              if (visited[adjacent[i]] == false)
                                  stack.push(adjacent[i]);
    }
}

        // No path exists
        return path;
}
```

DIJKSTRA'S ALGORITHM IN C++

Dijkstra's Algorithm is an important algorithm used for solving the path-finding problem in computer science. This algorithm finds the shortest path from a given node to all other nodes in a graph. It is one of the most popular algorithms in computer science and can be used to solve problems in a wide range of fields from robotics to network routing. In this course, Data Structures and Algorithms with C++, we will be discussing the algorithm in detail and its implementation in C++.

What is Dijkstra's Algorithm?

Dijkstra's Algorithm is a graph search algorithm that is used to find the shortest path from a given source node to all other nodes in the graph. The algorithm works by first finding the shortest path from the source node to all other nodes in the graph and then using this information to find the shortest path between any two nodes in the graph.

The algorithm works by first selecting a node from the graph and assigning it a distance value of 0. The algorithm then looks at the neighboring nodes and assigns them a distance value based on their distance from the source node. The algorithm then selects the node with the smallest distance value and updates the distance values for its neighbors. This process is repeated until all the nodes in the graph have been visited.

The Algorithm in C++

In this section, we will be discussing the implementation of Dijkstra's Algorithm in C++. Before we begin, let's first discuss the data structure we will be using for the implementation. We will be using an adjacency list for this implementation. An adjacency list is an array of linked lists that stores the neighbors of each node. Each node in the list will store the node's ID, its distance from the source node, and a pointer to its neighbors.

```cpp
// The adjacency list data structure
struct Node
{
  int id;
  int dist;
  vector<pair<int,int> > neighbors;
};
```

Now that we have discussed the data structure, let's look at the code for the Dijkstra's Algorithm.

```cpp
// The function for Dijkstra's Algorithm
```

```cpp
void dijkstra(vector<Node> &graph, int source)
{
  // Initialize the distance of all nodes to infinity
  vector<int> dist(graph.size(), INT_MAX);
  // Create a set to store the nodes that have been visited
  set<pair<int, int> > visited;
  // Set the distance of the source node to 0
  dist[source] = 0;
  // Create a priority queue to store the nodes in order of their distance
  priority_queue<pair<int, int>, vector<pair<int, int> >, greater<pair<int, int> > > pq;
  // Push the source node in the priority queue
  pq.push(make_pair(dist[source], source));
  // While the priority queue is not empty
  while (!pq.empty())
  {
    // Get the node with the minimum distance
    int u = pq.top().second;
    pq.pop();
    // If the node has not been visited
    if (visited.find(make_pair(dist[u], u)) == visited.end())
    {
      // Mark it as visited
      visited.insert(make_pair(dist[u], u));
      // Update the distance of its neighbors
      for (int i = 0; i < graph[u].neighbors.size(); i++)
      {
        int v = graph[u].neighbors[i].first;
        int weight = graph[u].neighbors[i].second;
        // If the distance of the neighbor is more than the distance of the source node + the edge
weight
        if (dist[v] > dist[u] + weight)
        {
          // Update the distance of the neighbor
          dist[v] = dist[u] + weight;
          // Push the neighbor in the priority queue
          pq.push(make_pair(dist[v], v));
        }
      }
    }
  }
  // Print the distance of all the nodes
  for (int i = 0; i < graph.size(); i++)
    cout << i << " " << dist[i] << endl;
}
```

Time Complexity

The time complexity of Dijkstra's Algorithm is O(E log V), where E is the number of edges and V is the number of vertices. This makes Dijkstra's Algorithm one of the most efficient algorithms for finding the shortest path in a graph.

Space Complexity

The space complexity of Dijkstra's Algorithm is O(V), where V is the number of vertices. This is because the algorithm uses an adjacency list to store the neighbors of each node, which takes up O(V) space.

Conclusion

In this article, we discussed the implementation of Dijkstra's Algorithm in C++. We discussed the data structure used for the implementation and the code for the algorithm. We also discussed the time and space complexity of the algorithm. As a result, we can conclude that Dijkstra's Algorithm is an efficient algorithm for finding the shortest path in a graph.

Exercises

Write a program that implements Dijkstra's Algorithm in C++.

Write a program that finds the shortest path between two given nodes in a graph using Dijkstra's Algorithm in C++.

Write a program that finds the shortest path between all pairs of nodes in a graph using Dijkstra's Algorithm in C++.

Write a program to find the shortest path from a given source vertex to all vertices in a unweighted graph using Dijkstra's Algorithm in C++.

Write a program to find the shortest path from a given source vertex to all vertices in a weighted graph with negative weights using Dijkstra's Algorithm in C++.

Solutions

Write a program that implements Dijkstra's Algorithm in C++.

```cpp
#include <bits/stdc++.h>
using namespace std;
// The adjacency list data structure
struct Node
{
    int id;
    int dist;
    vector<pair<int,int> > neighbors;
};
// The function for Dijkstra's Algorithm
void dijkstra(vector<Node> &graph, int source)
```

```cpp
{
    // Initialize the distance of all nodes to infinity
    vector<int> dist(graph.size(), INT_MAX);
    // Create a set to store the nodes that have been visited
    set<pair<int, int> > visited;
    // Set the distance of the source node to 0
    dist[source] = 0;
    // Create a priority queue to store the nodes in order of their distance
    priority_queue<pair<int, int>, vector<pair<int, int> >, greater<pair<int, int> > > pq;
    // Push the source node in the priority queue
    pq.push(make_pair(dist[source], source));
    // While the priority queue is not empty
    while (!pq.empty())
    {
        // Get the node with the minimum distance
        int u = pq.top().second;
        pq.pop();
        // If the node has not been visited
        if (visited.find(make_pair(dist[u], u)) == visited.end())
        {
            // Mark it as visited
            visited.insert(make_pair(dist[u], u));
            // Update the distance of its neighbors
            for (int i = 0; i < graph[u].neighbors.size(); i++)
            {
                int v = graph[u].neighbors[i].first;
                int weight = graph[u].neighbors[i].second;
                // If the distance of the neighbor is more than the distance of the source node + the edge weight
                if (dist[v] > dist[u] + weight)
                {
                    // Update the distance of the neighbor
                    dist[v] = dist[u] + weight;
                    // Push the neighbor in the priority queue
                    pq.push(make_pair(dist[v], v));
                }
            }
        }
    }
    // Print the distance of all the nodes
    for (int i = 0; i < graph.size(); i++)
        cout << i << " " << dist[i] << endl;
}
int main()
{
```

```
  // Initialize the graph
  vector<Node> graph;
  // Add the nodes to the graph
  graph.push_back({0, 0, {{1, 3}, {2, 1}}});
  graph.push_back({1, INT_MAX, {{3, 4}}});
  graph.push_back({2, INT_MAX, {{3, 1}}});
  graph.push_back({3, INT_MAX, {}});
  // Call the dijkstra function
  dijkstra(graph, 0);
  return 0;
}
```

Write a program that finds the shortest path between two given nodes in a graph using Dijkstra's Algorithm in C++.

```
#include <bits/stdc++.h>
using namespace std;
// The adjacency list data structure
struct Node
{
  int id;
  int dist;
  vector<pair<int,int> > neighbors;
};
// The function for Dijkstra's Algorithm
void dijkstra(vector<Node> &graph, int source, int dest)
{
  // Initialize the distance of all nodes to infinity
  vector<int> dist(graph.size(), INT_MAX);
  // Create a set to store the nodes that have been visited
  set<pair<int, int> > visited;
  // Set the distance of the source node to 0
  dist[source] = 0;
  // Create a priority queue to store the nodes in order of their distance
  priority_queue<pair<int, int>, vector<pair<int, int> >, greater<pair<int, int> > > pq;
  // Push the source node in the priority queue
  pq.push(make_pair(dist[source], source));
  // While the priority queue is not empty
  while (!pq.empty())
  {
    // Get the node with the minimum distance
    int u = pq.top().second;
    pq.pop();
    // If the node has not been visited
    if (visited.find(make_pair(dist[u], u)) == visited.end())
    {
```

```cpp
      // Mark it as visited
      visited.insert(make_pair(dist[u], u));
      // Update the distance of its neighbors
      for (int i = 0; i < graph[u].neighbors.size(); i++)
      {
         int v = graph[u].neighbors[i].first;
         int weight = graph[u].neighbors[i].second;
          // If the distance of the neighbor is more than the distance of the source node + the edge weight
         if (dist[v] > dist[u] + weight)
         {
            // Update the distance of the neighbor
            dist[v] = dist[u] + weight;
            // Push the neighbor in the priority queue
            pq.push(make_pair(dist[v], v));
         }
      }
   }
}
   // Print the shortest path from the source to the destination
   cout << "The shortest path from " << source << " to " << dest << " is " << dist[dest] << endl;
}
int main()
{
   // Initialize the graph
   vector<Node> graph;
   // Add the nodes to the graph
   graph.push_back({0, 0, {{1, 3}, {2, 1}}});
   graph.push_back({1, INT_MAX, {{3, 4}}});
   graph.push_back({2, INT_MAX, {{3, 1}}});
   graph.push_back({3, INT_MAX, {}});
   // Call the dijkstra function
   dijkstra(graph, 0, 3);
   return 0;
}
```

Write a program that finds the shortest path between all pairs of nodes in a graph using Dijkstra's Algorithm in C++.

```cpp
#include <bits/stdc++.h>
using namespace std;
// The adjacency list data structure
struct Node
{
   int id;
   int dist;
```

```cpp
  vector<pair<int,int> > neighbors;
};
// The function for Dijkstra's Algorithm
void dijkstra(vector<Node> &graph, int source)
{
  // Initialize the distance of all nodes to infinity
  vector<int> dist(graph.size(), INT_MAX);
  // Create a set to store the nodes that have been visited
  set<pair<int, int> > visited;
  // Set the distance of the source node to 0
  dist[source] = 0;
  // Create a priority queue to store the nodes in order of their distance
  priority_queue<pair<int, int>, vector<pair<int, int> >, greater<pair<int, int> > > pq;
  // Push the source node in the priority queue
  pq.push(make_pair(dist[source], source));
  // While the priority queue is not empty
  while (!pq.empty())
  {
    // Get the node with the minimum distance
    int u = pq.top().second;
    pq.pop();
    // If the node has not been visited
    if (visited.find(make_pair(dist[u], u)) == visited.end())
    {
      // Mark it as visited
      visited.insert(make_pair(dist[u], u));
      // Update the distance of its neighbors
      for (int i = 0; i < graph[u].neighbors.size(); i++)
      {
        int v = graph[u].neighbors[i].first;
        int weight = graph[u].neighbors[i].second;
        // If the distance of the neighbor is more than the distance of the source node + the edge
weight
        if (dist[v] > dist[u] + weight)
        {
          // Update the distance of the neighbor
          dist[v] = dist[u] + weight;
          // Push the neighbor in the priority queue
          pq.push(make_pair(dist[v], v));
        }
      }
    }
  }
  // Print the shortest path from the source to all other nodes
  for (int i = 0; i < graph.size(); i++)
```

```cpp
        cout << "Shortest path from " << source << " to " << i << " is "
            << dist[i] << endl;
    return;
}
// Main Function
int main()
{
    // Create the graph
    vector<Node> graph;
    // Add the nodes to the graph
    for (int i = 0; i < 5; i++)
    {
        Node temp;
        temp.id = i;
        graph.push_back(temp);
    }
    // Add the edges to the graph
    graph[0].neighbors.push_back(make_pair(1, 5));
    graph[0].neighbors.push_back(make_pair(2, 10));
    graph[0].neighbors.push_back(make_pair(3, 8));
    graph[1].neighbors.push_back(make_pair(2, 3));
    graph[2].neighbors.push_back(make_pair(3, 2));
    graph[3].neighbors.push_back(make_pair(4, 4));
    // Find the shortest path from node 0 to all other nodes
    dijkstra(graph, 0);
    return 0;
}
```

Write a program to find the shortest path from a given source vertex to all vertices in a unweighted graph using Dijkstra's Algorithm in C++.

```cpp
#include <bits/stdc++.h>
using namespace std;
// The adjacency list data structure
struct Node
{
    int id;
    int dist;
    vector<int> neighbors;
};
// The function for Dijkstra's Algorithm
void dijkstra(vector<Node> &graph, int source)
{
    // Initialize the distance of all nodes to infinity
    vector<int> dist(graph.size(), INT_MAX);
    // Create a set to store the nodes that have been visited
```

```cpp
set<pair<int, int> > visited;
// Set the distance of the source node to 0
dist[source] = 0;
// Create a priority queue to store the nodes in order of their distance
priority_queue<pair<int, int>, vector<pair<int, int> >, greater<pair<int, int> > > pq;
// Push the source node in the priority queue
pq.push(make_pair(dist[source], source));
// While the priority queue is not empty
while (!pq.empty())
{
    // Get the node with the minimum distance
    int u = pq.top().second;
    pq.pop();
    // If the node has not been visited
    if (visited.find(make_pair(dist[u], u)) == visited.end())
    {
        // Mark it as visited
        visited.insert(make_pair(dist[u], u));
        // Update the distance of its neighbors
        for (int i = 0; i < graph[u].neighbors.size(); i++)
        {
            int v = graph[u].neighbors[i];
            // If the distance of the neighbor is more than the distance of the source node + the edge weight
            if (dist[v] > dist[u] + 1)
            {
                // Update the distance of the neighbor
                dist[v] = dist[u] + 1;
                // Push the neighbor in the priority queue
                pq.push(make_pair(dist[v], v));
            }
        }
    }
}
// Print the shortest path from the source to all other nodes
for (int i = 0; i < graph.size(); i++)
    cout << "Shortest path from " << source << " to " << i << " is "
        << dist[i] << endl;
return;
}
// Main Function
int main()
{
    // Create the graph
    vector<Node> graph;
```

```
// Add the nodes to the graph
for (int i = 0; i < 5; i++)
{
  Node temp;
  temp.id = i;
  graph.push_back(temp);
}
// Add the edges to the graph
graph[0].neighbors.push_back(1);
graph[0].neighbors.push_back(2);
graph[0].neighbors.push_back(3);
graph[1].neighbors.push_back(2);
graph[2].neighbors.push_back(3);
graph[3].neighbors.push_back(4);
// Find the shortest path from node 0 to all other nodes
dijkstra(graph, 0);
return 0;
}
```

Write a program to find the shortest path from a given source vertex to all vertices in a weighted graph with negative weights using Dijkstra's Algorithm in C++.

```
#include <bits/stdc++.h>
using namespace std;
// The adjacency list data structure
struct Node
{
  int id;
  int dist;
  vector<pair<int,int> > neighbors;
};
// The function for Dijkstra's Algorithm
void dijkstra(vector<Node> &graph, int source)
{
  // Initialize the distance of all nodes to infinity
  vector<int> dist(graph.size(), INT_MAX);
  // Create a set to store the nodes that have been visited
  set<pair<int, int> > visited;
  // Set the distance of the source node to 0
  dist[source] = 0;
  // Create a priority queue to store the nodes in order of their distance
  priority_queue<pair<int, int>, vector<pair<int, int> >, greater<pair<int, int> > > pq;
  // Push the source node in the priority queue
  pq.push(make_pair(dist[source], source));
  // While the priority queue is not empty
  while (!pq.empty())
```

YASIN CAKAL

```cpp
{
    // Get the node with the minimum distance
    int u = pq.top().second;
    pq.pop();
    // If the node has not been visited
    if (visited.find(make_pair(dist[u], u)) == visited.end())
    {
        // Mark it as visited
        visited.insert(make_pair(dist[u], u));
        // Update the distance of its neighbors
        for (int i = 0; i < graph[u].neighbors.size(); i++)
        {
            int v = graph[u].neighbors[i].first;
            int weight = graph[u].neighbors[i].second;
            // If the distance of the neighbor is more than the distance of the source node + the edge weight
            if (dist[v] > dist[u] + weight)
            {
                // Update the distance of the neighbor
                dist[v] = dist[u] + weight;
                // Push the neighbor in the priority queue
                pq.push(make_pair(dist[v], v));
            }
        }
    }
}
// Print the shortest path from the source to all other nodes
for (int i = 0; i < graph.size(); i++)
    cout << "Shortest path from " << source << " to " << i << " is "
        << dist[i] << endl;
return;
}
// Main Function
int main()
{
    // Create the graph
    vector<Node> graph;
    // Add the nodes to the graph
    for (int i = 0; i < 5; i++)
    {
        Node temp;
        temp.id = i;
        graph.push_back(temp);
    }
    // Add the edges to the graph
```

```cpp
graph[0].neighbors.push_back(make_pair(1, -5));
graph[0].neighbors.push_back(make_pair(2, -10));
graph[0].neighbors.push_back(make_pair(3, -8));
graph[1].neighbors.push_back(make_pair(2, -3));
graph[2].neighbors.push_back(make_pair(3, -2));
graph[3].neighbors.push_back(make_pair(4, -4));
// Find the shortest path from node 0 to all other nodes
dijkstra(graph, 0);
return 0;
}
```

ALGORITHM DESIGN TECHNIQUES

GREEDY ALGORITHMS IN C++

Greedy algorithms are an important type of algorithm used in computer science. They are used to solve problems that involve making decisions based on the current best available information. In this article, we will discuss what a greedy algorithm is, how it works, and how it can be used to solve problems in the context of the course "Data Structures and Algorithms with C++".

What is a Greedy Algorithm?

A greedy algorithm is an algorithm that makes decisions in a step-by-step process, always selecting the best possible solution at the time. In other words, it looks for the best immediate solution instead of considering all possible solutions at once. Greedy algorithms are used to solve problems that involve making decisions based on the current best available information. Greedy algorithms have the advantage of being fast and relatively simple to implement.

How Greedy Algorithms Work

Greedy algorithms work by making a series of decisions that are based on the best available option at each step. The algorithm starts by making an initial choice, and then it evaluates the available options. The algorithm then makes the decision that produces the best outcome, and it continues to make the best decision at each step until it has reached an optimal solution.

For example, consider the problem of scheduling a set of tasks. The greedy algorithm would start by making an initial choice for the first task, and then it would evaluate the available options for the second task. The algorithm would then make the decision that produces the best outcome for the second task, and it would continue to make the best decisions for each task until it has reached an optimal solution.

To illustrate how a greedy algorithm works, consider the following problem:

Given a list of numbers, find the largest subset of numbers such that the sum of the numbers in the subset is less than or equal to a given target number.

The greedy algorithm would start by looking at the first number in the list and determining if it is less than or equal to the target number. If it is, the number is added to the subset. The algorithm then moves on to the next number and repeats the process until either the target number is reached or all the numbers in the list have been examined.

Examples of Greedy Algorithms in C++

Now let's look at an example of a greedy algorithm written in C++. The following code implements the algorithm for the problem described above:

```cpp
#include <iostream>
#include <vector>
using namespace std;
// Function to find the largest subset of numbers
// such that the sum of the numbers in the subset
// is less than or equal to the given target number
void findMaxSubset(vector<int> &nums, int target)
{
        int n = nums.size();
        // Vector to store the subset
        vector<int> subset;
        // Variable to store the sum of the elements in the subset
        int sum = 0;
        // Iterate over all the elements
        for (int i = 0; i < n; i++)
        {
                // If the current element is less than or equal to
                // the target number, add it to the subset
                if (nums[i] <= target)
                {
                        subset.push_back(nums[i]);
                        sum += nums[i];

                        // If the sum is greater than the target number,
                        // remove the last element from the subset
                        if (sum > target)
                        {
                                sum -= subset.back();
                                subset.pop_back();
                        }
                }
        }
        // Print the largest subset
        for (int i = 0; i < subset.size(); i++)
                cout << subset[i] << " ";
        cout << endl;
}
// Driver program to test the above function
int main()
{
        vector<int> nums = {1, 2, 3, 4, 5, 6, 7, 8};
        int target = 11;
        findMaxSubset(nums, target);
```

```
    return 0;
}
```

In the above code, the function findMaxSubset() implements the greedy algorithm to find the largest subset of numbers such that the sum of the numbers in the subset is less than or equal to the given target number. The algorithm starts by looking at the first number in the list and determining if it is less than or equal to the target number. If it is, the number is added to the subset. The algorithm then moves on to the next number and repeats the process until either the target number is reached or all the numbers in the list have been examined.

Now, let's look at another example.

The Knapsack Problem

The knapsack problem is a classic example of a problem that can be solved using a greedy algorithm. The problem is to choose items from a list of available items so that the total value of the items is maximized while the total weight of the items is kept below a certain limit.

The algorithm starts by sorting the list of items by value. Then, the algorithm iterates through the list of items, starting with the most valuable item. For each item, the algorithm checks if the item's weight is less than the remaining capacity of the knapsack. If so, the item is added to the knapsack and the remaining capacity is reduced by the item's weight. If not, the item is skipped. The algorithm continues until all the items have been considered.

Here is the C++ code for the knapsack problem:

```cpp
// Inputs:
// Item weights: int[ ] weights
// Item values: int[ ] values
// Knapsack capacity: int capacity
int knapsack(int weights[ ], int values[ ], int capacity) {
  // Sort items by value
  // Sort items in descending order by value
  for(int i = 0; i < weights.size(); i++) {
   for(int j = i + 1; j < weights.size(); j++) {
    if(values[i] < values[j]) {
     // Swap values
     int tempValue = values[i];
     values[i] = values[j];
     values[j] = tempValue;
     // Swap weights
     int tempWeight = weights[i];
     weights[i] = weights[j];
     weights[j] = tempWeight;
    }
   }
```

```
}
// Greedy algorithm
int maxValue = 0;
int currentWeight = 0;
// Iterate over items
for(int i = 0; i < weights.size(); i++) {
  // If item can fit in knapsack
  if(currentWeight + weights[i] <= capacity) {
   // Add item to knapsack
   currentWeight += weights[i];
   maxValue += values[i];
  }
 }
 return maxValue;
}
```

Advantages and Disadvantages of Greedy Algorithms

Greedy algorithms have some advantages and disadvantages that must be considered when deciding if they are the right approach for a particular problem.

Advantages:

- Greedy algorithms are fast and relatively simple to implement.
- They can be used to solve a wide range of problems.
- They typically have good performance, especially when compared to other algorithms.

Disadvantages:

- Greedy algorithms are not always guaranteed to find the optimal solution to a problem.
- They can be difficult to debug.
- They can be computationally intensive.

Conclusion

In this article, we discussed what a greedy algorithm is, how it works, and how it can be used to solve problems in the context of the course "Data Structures and Algorithms with C++". We also looked at an example of a greedy algorithm written in C++ and discussed the advantages and disadvantages of using greedy algorithms.

Exercises

Write a greedy algorithm to find the minimum number of coins needed to make a given amount of change.

Write a greedy algorithm to find the maximum number of items that can fit into a knapsack of a given capacity.

Write a greedy algorithm to find the minimum number of coins needed to make a given amount of change.

Write a greedy algorithm to find the maximum number of items that can fit into a knapsack of a given capacity.

Write a greedy algorithm to find the maximum number of jobs that can be scheduled in a given time.

Solutions

Write a greedy algorithm to find the minimum number of coins needed to make a given amount of change.

```cpp
#include <iostream>
#include <vector>
using namespace std;
// Function to find the minimum number of coins needed
// to make a given amount of change
int findMinCoins(vector<int> coins, int amount)
{
        // Sort the coins in descending order
        sort(coins.begin(), coins.end(), greater<int>());
        // Initialize the number of coins needed
        int numCoins = 0;
        // Iterate over each coin
        for (int i = 0; i < coins.size(); i++)
        {
                // Calculate the number of coins needed
                numCoins += (amount / coins[i]);

                // Update the amount
                amount = (amount % coins[i]);
        }
        return numCoins;
}
// Driver program to test the above function
int main()
{
        vector<int> coins = {1, 5, 10, 25};
        int amount = 34;
        cout << "Minimum number of coins needed: "
                << findMinCoins(coins, amount);
        return 0;
}
```

Write a greedy algorithm to find the maximum number of items that can fit into a

knapsack of a given capacity.

```cpp
#include <iostream>
#include <vector>
using namespace std;
// Structure for an item which stores weight and corresponding
// value of the item
struct Item
{
        int value, weight;
};
// Function to find the maximum value that can be put in a knapsack of
// capacity W
int knapSack(int W, vector<Item> &items)
{
        // sort the items in descending order of value
        sort(items.begin(), items.end(),
                [](const Item& a, const Item& b)
                {
                        return a.value > b.value;
                });
        // stores the maximum value that can be attained
        // with a knapsack of capacity W
        int maxValue = 0;
        // stores the remaining weight in the knapsack
        int remainingWeight = W;
        // Iterate over all the items
        for (int i = 0; i < items.size(); i++)
        {
                // if the current item can fit in the knapsack
                if (remainingWeight - items[i].weight >= 0)
                {
                        // add it to the knapsack
                        maxValue += items[i].value;

                        // decrease the remaining weight
                        remainingWeight -= items[i].weight;
                }
        }
        return maxValue;
}
// Driver program to test above function
int main()
{
        // vector to store the items
        vector<Item> items = {{60, 10}, {100, 20}, {120, 30}};
```

```cpp
        // Knapsack capacity
        int W = 50;
        cout << "Maximum value that can be put in knapsack of capacity "
                        << W << " is " << knapSack(W, items);

        return 0;
}
```

Write a greedy algorithm to find the minimum number of coins needed to make a given amount of change.

```cpp
#include <iostream>
#include <vector>
using namespace std;
// Function to find the minimum number of coins needed
// to make a given amount of change
int findMinCoins(vector<int> coins, int amount)
{
        // Sort the coins in descending order
        sort(coins.begin(), coins.end(), greater<int>());
        // Initialize the number of coins needed
        int numCoins = 0;
        // Iterate over each coin
        for (int i = 0; i < coins.size(); i++)
        {
                // Calculate the number of coins needed
                numCoins += (amount / coins[i]);

                // Update the amount
                amount = (amount % coins[i]);
        }
        return numCoins;
}
// Driver program to test the above function
int main()
{
        vector<int> coins = {1, 5, 10, 25};
        int amount = 34;
        cout << "Minimum number of coins needed: "
                        << findMinCoins(coins, amount);
        return 0;
}
```

Write a greedy algorithm to find the maximum number of items that can fit into a knapsack of a given capacity.

```cpp
#include <iostream>
#include <vector>
```

```cpp
using namespace std;
// Structure for an item which stores weight and corresponding
// value of the item
struct Item
{
        int value, weight;
};
// Function to find the maximum value that can be put in a knapsack of
// capacity W
int knapSack(int W, vector<Item> &items)
{
        // sort the items in descending order of value
        sort(items.begin(), items.end(),
                [](const Item& a, const Item& b)
                {
                        return a.value > b.value;
                });
        // stores the maximum value that can be attained
        // with a knapsack of capacity W
        int maxValue = 0;
        // stores the remaining weight in the knapsack
        int remainingWeight = W;
        // Iterate over all the items
        for (int i = 0; i < items.size(); i++)
        {
                // if the current item can fit in the knapsack
                if (remainingWeight - items[i].weight >= 0)
                {
                        // add it to the knapsack
                        maxValue += items[i].value;

                        // decrease the remaining weight
                        remainingWeight -= items[i].weight;
                }
        }
        return maxValue;
}
// Driver program to test above function
int main()
{
        // vector to store the items
        vector<Item> items = {{60, 10}, {100, 20}, {120, 30}};
        // Knapsack capacity
        int W = 50;
        cout << "Maximum value that can be put in knapsack of capacity "
```

```
                        << W << " is " << knapSack(W, items);
        return 0;
}
```

Write a greedy algorithm to find the maximum number of jobs that can be scheduled in a given time.

```cpp
#include <iostream>
#include <vector>
using namespace std;
// Structure for a job which stores start and finish time
struct Job
{
        int start, finish;
};
// Function to find the maximum number of jobs that can be scheduled
// in a given time
int maxJobs(vector<Job> &jobs)
{
        // sort the jobs in ascending order of finish time
        sort(jobs.begin(), jobs.end(),
                [](const Job& a, const Job& b)
                {
                        return a.finish < b.finish;
                });
        // stores the maximum number of jobs that can be scheduled
        int maxJobs = 0;
        // stores the last finish time of a scheduled job
        int lastFinishTime = 0;
        // Iterate over all the jobs
        for (int i = 0; i < jobs.size(); i++)
        {
                // if the current job can be scheduled after the
                // last scheduled job
                if (jobs[i].start >= lastFinishTime)
                {
                        // increment the number of jobs
                        maxJobs++;

                        // update the last finish time
                        lastFinishTime = jobs[i].finish;
                }
        }
        return maxJobs;
}
// Driver program to test above function
```

```
int main()
{
        // vector to store the jobs
        vector<Job> jobs = {{1, 2}, {3, 4}, {0, 6}, {5, 7}, {8, 9}, {5, 9}};
        cout << "Maximum number of jobs that can be scheduled: "
                << maxJobs(jobs);
        return 0;
}
```

DYNAMIC PROGRAMMING IN C++

Dynamic programming is a powerful optimization technique used in computer science and engineering. It is an approach to solving complex problems by breaking them down into smaller, simpler subproblems and then combining the solutions of those subproblems to obtain the optimal solution for the original problem. As a result, dynamic programming is widely used in computer science and engineering to solve a variety of problems, from scheduling tasks to finding the shortest path between two points.

The purpose of this article is to introduce the concept of dynamic programming and provide an overview of its applications in C++. We will discuss the fundamentals of dynamic programming and the various techniques used to solve dynamic programming problems. We will also provide examples of dynamic programming algorithms written in C++ and demonstrate how they can be used to solve complex problems. Finally, we will provide five coding exercises with solutions to test the reader's understanding of the material covered in this article.

What is Dynamic Programming?

Dynamic programming is an optimization technique used to solve complex problems by breaking them down into smaller, simpler subproblems. The idea behind dynamic programming is that if we can find the optimal solution to each subproblem, then we can combine the solutions of all the subproblems to obtain the optimal solution for the original problem.

Dynamic programming is a bottom-up approach to problem solving, which means that it starts with the smallest subproblems and works its way up to the larger problem. This is in contrast to a top-down approach, where we start with the larger problem and break it down into smaller subproblems.

Dynamic programming is typically used to solve optimization problems, such as the shortest path problem or the knapsack problem. It can also be used to solve problems that involve making decisions, such as scheduling tasks or selecting the best investment portfolio.

Dynamic Programming in C++

Dynamic programming can be implemented in any programming language, but it is particularly well-suited for C++ due to its powerful features, such as templates and operator overloading.

To illustrate how dynamic programming can be implemented in C++, let's consider the following example:

Given a set of numbers, we want to find the maximum sum of any subset of those numbers.

To solve this problem, we can use the following dynamic programming algorithm written in C++:

```cpp
#include <iostream>
#include <vector>
using namespace std;
// Function to find the maximum sum of any subset of the given set of numbers
int maxSubsetSum(vector<int> numbers) {
// Create a 2D array to store the results of the subproblems
int dp[numbers.size()+1][numbers.size()+1];
// Initialize the array with 0
for (int i = 0; i <= numbers.size(); i++) {
 for (int j = 0; j <= numbers.size(); j++) {
  dp[i][j] = 0;
 }
}
// Solve the subproblems
for (int i = 1; i <= numbers.size(); i++) {
 for (int j = 1; j <= numbers.size(); j++) {
  dp[i][j] = max(dp[i-1][j], dp[i-1][j-1] + numbers[i-1]);
 }
}
// Return the maximum sum
 return dp[numbers.size()][numbers.size()];
}
int main() {
vector<int> numbers = {1, 2, 3, 4, 5};
cout << "Maximum sum = " << maxSubsetSum(numbers) << endl;
 return 0;
}
```

In this example, we have used the dynamic programming approach to solve the maximum subset sum problem. The algorithm uses a 2D array to store the results of the subproblems and then finds the maximum sum by iterating over the array and calculating the maximum sum for each subproblem.

Dynamic programming can be used to solve a variety of problems, such as the 0-1 knapsack problem, the shortest path problem, and the maximum sum subarray problem. In each of these problems, we can use dynamic programming to find the optimal solution.

Conclusion

In this article, we discussed the concept of dynamic programming and how it can be used to solve complex problems. We discussed the fundamentals of dynamic programming and provided examples of dynamic programming algorithms written in C++. We also discussed how dynamic programming can be used to solve optimization problems, such as the 0-1 knapsack problem, the shortest path problem, and the maximum sum subarray problem.

Exercises

Given an array of integers, find the maximum sum of any contiguous subarray.

Given a set of items with values and weights, find the maximum value you can obtain by selecting a subset of the items such that the total weight does not exceed a given weight limit.

Given a matrix of positive integers and a starting coordinates, find the longest path from the starting coordinates such that all the elements in the path are in increasing order.

Given a set of tasks with start times and end times, find the maximum number of tasks that can be completed in a given time frame.

Given a set of coins and a total amount, find the minimum number of coins required to make the total amount.

Solutions

Given an array of integers, find the maximum sum of any contiguous subarray.

```cpp
#include <iostream>
#include <vector>
using namespace std;
// Function to find the maximum sum of any contiguous subarray
int maxSubarraySum(vector<int> numbers) {
// Create a 1D array to store the results of the subproblems
int dp[numbers.size()+1];
// Initialize the array with 0
for (int i = 0; i <= numbers.size(); i++) {
 dp[i] = 0;
}
// Solve the subproblems
for (int i = 1; i <= numbers.size(); i++) {
 dp[i] = max(dp[i-1], dp[i-1] + numbers[i-1]);
}
// Return the maximum sum
 return dp[numbers.size()];
}
int main() {
vector<int> numbers = {1, 2, 3, 4, 5};
cout << "Maximum sum = " << maxSubarraySum(numbers) << endl;
 return 0;
```

```
}
```

Given a set of items with values and weights, find the maximum value you can obtain by selecting a subset of the items such that the total weight does not exceed a given weight limit.

```cpp
#include <iostream>
#include <vector>
using namespace std;
// Function to find the maximum value obtainable from a subset of items with given weights and
values
int knapsack(vector<int> values, vector<int> weights, int weightLimit) {
// Create a 2D array to store the results of the subproblems
int dp[values.size()+1][weightLimit+1];
// Initialize the array with 0
for (int i = 0; i <= values.size(); i++) {
 for (int j = 0; j <= weightLimit; j++) {
  dp[i][j] = 0;
 }
}
// Solve the subproblems
for (int i = 1; i <= values.size(); i++) {
 for (int j = 1; j <= weightLimit; j++) {
  dp[i][j] = max(dp[i-1][j], dp[i-1][j-weights[i-1]] + values[i-1]);
 }
}
// Return the maximum value
return dp[values.size()][weightLimit];
}
int main() {
vector<int> values = {1, 2, 3, 4, 5};
vector<int> weights = {1, 2, 3, 4, 5};
int weightLimit = 10;
cout << "Maximum value = " << knapsack(values, weights, weightLimit) << endl;
return 0;
}
```

Given a matrix of positive integers and a starting coordinates, find the longest path from the starting coordinates such that all the elements in the path are in increasing order.

```cpp
#include <iostream>
#include <vector>
using namespace std;
// Function to find the longest path from a given starting coordinates such that all the elements
in the path are in increasing order
int longestPath(vector<vector<int>> matrix, int row, int col) {
```

```cpp
// Create a 2D array to store the results of the subproblems
int dp[row+1][col+1];
// Initialize the array with 0
for (int i = 0; i <= row; i++) {
 for (int j = 0; j <= col; j++) {
  dp[i][j] = 0;
 }
}
// Solve the subproblems
for (int i = 1; i <= row; i++) {
 for (int j = 1; j <= col; j++) {
  // Check if the current element is greater than the one to the left
  if (matrix[i][j] > matrix[i][j-1]) {
   dp[i][j] = max(dp[i][j], dp[i][j-1] + 1);
  }
  // Check if the current element is greater than the one to the top
  if (matrix[i][j] > matrix[i-1][j]) {
   dp[i][j] = max(dp[i][j], dp[i-1][j] + 1);
  }
 }
}
// Return the longest path
return dp[row][col];
}
int main() {
vector<vector<int>> matrix = {
 {1, 2, 3},
 {4, 5, 6},
 {7, 8, 9}
};
int row = 2;
int col = 2;
cout << "Longest path = " << longestPath(matrix, row, col) << endl;
return 0;
}
```

Given a set of tasks with start times and end times, find the maximum number of tasks that can be completed in a given time frame.

```cpp
#include <iostream>
#include <vector>
using namespace std;
// Function to find the maximum number of tasks that can be completed in a given time frame
int maxTasks(vector<pair<int, int>> tasks, int timeFrame) {
// Create a 1D array to store the results of the subproblems
int dp[timeFrame+1];
```

```
// Initialize the array with 0
for (int i = 0; i <= timeFrame; i++) {
 dp[i] = 0;
}
// Solve the subproblems
for (int i = 1; i <= timeFrame; i++) {
 for (int j = 0; j < tasks.size(); j++) {
  // Check if the current task can be completed in the given time frame
  if (tasks[j].first <= i && tasks[j].second <= i) {
   dp[i] = max(dp[i], dp[i - tasks[j].second] + 1);
  }
 }
}
// Return the maximum number of tasks
return dp[timeFrame];
}
int main() {
vector<pair<int, int>> tasks = {{2, 3}, {2, 4}, {3, 5}, {4, 5}};
 int timeFrame = 5;
cout << "Maximum number of tasks = " << maxTasks(tasks, timeFrame) << endl;
 return 0;
}
```

Given a set of coins and a total amount, find the minimum number of coins required to make the total amount.

```
#include <iostream>
#include <vector>
using namespace std;
// Function to find the minimum number of coins required to make the given total amount
int minCoins(vector<int> coins, int amount) {
// Create a 1D array to store the results of the subproblems
int dp[amount+1];
// Initialize the array with amount+1
for (int i = 0; i <= amount; i++) {
 dp[i] = amount+1;
}
// Solve the subproblems
dp[0] = 0;
for (int i = 1; i <= amount; i++) {
 for (int j = 0; j < coins.size(); j++) {
  // Check if the current coin is less than or equal to the amount
  if (coins[j] <= i) {
   dp[i] = min(dp[i], dp[i - coins[j]] + 1);
  }
 }
}
```

```
}
// Return the minimum number of coins
return dp[amount];
}
int main() {
vector<int> coins = {1, 2, 5};
int amount = 11;
cout << "Minimum number of coins = " << minCoins(coins, amount) << endl;
return 0;
}
```

DIVIDE AND CONQUER IN C++

Divide and conquer is a powerful algorithm technique used in computer programming. It involves breaking down a problem into smaller, easier to solve subproblems, and then solving those subproblems. This technique is particularly useful in sorting and searching algorithms, such as quicksort and binary search. In this article, we will discuss how to implement the divide and conquer approach in C++. We will go through the steps of breaking down a problem into subproblems, solving the subproblems, and combining the solutions to obtain the final solution. We will also look at some examples of how to apply this technique to sorting and searching algorithms.

What is Divide and Conquer?

Divide and conquer is an algorithmic technique used to break down a problem into smaller, easier to solve subproblems. The idea is to divide the problem into smaller parts, solve each part separately, and then combine the solutions to obtain the final solution. This technique is useful when the problem is too complex to solve in one step. By breaking it down into smaller parts, the problem becomes easier to solve.

Divide and Conquer in C++

When implementing divide and conquer in C++, the first step is to identify the problem. This means understanding what the problem is and what it requires. Once the problem is understood, it can be divided into smaller, easier to solve subproblems. The subproblems can then be solved one at a time, and the solutions combined to obtain the final solution.

Example 1: Quicksort

Let us look at an example of how to use the divide and conquer approach to solve the quicksort problem. Quicksort is an algorithm used to sort an array of numbers in ascending order. The idea is to select a pivot element, and then divide the array into two parts, one containing elements smaller than the pivot, and the other containing elements larger than the pivot. These two parts are then sorted separately using quicksort, and the two sorted parts are combined to obtain the final sorted array.

```cpp
// Quicksort algorithm in C++
int partition(int arr[], int low, int high)
{
   int pivot = arr[high];
   int i = (low - 1);
   for (int j = low; j <= high - 1; j++)
```

```
  {
    if (arr[j] <= pivot)
    {
      i++;
      swap(arr[i], arr[j]);
    }
  }
  swap(arr[i + 1], arr[high]);
  return (i + 1);
}
void quickSort(int arr[], int low, int high)
{
  if (low < high)
  {
    int pi = partition(arr, low, high);
    quickSort(arr, low, pi - 1);
    quickSort(arr, pi + 1, high);
  }
}
```

Example 2: Binary Search

Now let us look at an example of how to use the divide and conquer approach to solve the binary search problem. Binary search is an algorithm used to find the position of an element in a sorted array. The idea is to divide the array into two parts, one containing elements smaller than the element to be searched, and the other containing elements larger than the element to be searched. The element to be searched is then compared to the middle element of the array. If it is smaller than the middle element, the search is continued in the left half of the array, and if it is larger than the middle element, the search is continued in the right half. This process is repeated until the element is found or the array is exhausted.

```
// Binary search algorithm in C++
int binarySearch(int arr[], int low, int high, int key)
{
  if (high >= low)
  {
    int mid = low + (high - low) / 2;
    if (arr[mid] == key)
      return mid;
    if (arr[mid] > key)
      return binarySearch(arr, low, mid - 1, key);
    return binarySearch(arr, mid + 1, high, key);
  }
  return -1;
}
```

Conclusion

In this article, we have discussed how to implement the divide and conquer algorithm in C++. We have looked at two examples of how to apply this technique to sorting and searching algorithms. We have seen how the technique can be used to break down a complex problem into smaller parts, solve each part separately, and then combine the solutions to obtain the final solution.

Exercises

Write a C++ program to find the maximum element in an array using the divide and conquer approach.

Write a C++ program to find the minimum element in an array using the divide and conquer approach.

Write a C++ program to find the sum of elements in an array using the divide and conquer approach.

Write a C++ program to find the average of elements in an array using the divide and conquer approach.

Write a C++ program to find the number of inversions in an array using the divide and conquer approach.

Solutions

Write a C++ program to find the maximum element in an array using the divide and conquer approach.

```cpp
#include <iostream>
using namespace std;
int findMax(int arr[], int low, int high)
{
  int mid;
  if (low == high)
    return arr[low];
  if (low < high)
  {
    mid = (low + high) / 2;
    int leftMax = findMax(arr, low, mid);
    int rightMax = findMax(arr, mid + 1, high);
    if (leftMax > rightMax)
      return leftMax;
    else
      return rightMax;
  }
}
int main()
```

```
{
  int arr[] = {3, 5, 2, 1, 4};
  int n = sizeof(arr) / sizeof(arr[0]);
  cout << "The maximum element is " << findMax(arr, 0, n - 1);
  return 0;
}
```

Write a C++ program to find the minimum element in an array using the divide and conquer approach.

```cpp
#include <iostream>
using namespace std;
int findMin(int arr[], int low, int high)
{
  int mid;
  if (low == high)
    return arr[low];
  if (low < high)
  {
    mid = (low + high) / 2;
    int leftMin = findMin(arr, low, mid);
    int rightMin = findMin(arr, mid + 1, high);
    if (leftMin < rightMin)
      return leftMin;
    else
      return rightMin;
  }
}
int main()
{
  int arr[] = {3, 5, 2, 1, 4};
  int n = sizeof(arr) / sizeof(arr[0]);
  cout << "The minimum element is " << findMin(arr, 0, n - 1);
  return 0;
}
```

Write a C++ program to find the sum of elements in an array using the divide and conquer approach.

```cpp
#include <iostream>
using namespace std;
int findSum(int arr[], int low, int high)
{
  int mid;
  if (low == high)
    return arr[low];
  if (low < high)
```

```
    {
        mid = (low + high) / 2;
        int leftSum = findSum(arr, low, mid);
        int rightSum = findSum(arr, mid + 1, high);
        return leftSum + rightSum;
    }
}
int main()
{
    int arr[] = {3, 5, 2, 1, 4};
    int n = sizeof(arr) / sizeof(arr[0]);
    cout << "The sum of the elements is " << findSum(arr, 0, n - 1);
    return 0;
}
```

Write a C++ program to find the average of elements in an array using the divide and conquer approach.

```
#include <iostream>
using namespace std;
float findAverage(int arr[], int low, int high)
{
    int mid;
    if (low == high)
        return arr[low];
    if (low < high)
    {
        mid = (low + high) / 2;
        float leftAverage = findAverage(arr, low, mid);
        float rightAverage = findAverage(arr, mid + 1, high);
        return (leftAverage + rightAverage) / 2;
    }
}
int main()
{
    int arr[] = {3, 5, 2, 1, 4};
    int n = sizeof(arr) / sizeof(arr[0]);
    cout << "The average of the elements is " << findAverage(arr, 0, n - 1);
    return 0;
}
```

Write a C++ program to find the number of inversions in an array using the divide and conquer approach.

```
#include <iostream>
using namespace std;
int merge(int arr[], int temp[], int left, int mid, int right)
```

```cpp
{
  int i, j, k;
  int inv_count = 0;
  i = left;
  j = mid;
  k = left;
  while ((i <= mid - 1) && (j <= right))
  {
    if (arr[i] <= arr[j])
    {
      temp[k++] = arr[i++];
    }
    else
    {
      temp[k++] = arr[j++];
      inv_count += (mid - i);
    }
  }
  while (i <= mid - 1)
    temp[k++] = arr[i++];
  while (j <= right)
    temp[k++] = arr[j++];
  for (i=left; i <= right; i++)
    arr[i] = temp[i];
  return inv_count;
}
int _mergeSort(int arr[], int temp[], int left, int right)
{
  int mid, inv_count = 0;
  if (right > left)
  {
    mid = (right + left)/2;
    inv_count  = _mergeSort(arr, temp, left, mid);
    inv_count += _mergeSort(arr, temp, mid+1, right);
    inv_count += merge(arr, temp, left, mid+1, right);
  }
  return inv_count;
}
int mergeSort(int arr[], int array_size)
{
  int temp[array_size];
  return _mergeSort(arr, temp, 0, array_size - 1);
}
int main()
{
```

```
int arr[] = {1, 20, 6, 4, 5};
int n = sizeof(arr)/sizeof(arr[0]);
int ans = mergeSort(arr, n);
cout << "Number of inversions are " << ans;
return 0;
}
```

BACKTRACKING IN C++

Welcome to this guide on backtracking in C++. Backtracking is an important algorithm used in computer science and is critical to understand for anyone studying data structures and algorithms with C++. This guide will provide an in-depth look at backtracking, including the definition, examples, and how to implement it in C++. By the end of this article, you should have a firm understanding of backtracking in C++, and be able to apply backtracking to solve your own problems.

What is Backtracking?

Backtracking is a type of algorithm used to solve a problem by exploring all possible solutions. It works by incrementally building a solution and then backtracking to the previous step if the solution does not work. The backtracking algorithm is an effective way to solve complex problems which may otherwise be difficult or impossible to solve.

Backtracking can be used for a wide range of applications, such as solving puzzles or maze problems, or finding the most optimal solution for a problem. It is often used in combination with other algorithms, such as dynamic programming or branch and bound, to further optimize the solution.

Backtracking can also be used to solve problems with multiple solutions. This is because the algorithm can generate all possible solutions and then select the best one.

How Does Backtracking Work?

Backtracking algorithms work by incrementally building a solution, and then backtracking to the previous step if the solution does not work. This process is repeated until a valid solution is found.

The algorithm starts by setting a variable to the initial state. It then begins to explore all possible solutions, starting with the initial state. If the solution is valid, the algorithm will continue to the next step, otherwise it will backtrack to the previous state and try a different solution. This process is repeated until a valid solution is found, or all possible solutions have been explored.

The backtracking algorithm is an efficient way to solve a problem with multiple solutions, as it is able to generate all possible solutions and then select the best one.

Example of Backtracking

The following example will demonstrate how the backtracking algorithm works.

The problem we will solve is to find the sum of all possible combinations of numbers from a given set of numbers.

For example, given the set {1, 2, 3}, the algorithm should return the sum of all possible combinations:

- 1 + 2 + 3 = 6
- 1 + 3 + 2 = 6
- 2 + 1 + 3 = 6
- 2 + 3 + 1 = 6
- 3 + 1 + 2 = 6
- 3 + 2 + 1 = 6

The solution to this problem can be solved using the backtracking algorithm.

We start by setting a variable to the initial state. In this case, the initial state is an empty set. We then begin to explore all possible solutions, starting with the empty set.

If the empty set is valid, we add the first number to the set. In this case, the first number is 1. We then check to see if the set is valid. If it is valid, we add the second number to the set. In this case, the second number is 2. We then check to see if the set is valid. If it is valid, we add the third number to the set. In this case, the third number is 3. We then check to see if the set is valid.

If the set is valid, we have found a valid solution and can return the sum of the set (1 + 2 + 3 = 6). If the set is not valid, we backtrack to the previous state (the set with two numbers) and try a different solution. This process is repeated until a valid solution is found, or all possible solutions have been explored.

Implementing Backtracking in C++

Now that we understand how backtracking works, let's take a look at how to implement it in C++.

The first step is to create a function that takes in the set of numbers and returns the sum of all possible combinations. This function will be the entry point for our backtracking algorithm.

```cpp
// Function to find the sum of all possible combinations
int sumOfCombinations(vector<int>& nums)
{
  // Initialize sum to 0
  int sum = 0;
  // Call the backtracking function
  backtrack(nums, 0, sum);
  // Return the sum
  return sum;
}
```

Next, we will create the backtracking function. This function will take in the set of numbers, the current index, and the sum.

```cpp
// Backtracking function
void backtrack(vector<int>& nums, int index, int& sum)
```

```
{
  // If the index is equal to the size of the set,
  // we have reached the end of the set and can
  // return the sum
  if (index == nums.size())
  {
    sum += accumulate(nums.begin(), nums.end(), 0);
    return;
  }
  // Loop through the set and add each number
  // to the sum
  for (int i = index; i < nums.size(); i++)
  {
    // Add the number to the sum
    sum += nums[i];
    // Call the backtracking function
    backtrack(nums, i + 1, sum);
    // Subtract the number from the sum
    sum -= nums[i];
  }
}
```

The backtracking function works by looping through the set of numbers and adding each number to the sum. It then calls the backtracking function with the next index and the updated sum. If the index is equal to the size of the set, we have reached the end of the set and can return the sum.

Conclusion

In this article, we discussed backtracking in C++, including the definition, how it works, and how to implement it in C++. We also provided an example of backtracking and discussed the advantages of using the algorithm. Backtracking is a powerful algorithm for solving complex problems and is often used in combination with other algorithms to further optimize the solution.

Exercises

Create a function that takes in a string and returns all possible permutations of the string. (Hint: Use backtracking)

Create a function that takes in a 2D array and returns all possible paths from the top-left corner to the bottom-right corner. (Hint: Use backtracking)

Create a function that takes in a binary tree and returns all possible paths from the root to the leaf nodes. (Hint: Use backtracking)

Create a function that takes in a string and returns all possible subsequences of the string. (Hint: Use backtracking)

Create a function that takes in a 2D array and returns all possible subsets of the array.

(Hint: Use backtracking)

Solutions

Create a function that takes in a string and returns all possible permutations of the string. (Hint: Use backtracking)

```cpp
// Function to return all possible permutations of a string
vector<string> permute(string s)
{
  // Vector to store the permutations
  vector<string> perms;
  // Call the backtracking function
  backtrack(s, 0, perms);
  // Return the vector
  return perms;
}
// Backtracking function
void backtrack(string s, int index, vector<string>& perms)
{
  // If the index is equal to the size of the string,
  // we have reached the end of the string and can add
  // the string to the vector
  if (index == s.size())
  {
    perms.push_back(s);
    return;
  }
  // Loop through the string and swap each character
  // with the character at the current index
  for (int i = index; i < s.size(); i++)
  {
    // Swap the characters
    swap(s[index], s[i]);
    // Call the backtracking function
    backtrack(s, index + 1, perms);
    // Swap the characters back
    swap(s[index], s[i]);
  }
}
```

Create a function that takes in a 2D array and returns all possible paths from the top-left corner to the bottom-right corner. (Hint: Use backtracking)

```cpp
// Function to return all possible paths from the top-left
// corner to the bottom-right corner of a 2D array
vector<vector<int>> findPaths(vector<vector<int>>& arr)
```

```cpp
{
  // Vector to store the paths
  vector<vector<int>> paths;
  // Call the backtracking function
  backtrack(arr, 0, 0, paths);
  // Return the vector
  return paths;
}
// Backtracking function
void backtrack(vector<vector<int>>& arr, int row, int col, vector<vector<int>>& paths)
{
  // If the row and column indices are equal to the size
  // of the array, we have reached the bottom-right corner
  // and can add the path to the vector
  if (row == arr.size() - 1 && col == arr[0].size() - 1)
  {
    paths.push_back(arr[row][col]);
    return;
  }
  // Check if the row and column indices are valid
  if (row >= 0 && row < arr.size() &&
    col >= 0 && col < arr[0].size())
  {
    // Add the current element to the path
    paths.push_back(arr[row][col]);
    // Call the backtracking function
    backtrack(arr, row + 1, col, paths);
    backtrack(arr, row, col + 1, paths);
    // Remove the last element from the path
    paths.pop_back();
  }
}
```

Create a function that takes in a binary tree and returns all possible paths from the root to the leaf nodes. (Hint: Use backtracking)

```cpp
// Function to return all possible paths from the root
// to the leaf nodes of a binary tree
vector<vector<int>> findPaths(TreeNode* root)
{
  // Vector to store the paths
  vector<vector<int>> paths;
  // Call the backtracking function
  backtrack(root, paths);
  // Return the vector
  return paths;
```

```
}
// Backtracking function
void backtrack(TreeNode* node, vector<vector<int>>& paths)
{
  // If the node is null, we have reached the end
  // of a path and can add the path to the vector
  if (node == nullptr)
  {
    paths.push_back({});
    return;
  }
  // Add the current node to the path
  paths.back().push_back(node->val);
  // Call the backtracking function
  backtrack(node->left, paths);
  backtrack(node->right, paths);
  // Remove the last element from the path
  paths.back().pop_back();
}
```

Create a function that takes in a string and returns all possible subsequences of the string. (Hint: Use backtracking)

```
// Function to return all possible subsequences of a string
vector<string> findSubsequences(string s)
{
  // Vector to store the subsequences
  vector<string> subsequences;
  // Call the backtracking function
  backtrack(s, 0, subsequences);
  // Return the vector
  return subsequences;
}
// Backtracking function
void backtrack(string s, int index, vector<string>& subsequences)
{
  // If the index is equal to the size of the string,
  // we have reached the end of the string and can
  // add the string to the vector
  if (index == s.size())
  {
    subsequences.push_back(s);
    return;
  }
  // Loop through the string and remove each character
  // at the current index
```

```cpp
for (int i = index; i < s.size(); i++)
{
    // Remove the character from the string
    s.erase(i, 1);
    // Call the backtracking function
    backtrack(s, i, subsequences);
    // Add the character back to the string
    s.insert(i, 1, s[i]);
}
}
```

Create a function that takes in a 2D array and returns all possible subsets of the array. (Hint: Use backtracking)

```cpp
// Function to return all possible subsets of a 2D array
vector<vector<int>> findSubsets(vector<vector<int>>& arr)
{
    // Vector to store the subsets
    vector<vector<int>> subsets;
    // Call the backtracking function
    backtrack(arr, 0, 0, subsets);
    // Return the vector
    return subsets;
}
// Backtracking function
void backtrack(vector<vector<int>>& arr, int row, int col, vector<vector<int>>& subsets)
{
    // If the row and column indices are equal to the size
    // of the array, we have reached the end of the array
    // and can add the subset to the vector
    if (row == arr.size() && col == arr[0].size())
    {
        subsets.push_back({});
        return;
    }
    // Check if the row and column indices are valid
    if (row >= 0 && row < arr.size() &&
        col >= 0 && col < arr[0].size())
    {
        // Add the current element to the subset
        subsets.back().push_back(arr[row][col]);
        // Call the backtracking function
        backtrack(arr, row + 1, col, subsets);
        backtrack(arr, row, col + 1, subsets);
        // Remove the last element from the subset
        subsets.back().pop_back();
```

```
    }
}
```

RANDOMIZED ALGORITHMS IN C++

Randomization is an important concept in the world of computer programming. Randomization allows for the development of algorithms that can solve problems more efficiently than non-randomized algorithms. Randomization is used in a variety of algorithms, including sorting, searching, and graph algorithms. In this article, we will discuss randomized algorithms in C++, and how they can be used to improve the efficiency of programs. We will cover the basics of using randomization in C++, as well as how to implement randomized algorithms in C++.

What are Randomized Algorithms?

Randomized algorithms are a type of algorithm that makes use of random input or random choices. Randomized algorithms are used to solve problems more efficiently than non-randomized algorithms. This is because randomization allows algorithms to make use of probabilistic methods, which can provide faster solutions to certain types of problems. Randomized algorithms can also provide more robust solutions than non-randomized algorithms, as they are less likely to be affected by certain types of errors.

The Role of Randomization in C++

Randomization is an important concept in C++ programming. Randomization allows for the development of efficient algorithms that can solve problems more quickly than non-randomized algorithms. Randomization can also be used to create algorithms that are more robust, as they are less likely to be affected by certain types of errors.

Randomization can be used in a variety of ways in C++. For example, randomization can be used to generate random numbers, or to create data structures that are randomized. Randomization can also be used to create algorithms that make use of probabilistic methods, which can provide faster solutions to certain types of problems.

Random Number Generation in C++

Random number generation is an important concept in C++ programming. Random number generation allows for the development of algorithms that make use of random numbers, which can be used to solve certain types of problems more efficiently than non-randomized algorithms.

In C++, random number generation can be achieved using the rand() function. The rand() function takes a single parameter, which is the maximum value that can be generated. For example, if you wanted to generate a random number between 0 and 10, you could call the rand() function like this:

```
int randomNumber = rand(10);
```

The rand() function will return a random integer between 0 and the maximum value specified in the parameter.

Randomizing Data Structures in C++

Randomizing data structures is another important concept in C++ programming. Randomizing data structures allows for the development of algorithms that make use of random data structures, which can be used to solve certain types of problems more efficiently than non-randomized algorithms.

In C++, data structures can be randomized using the shuffle() function. The shuffle() function takes two parameters: an array of data, and a random number generator. The shuffle() function will randomly rearrange the elements of the array using the random number generator. For example, if you had an array of integers, you could call the shuffle() function like this:

```
// Create an array of integers
int myArray[] = {1, 2, 3, 4, 5, 6, 7, 8, 9, 10};
// Shuffle the array
shuffle(myArray, rand);
```

The shuffle() function will randomly rearrange the elements of the array using the rand() function.

Implementing Randomized Algorithms in C++

Now that we have discussed the basics of randomization in C++, let's look at how to implement randomized algorithms in C++. In order to implement a randomized algorithm in C++, you will need to make use of the rand() and shuffle() functions.

For example, let's say that we want to implement a randomized sorting algorithm in C++. We can do this by using the rand() and shuffle() functions. First, we will need to generate a random number using the rand() function. We can use this random number to randomly rearrange the elements in the array using the shuffle() function. Then, we can use a sorting algorithm such as insertion sort or quick sort to sort the array.

Conclusion

Randomized algorithms are an important concept in C++ programming. Randomization allows for the development of algorithms that can solve problems more efficiently than non-randomized algorithms. Randomization can be used in a variety of ways in C++, including random number generation and randomizing data structures. Randomization can also be used to create algorithms that make use of probabilistic methods, which can provide faster solutions to certain types of problems.

Exercises

Write a function in C++ that takes an integer array as input and randomly rearranges the elements using the shuffle() function.

Write a function in C++ that takes an array of integers and returns a randomly generated number.

Write a function in C++ that takes an array of integers and an integer k as input and returns the kth smallest element in the array using a randomized algorithm.

Write a function in C++ that takes an array of integers and an integer k as input and returns the kth largest element in the array using a randomized algorithm.

Write a function in C++ that takes an array of integers and an integer k as input and returns the kth smallest element in the array using a non-randomized algorithm.

Solutions

Write a function in C++ that takes an integer array as input and randomly rearranges the elements using the shuffle() function.

```cpp
#include <algorithm>
#include <random>
void shuffleArray(int array[], int size) {
    std::random_device rd;
    std::mt19937 mt(rd());
    std::shuffle(array, array + size, mt);
}
```

Write a function in C++ that takes an array of integers and returns a randomly generated number.

```cpp
#include <random>
int generateRandomNumber(int max) {
    std::random_device rd;
    std::mt19937 mt(rd());
    std::uniform_int_distribution<int> dist(0, max);
    return dist(mt);
}
```

Write a function in C++ that takes an array of integers and an integer k as input and returns the kth smallest element in the array using a randomized algorithm.

```cpp
#include <algorithm>
#include <random>
int findKthSmallest(int array[], int size, int k) {
    std::random_device rd;
    std::mt19937 mt(rd());
    std::shuffle(array, array + size, mt);
    std::sort(array, array + size);
    return array[k-1];
}
```

Write a function in C++ that takes an array of integers and an integer k as input and returns the kth largest element in the array using a randomized algorithm.

```cpp
#include <algorithm>
#include <random>
int findKthLargest(int array[], int size, int k) {
    std::random_device rd;
    std::mt19937 mt(rd());
    std::shuffle(array, array + size, mt);
    std::sort(array, array + size, std::greater<int>());
    return array[k-1];
}
```

Write a function in C++ that takes an array of integers and an integer k as input and returns the kth smallest element in the array using a non-randomized algorithm.

```cpp
#include <algorithm>
int findKthSmallest(int array[], int size, int k) {
    std::sort(array, array + size);
    return array[k-1];
}
```

CONCLUSION

RECAP OF DSA WITH C++

This course provided an in-depth look into the core concepts of data structures and algorithms, including various data structures such as arrays, stacks, queues, linked lists, skip lists, hash tables, binary search trees, Cartesian trees, B-trees, red-black trees, splay trees, AVL trees, and KD trees. In addition, learners were exposed to a variety of sorting and searching algorithms, as well as algorithm design techniques such as greedy algorithms, dynamic programming, divide and conquer, backtracking, and randomized algorithms.

Moreover, learners had the opportunity to understand the trade-offs between different data structures and algorithms through the study of Time and Space Complexity analysis, as well as apply their knowledge and practice their skills through a number of hands-on exercises and examples. After completing this course, learners gained the essential knowledge and abilities necessary to become proficient in data structures and algorithms.

This knowledge and understanding of data structures and algorithms can help learners to become better and more efficient developers, especially in the field of computer science and data science. We thank you for taking this course and encourage you to keep exploring and honing your data structures and algorithms skills, as well as continuing to expand your knowledge and grow as a programmer.

THANK YOU

Thank you again for choosing "Data Structures and Algorithms with C++". I hope it helps you in your journey to learn Data Structures and Algorithms with C++ and achieve your goals. Please take a small portion of your time and share this with your friends and family and write a review for this book. I hope your programming journey does not end here. If you are interested, check out other books that I have or find more coding challenges at: https://codeofcode.org